Jim Henson's™
LABYRINTH™
CORONATION

VOLUME TWO

Published by
ARCHAIA™

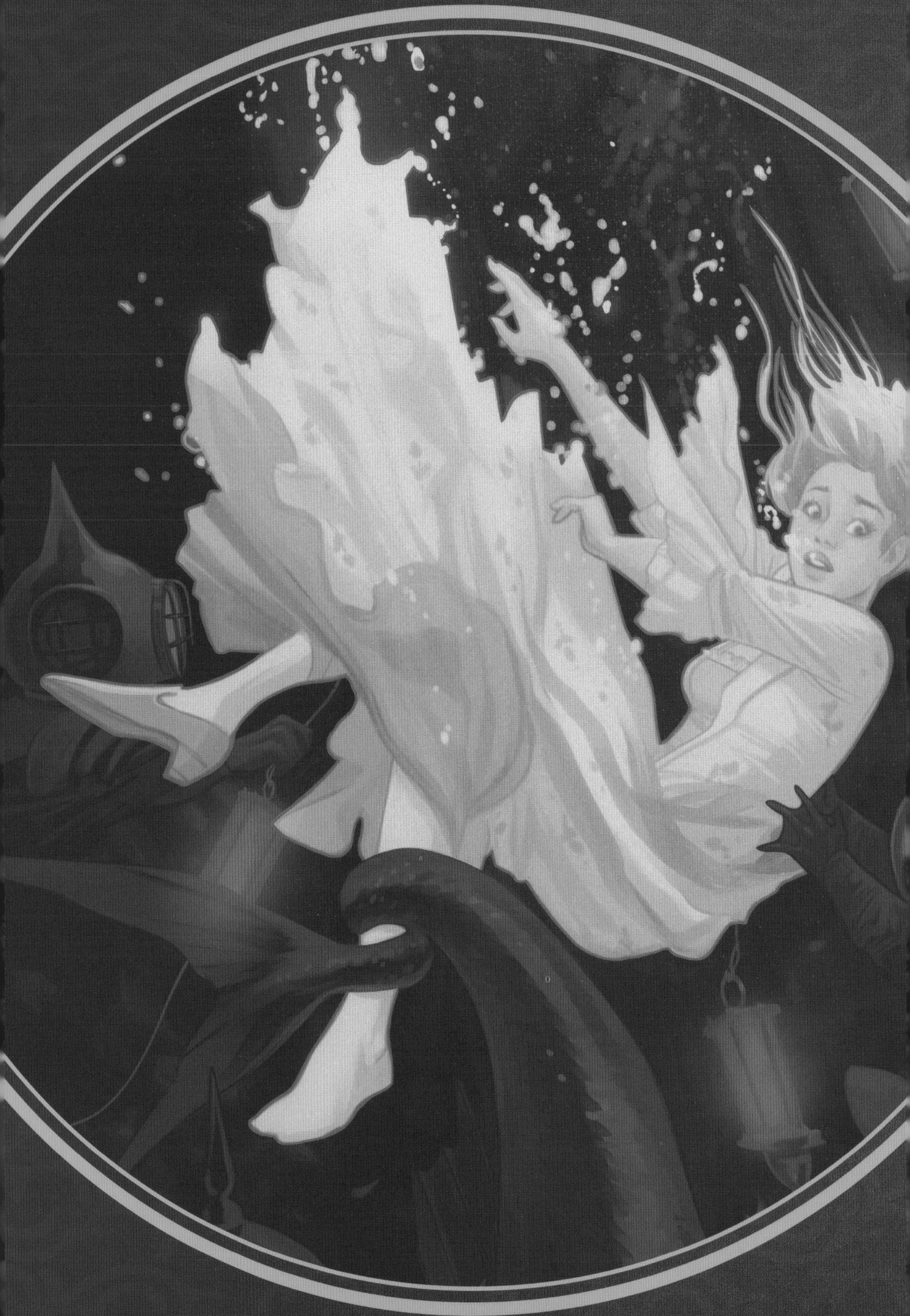

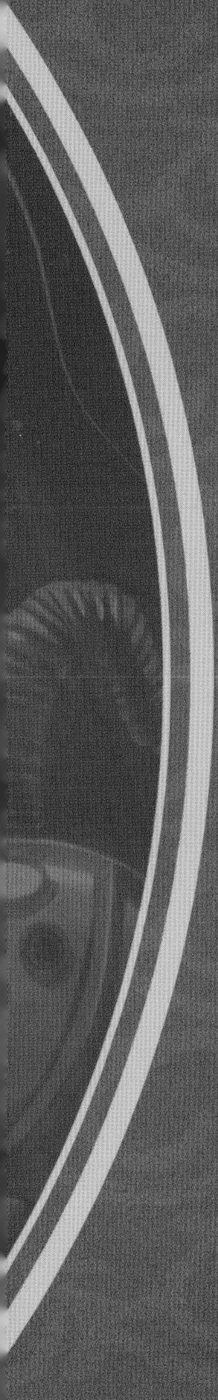

Jim Henson's™

LABYRINTH™

CORONATION

Written by **Simon Spurrier** and **Ryan Ferrier**

Illustrated by **Daniel Bayliss** with **Irene Flores**

Colored by **Dan Jackson** and **Joana Lafuente**

Lettered by **Jim Campbell**

Character Designs by **Kyla Vanderklugt** and **Daniel Bayliss**

Cover and Chapter Break Art by **Fiona Staples**

Series Designer **Michelle Ankley**

Collection Designer **Scott Newman**

Assistant Editor **Gavin Gronenthal**

Editor **Cameron Chittock**

Special Thanks to **Brian Henson, Lisa Henson, Jim Formanek,
Nicole Goldman, Carla DellaVedova, Karen Falk, Blanca Lista,
Shane Mang,** and the entire **Jim Henson Company team,
Wendy Froud, Brian Froud,** and **Sierra Hahn**

JIM HENSON'S LABYRINTH: CORONATION Volume Two, May 2019. Published by Archaia,
a division of Boom Entertainment, Inc. ™ & © 2019 The Jim Henson Company. JIM HENSON'S
mark & logo, LABYRINTH mark & logo, characters and elements are trademarks of The Jim Henson
Company. Motion Picture © 1986 Labyrinth Enterprises. Originally published in single magazine
form as JIM HENSON'S LABYRINTH: CORONATION No. 5-8. ™ & © 2018 The Jim Henson
Company. All Rights Reserved. Archaia™ and the Archaia logo are trademarks of Boom Entertainment,
Inc., registered in various countries and categories. All characters, events, and institutions depicted
herein are fictional. Any similarity between any of the names, characters, persons, events, and/or
institutions in this publication to actual names, characters, and persons, whether living or dead, events,
and/or institutions is unintended and purely coincidental.

BOOM! Studios, 5670 Wilshire Boulevard, Suite 400, Los Angeles, CA 90036-5679. Printed in
China. First Printing.

ISBN: 978-1-68415-358-9, eISBN: 978-1-64144-341-8

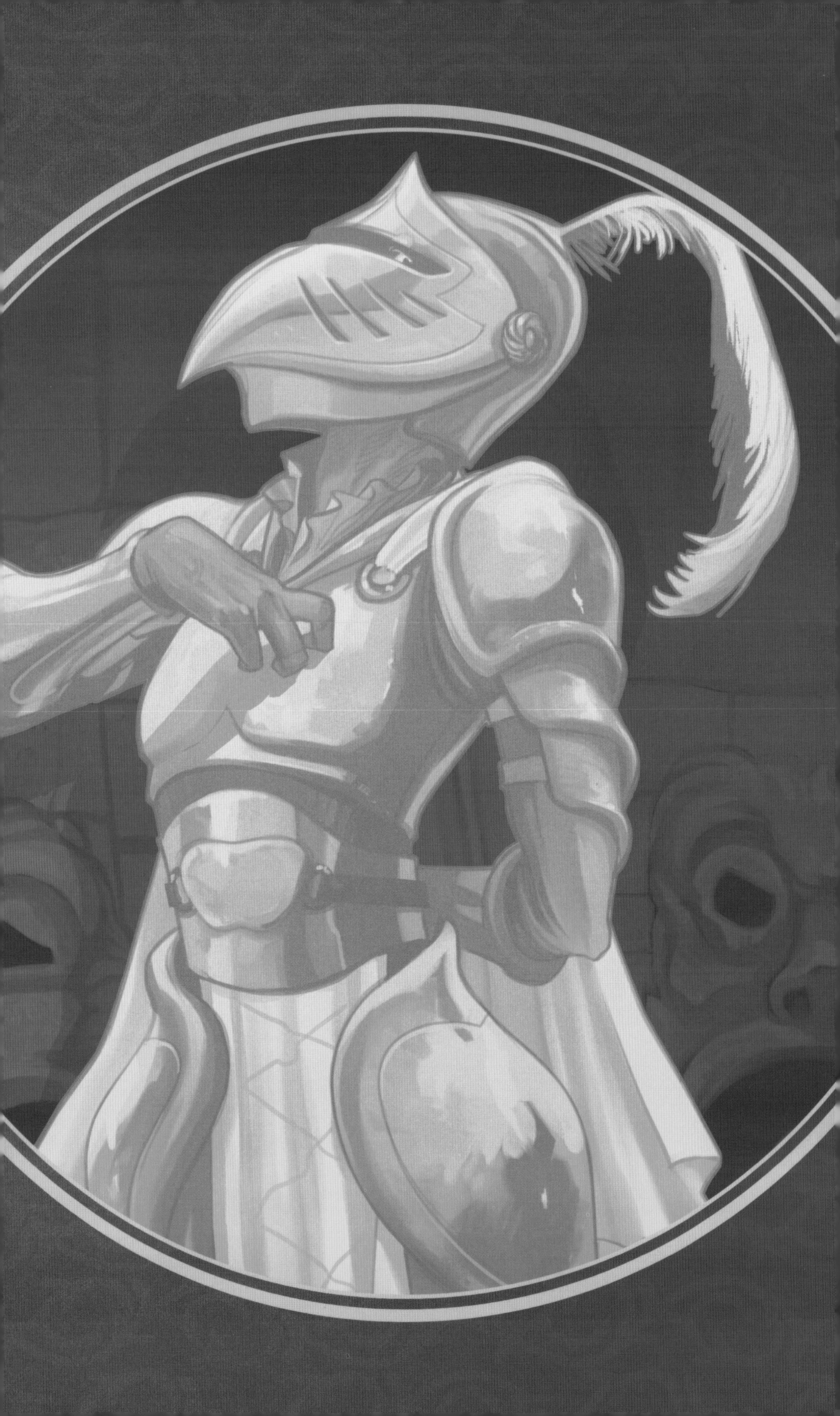

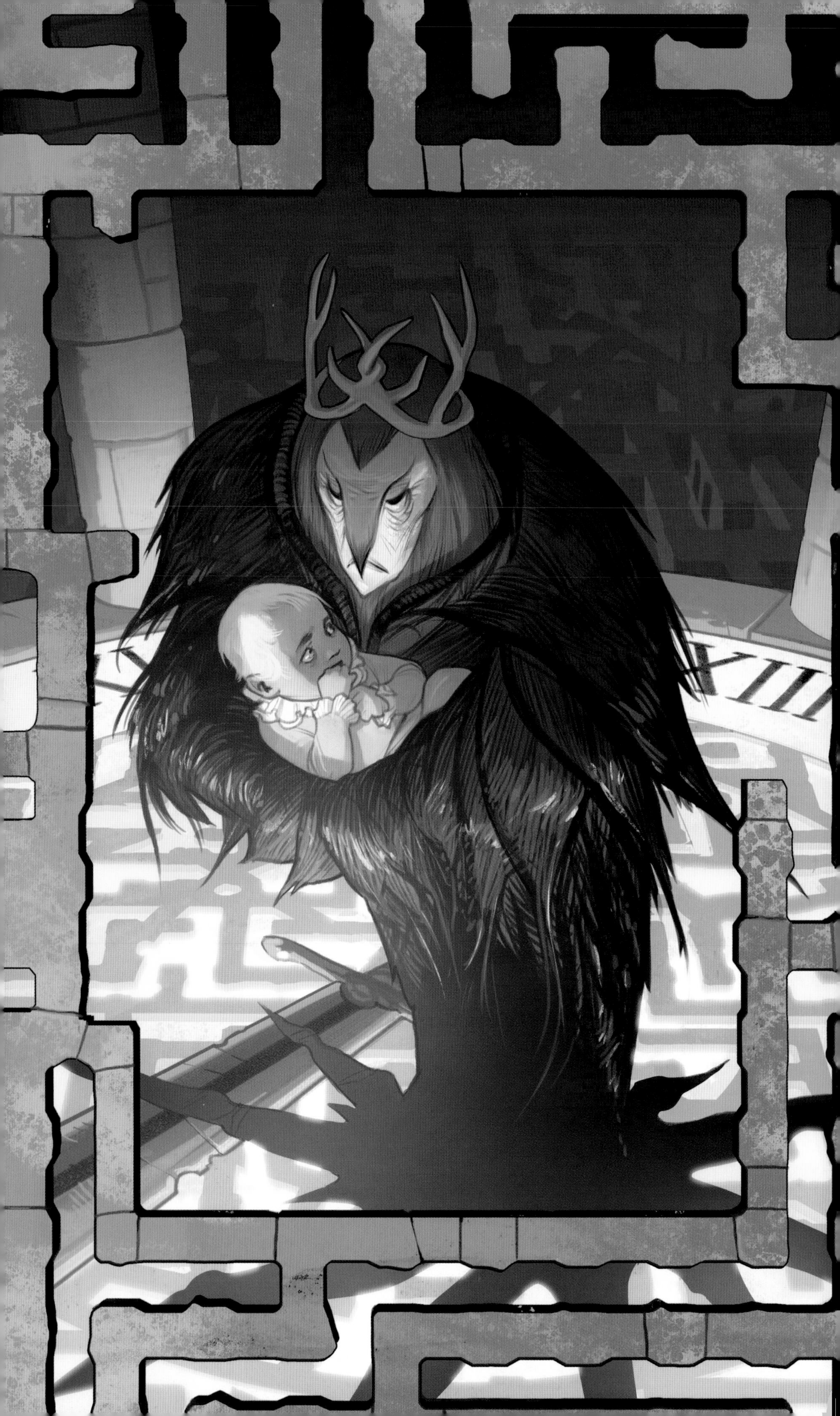

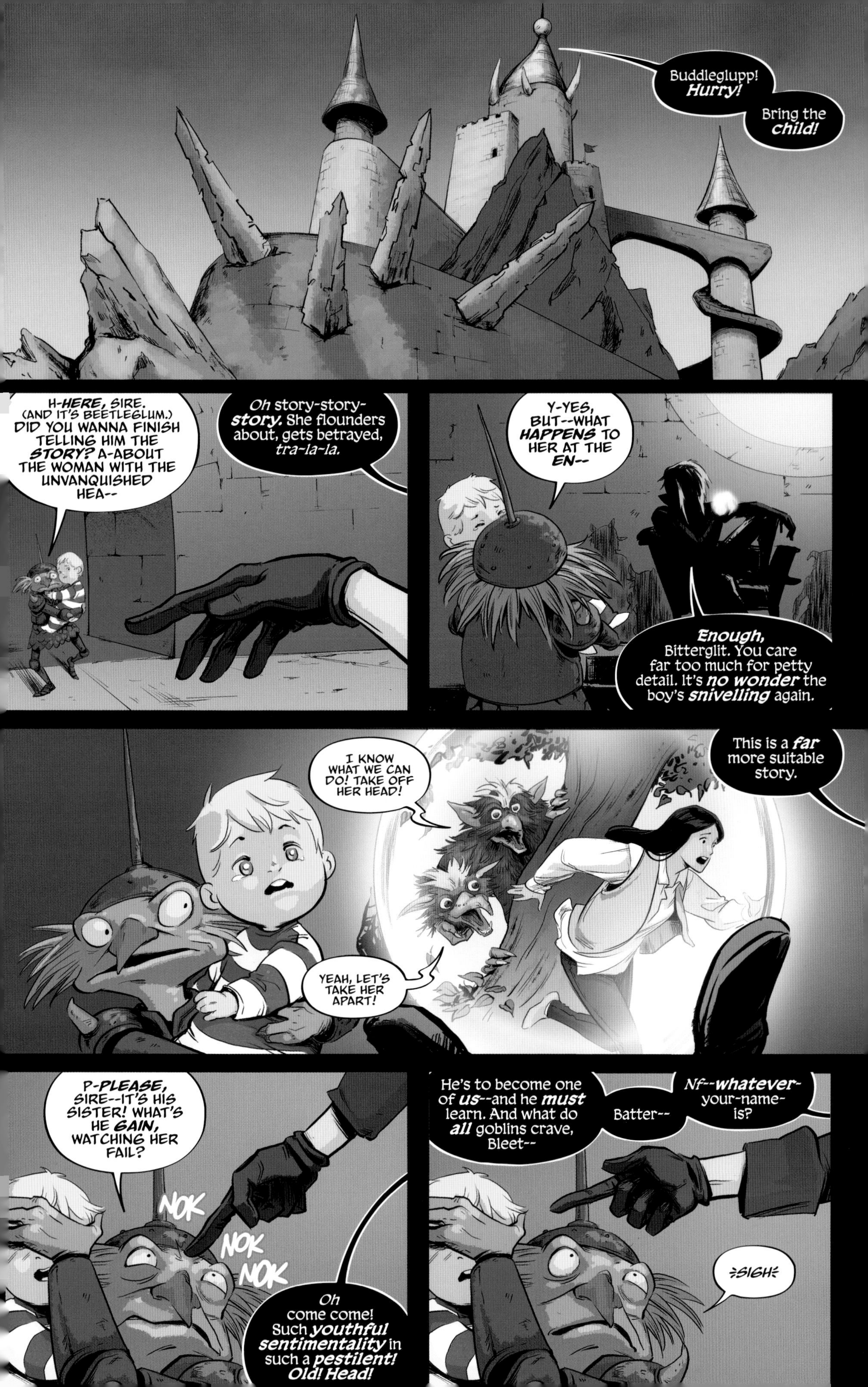
Buddleglupp! Hurry!
Bring the child!
H-HERE, SIRE. (AND IT'S BEETLEGLUM.) DID YOU WANNA FINISH TELLING HIM THE STORY? A-ABOUT THE WOMAN WITH THE UNVANQUISHED HEA--
Oh story-story-story. She flounders about, gets betrayed, tra-la-la.
Y-YES, BUT--WHAT HAPPENS TO HER AT THE EN--
Enough, Bitterglit. You care far too much for petty detail. It's no wonder the boy's snivelling again.
This is a far more suitable story.
I KNOW WHAT WE CAN DO! TAKE OFF HER HEAD!
YEAH, LET'S TAKE HER APART!
P-PLEASE, SIRE--IT'S HIS SISTER! WHAT'S HE GAIN, WATCHING HER FAIL?
NOK
NOK
NOK
Oh come come! Such youthful sentimentality in such a pestilent! Old! Head!
He's to become one of us--and he must learn. And what do all goblins crave, Bleet--
Batter--
Nf--whatever-your-name-is?
SIGH

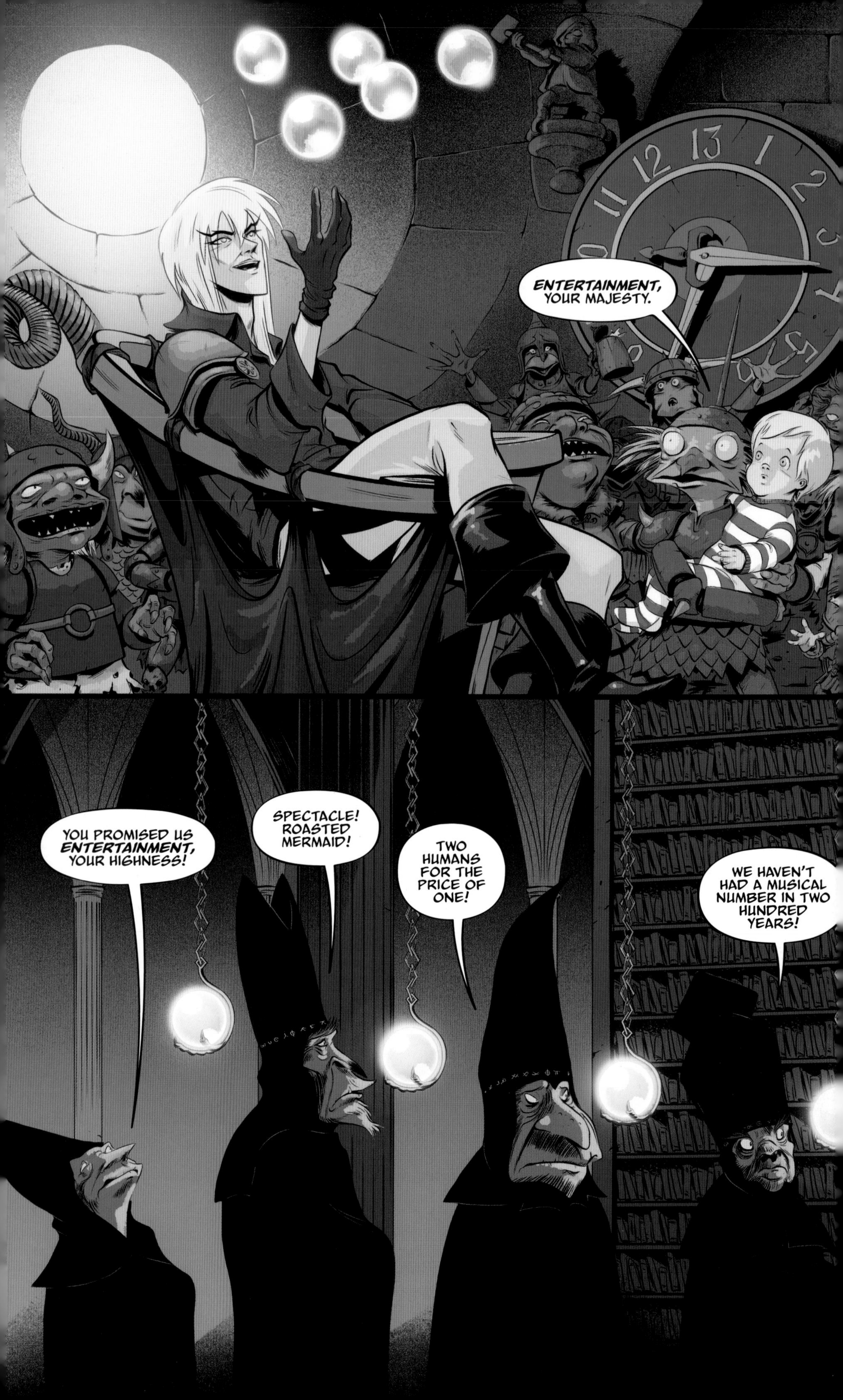

ENTERTAINMENT, YOUR MAJESTY.
YOU PROMISED US ENTERTAINMENT, YOUR HIGHNESS!
SPECTACLE! ROASTED MERMAID!
TWO HUMANS FOR THE PRICE OF ONE!
WE HAVEN'T HAD A MUSICAL NUMBER IN TWO HUNDRED YEARS!

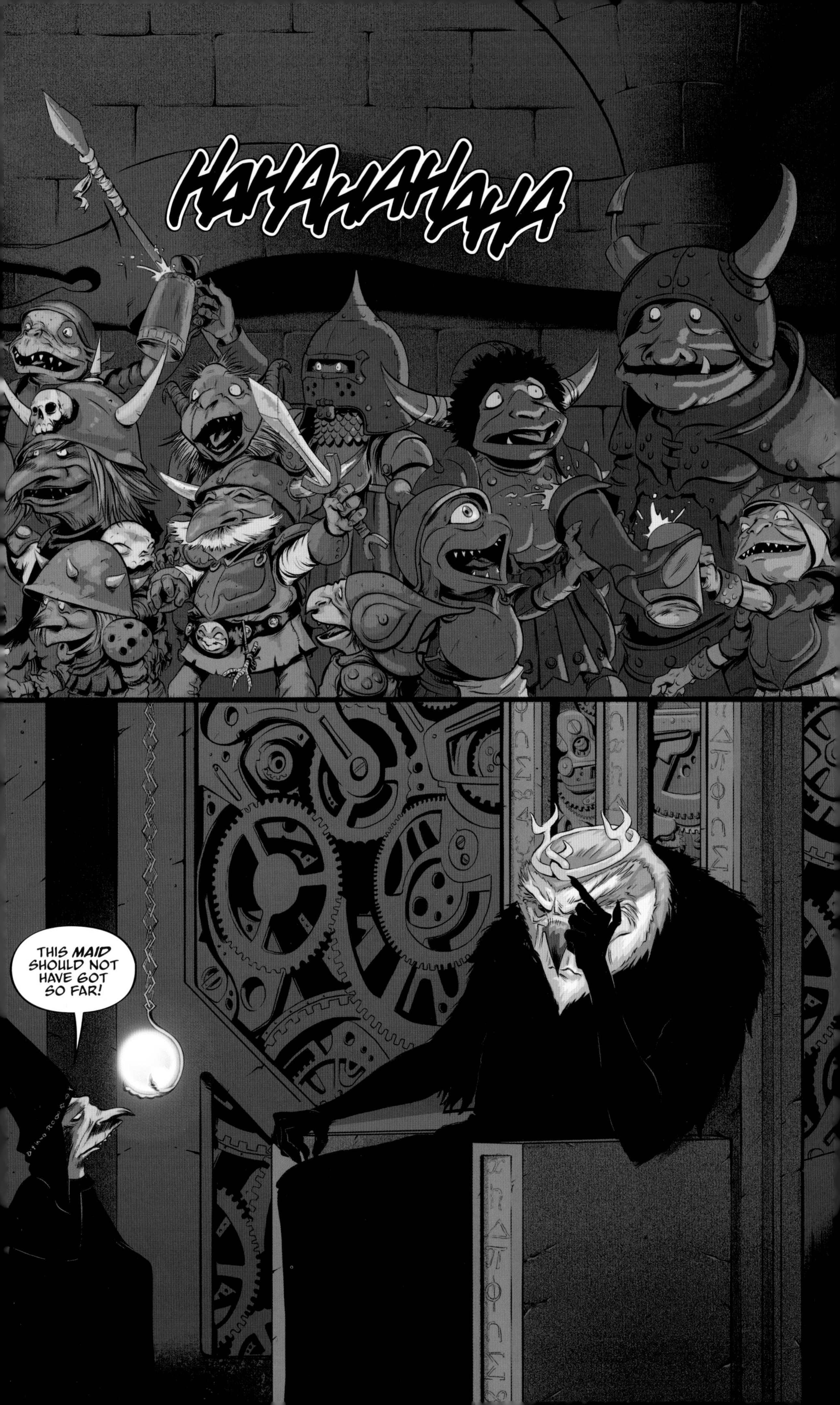
HAHAHAHAHAHAHA
THIS MAID SHOULD NOT HAVE GOT SO FAR!

...NNNNNNNNNSILENCE!

≥KOFF≥

MUTTER

MUTTER

MUTTER

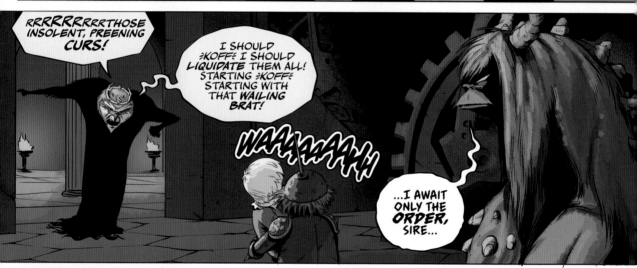

RRRRRRRRRTHOSE INSOLENT, PREENING CURS!

I SHOULD ≥KOFF≥ I SHOULD LIQUIDATE THEM ALL! STARTING ≥KOFF≥ STARTING WITH THAT WAILING BRAT!

WAAAAAAAH

...I AWAIT ONLY THE ORDER, SIRE...

≥HHKHH≥ TH-THANK YOU, SEPTIMUS. YOU ARE A TRUE AND LOYAL FIEND. BUT-- NO. I NEED THE BOY.

AND I CANNOT RISK A PURGE OF THE COURT. THERE'S ALREADY REBELLION IN THE AIR.

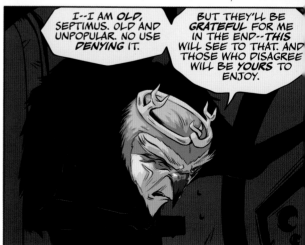

I--I AM OLD, SEPTIMUS. OLD AND UNPOPULAR. NO USE DENYING IT.

BUT THEY'LL BE GRATEFUL FOR ME IN THE END--THIS WILL SEE TO THAT. AND THOSE WHO DISAGREE WILL BE YOURS TO ENJOY.

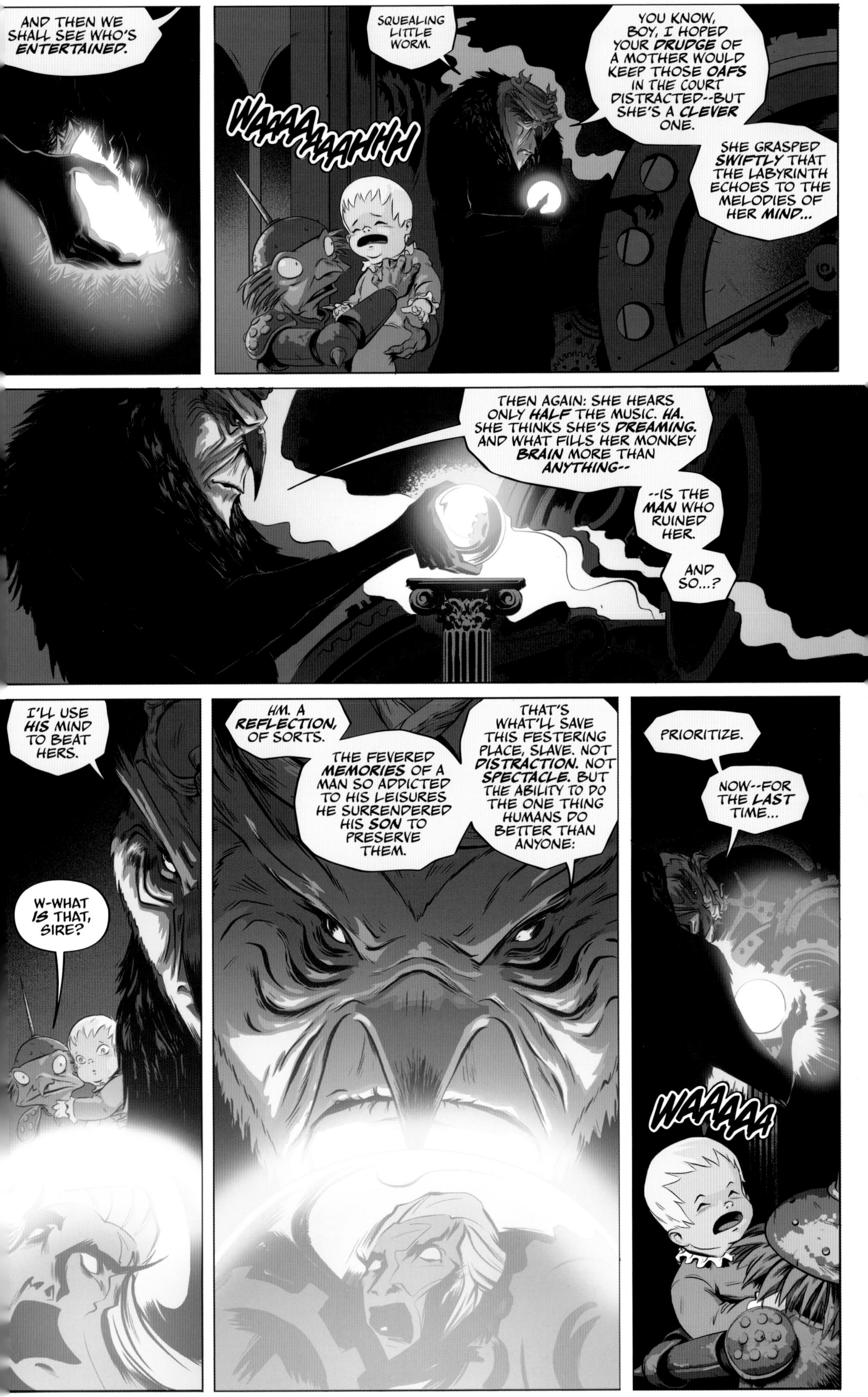
AND THEN WE SHALL SEE WHO'S ENTERTAINED.
SQUEALING LITTLE WORM.
WAAAAAAAHHH
YOU KNOW, BOY, I HOPED YOUR DRUDGE OF A MOTHER WOULD KEEP THOSE OAFS IN THE COURT DISTRACTED--BUT SHE'S A CLEVER ONE.
SHE GRASPED SWIFTLY THAT THE LABYRINTH ECHOES TO THE MELODIES OF HER MIND...
THEN AGAIN: SHE HEARS ONLY HALF THE MUSIC. HA. SHE THINKS SHE'S DREAMING. AND WHAT FILLS HER MONKEY BRAIN MORE THAN ANYTHING--
--IS THE MAN WHO RUINED HER.
AND SO...?
I'LL USE HIS MIND TO BEAT HERS.
W-WHAT IS THAT, SIRE?
HM. A REFLECTION, OF SORTS.
THE FEVERED MEMORIES OF A MAN SO ADDICTED TO HIS LEISURES HE SURRENDERED HIS SON TO PRESERVE THEM.
THAT'S WHAT'LL SAVE THIS FESTERING PLACE, SLAVE. NOT DISTRACTION. NOT SPECTACLE. BUT THE ABILITY TO DO THE ONE THING HUMANS DO BETTER THAN ANYONE:
PRIORITIZE.
NOW--FOR THE LAST TIME...
WAAAAA

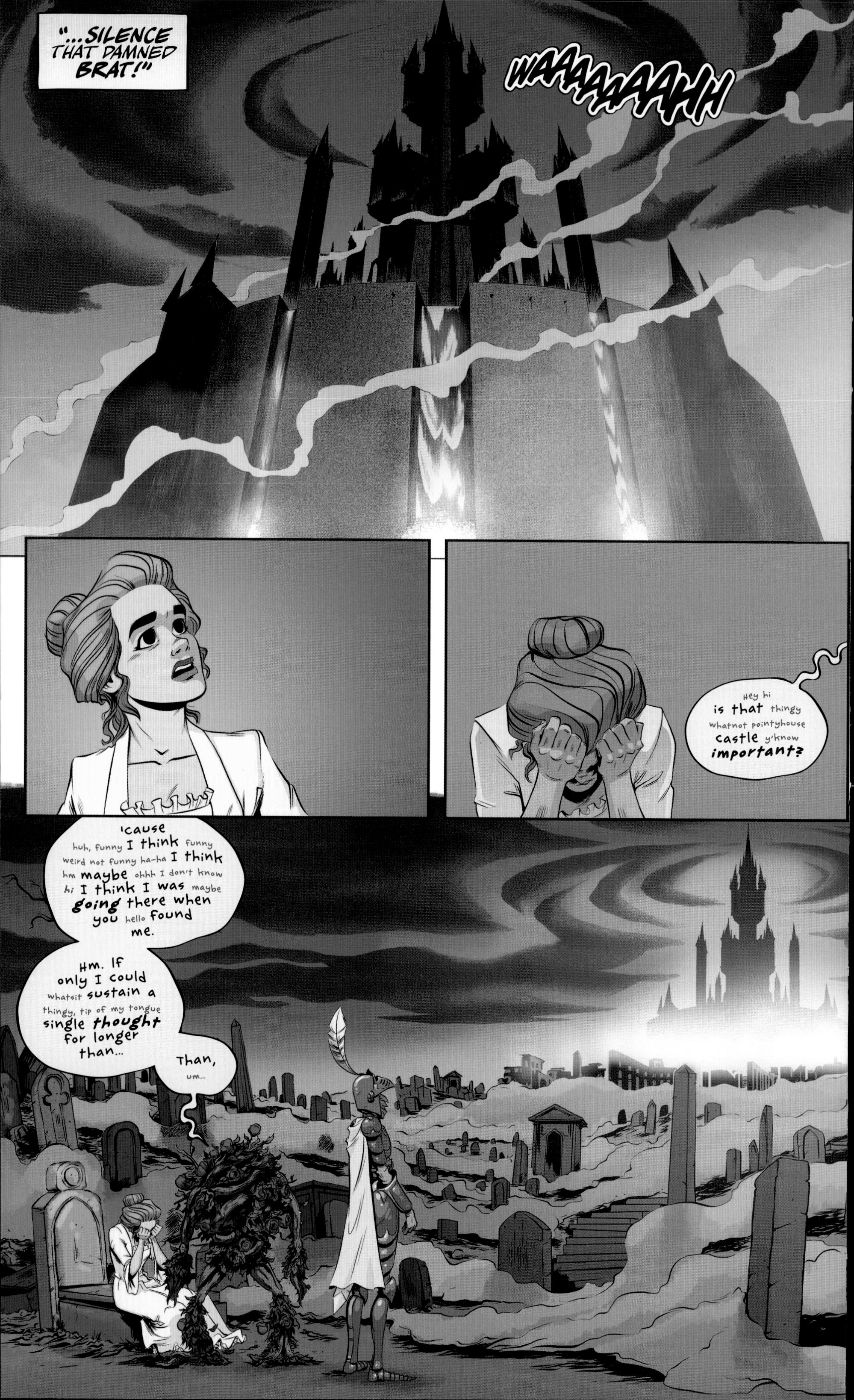
"...SILENCE THAT DAMNED BRAT!"
WAAAAAAAAHH
Hey hi is that thingy whatnot pointyhouse castle y'know important?
'cause huh, funny I think funny weird not funny ha-ha I think hm maybe ohhh I don't know hi I think I was maybe going there when you hello found me.
Hm. If only I could whatsit sustain a thingy, tip of my tongue single thought for longer than...
Than, um...

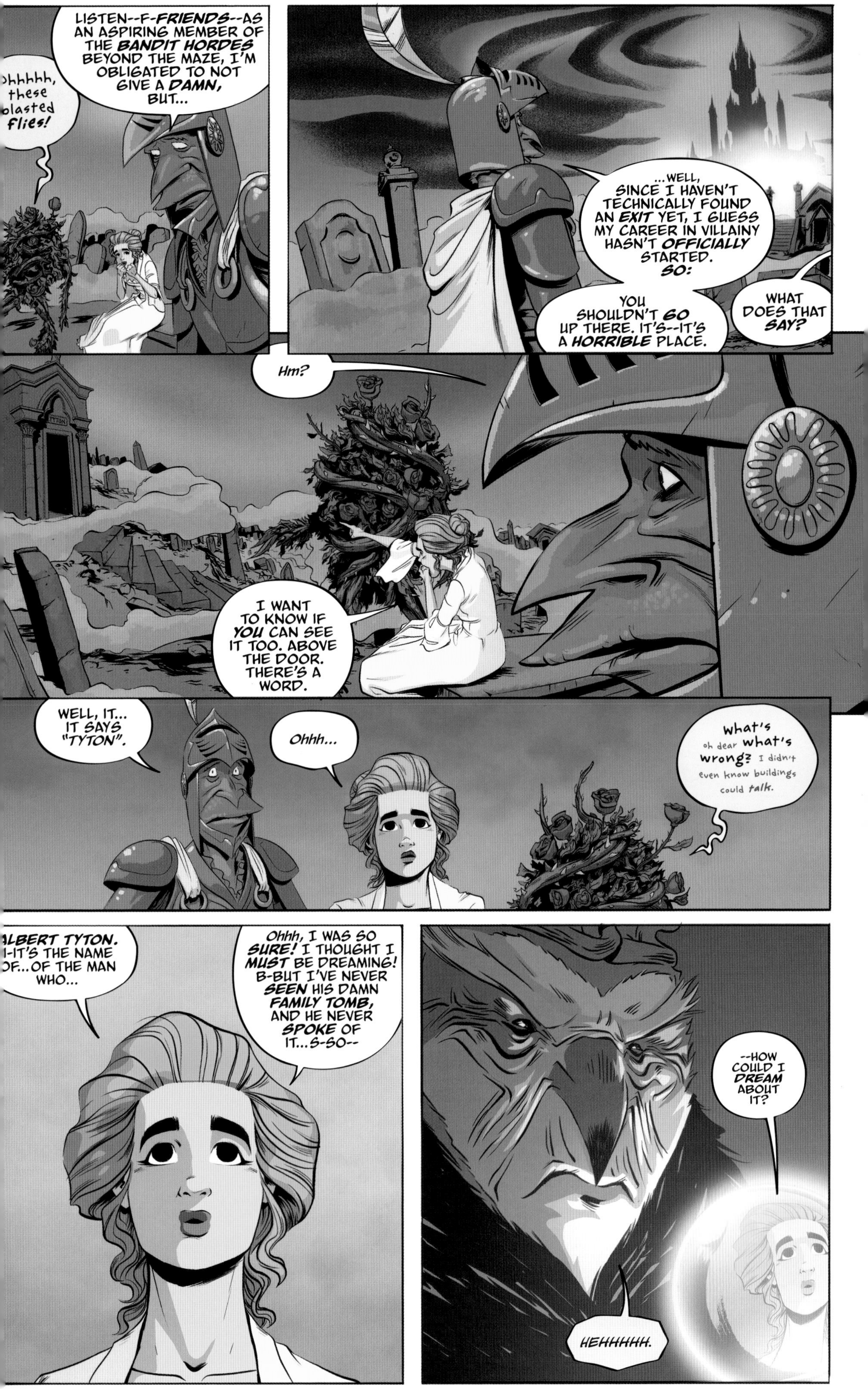

LISTEN--F-FRIENDS--AS AN ASPIRING MEMBER OF THE BANDIT HORDES BEYOND THE MAZE, I'M OBLIGATED TO NOT GIVE A DAMN, BUT...
hhhhh, these lasted flies!
...WELL, SINCE I HAVEN'T TECHNICALLY FOUND AN EXIT YET, I GUESS MY CAREER IN VILLAINY HASN'T OFFICIALLY STARTED. SO:
YOU SHOULDN'T GO UP THERE. IT'S--IT'S A HORRIBLE PLACE.
WHAT DOES THAT SAY?
Hm?
TYTON
I WANT TO KNOW IF YOU CAN SEE IT TOO. ABOVE THE DOOR. THERE'S A WORD.
WELL, IT... IT SAYS "TYTON".
Ohhh...
What's oh dear what's wrong? I didn't even know buildings could talk.
LBERT TYTON. -IT'S THE NAME F...OF THE MAN WHO...
Ohhh, I WAS SO SURE! I THOUGHT I MUST BE DREAMING! B-BUT I'VE NEVER SEEN HIS DAMN FAMILY TOMB, AND HE NEVER SPOKE OF IT...S-SO--
--HOW COULD I DREAM ABOUT IT?
HEHHHHH.

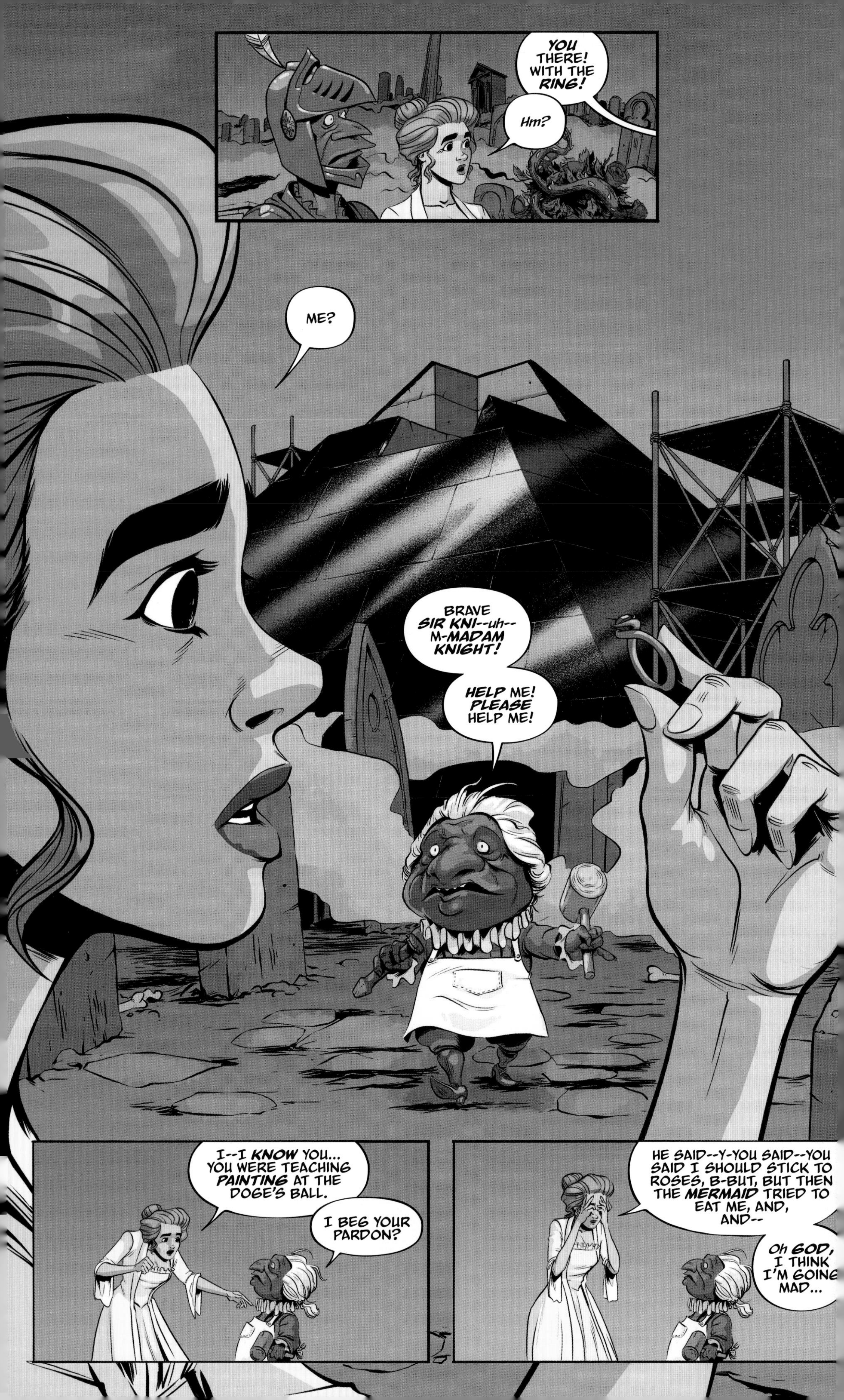
YOU THERE! WITH THE RING!
Hm?
ME?
BRAVE SIR KNI--uh-- M-MADAM KNIGHT!
HELP ME! PLEASE HELP ME!
I--I KNOW YOU... YOU WERE TEACHING PAINTING AT THE DOGE'S BALL.
I BEG YOUR PARDON?
HE SAID--Y-YOU SAID--YOU SAID I SHOULD STICK TO ROSES, B-BUT, BUT THEN THE MERMAID TRIED TO EAT ME, AND, AND--
Oh GOD, I THINK I'M GOING MAD...

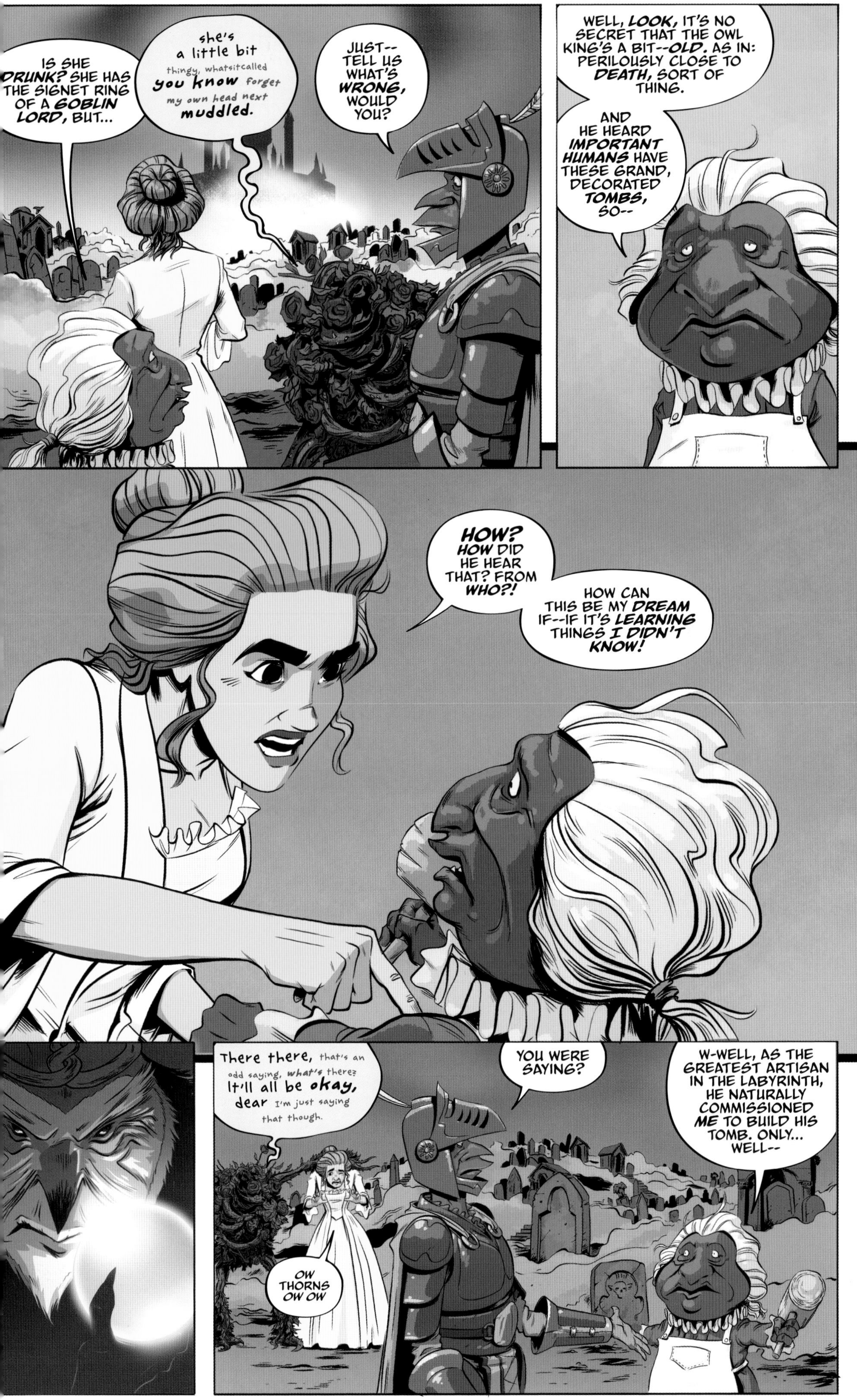

IS SHE DRUNK? SHE HAS THE SIGNET RING OF A GOBLIN LORD, BUT...
she's a little bit thingy, whatsitcalled you know forget my own head next muddled.
JUST-- TELL US WHAT'S WRONG, WOULD YOU?
WELL, LOOK, IT'S NO SECRET THAT THE OWL KING'S A BIT--OLD. AS IN: PERILOUSLY CLOSE TO DEATH, SORT OF THING.
AND HE HEARD IMPORTANT HUMANS HAVE THESE GRAND, DECORATED TOMBS, SO--
HOW? HOW DID HE HEAR THAT? FROM WHO?!
HOW CAN THIS BE MY DREAM IF--IF IT'S LEARNING THINGS I DIDN'T KNOW!
There there, that's an odd saying, what's there? It'll all be okay, dear I'm just saying that though.
YOU WERE SAYING?
W-WELL, AS THE GREATEST ARTISAN IN THE LABYRINTH, HE NATURALLY COMMISSIONED ME TO BUILD HIS TOMB. ONLY... WELL--
OW THORNS OW OW

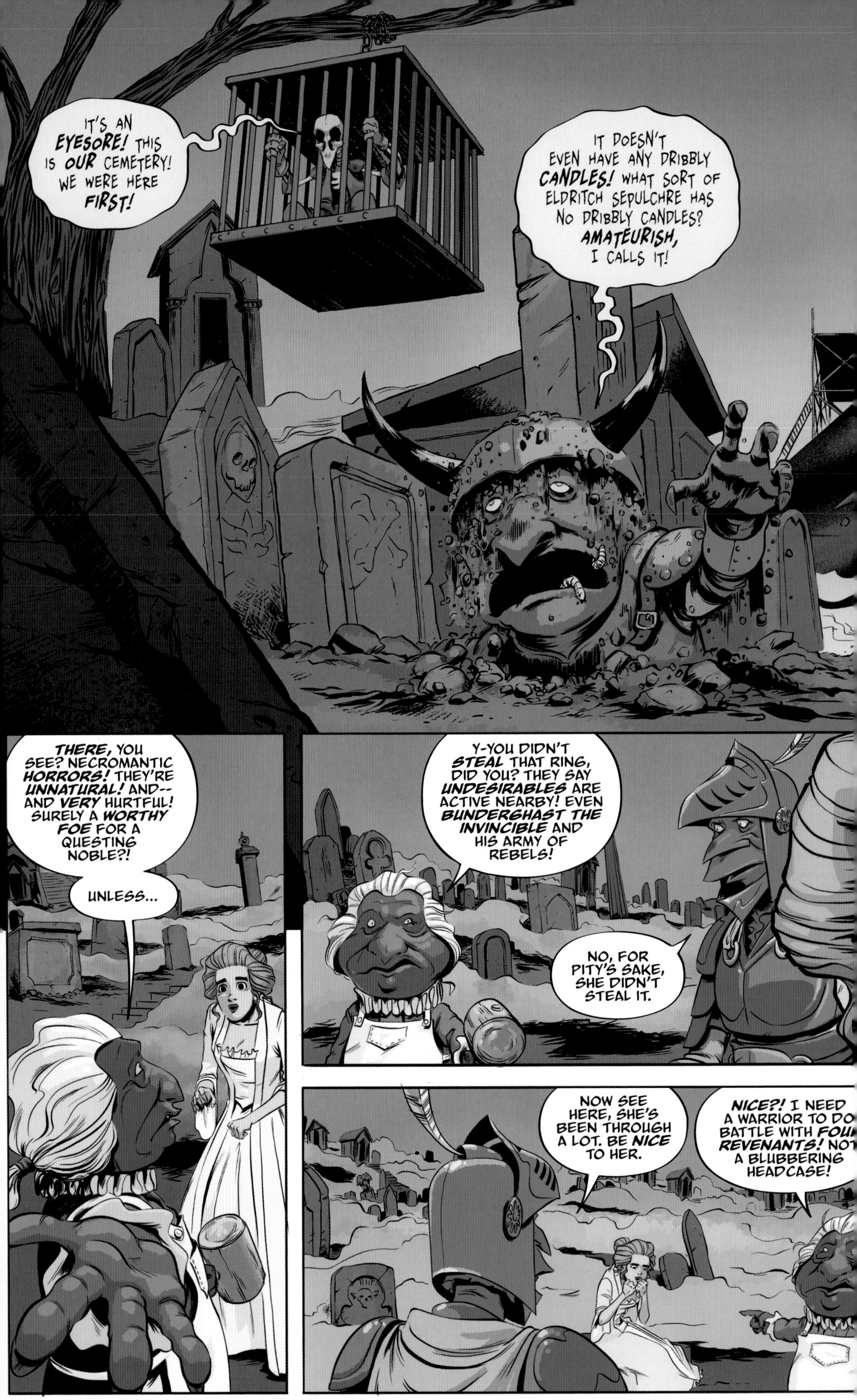

IT'S AN EYESORE! THIS IS OUR CEMETERY! WE WERE HERE FIRST!
IT DOESN'T EVEN HAVE ANY DRIBBLY CANDLES! WHAT SORT OF ELDRITCH SEPULCHRE HAS NO DRIBBLY CANDLES? AMATEURISH, I CALLS IT!
THERE, YOU SEE? NECROMANTIC HORRORS! THEY'RE UNNATURAL! AND--AND VERY HURTFUL! SURELY A WORTHY FOE FOR A QUESTING NOBLE?!
UNLESS...
Y-YOU DIDN'T STEAL THAT RING, DID YOU? THEY SAY UNDESIRABLES ARE ACTIVE NEARBY! EVEN BUNDERGHAST THE INVINCIBLE AND HIS ARMY OF REBELS!
NO, FOR PITY'S SAKE, SHE DIDN'T STEAL IT.
NOW SEE HERE, SHE'S BEEN THROUGH A LOT. BE NICE TO HER.
NICE?! I NEED A WARRIOR TO DO BATTLE WITH FOUR REVENANTS! NOT A BLUBBERING HEADCASE!

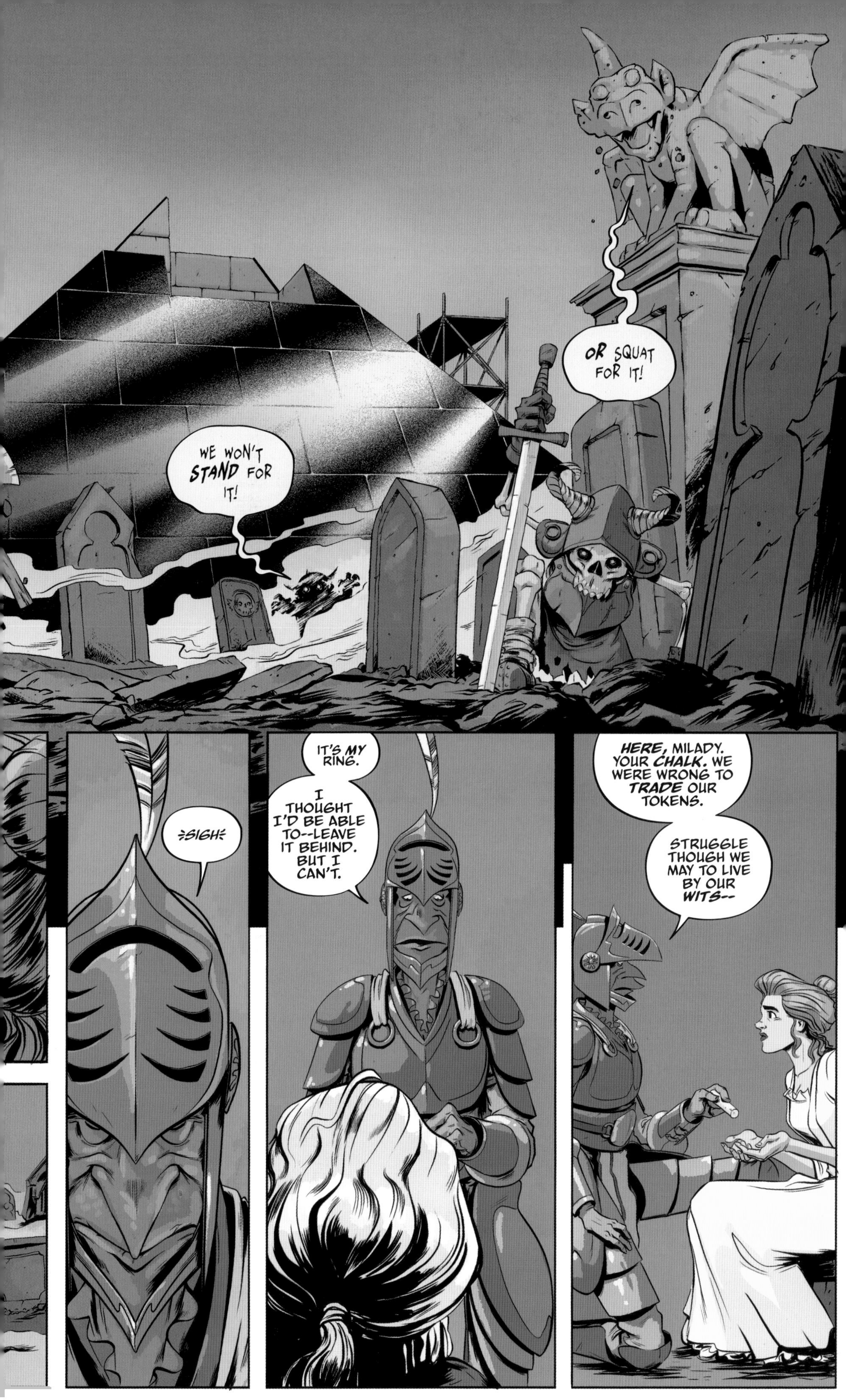
WE WON'T STAND FOR IT!
OR SQUAT FOR IT!
≈SIGH≈
IT'S MY RING.
I THOUGHT I'D BE ABLE TO--LEAVE IT BEHIND. BUT I CAN'T.
HERE, MILADY. YOUR CHALK. WE WERE WRONG TO TRADE OUR TOKENS.
STRUGGLE THOUGH WE MAY TO LIVE BY OUR WITS--

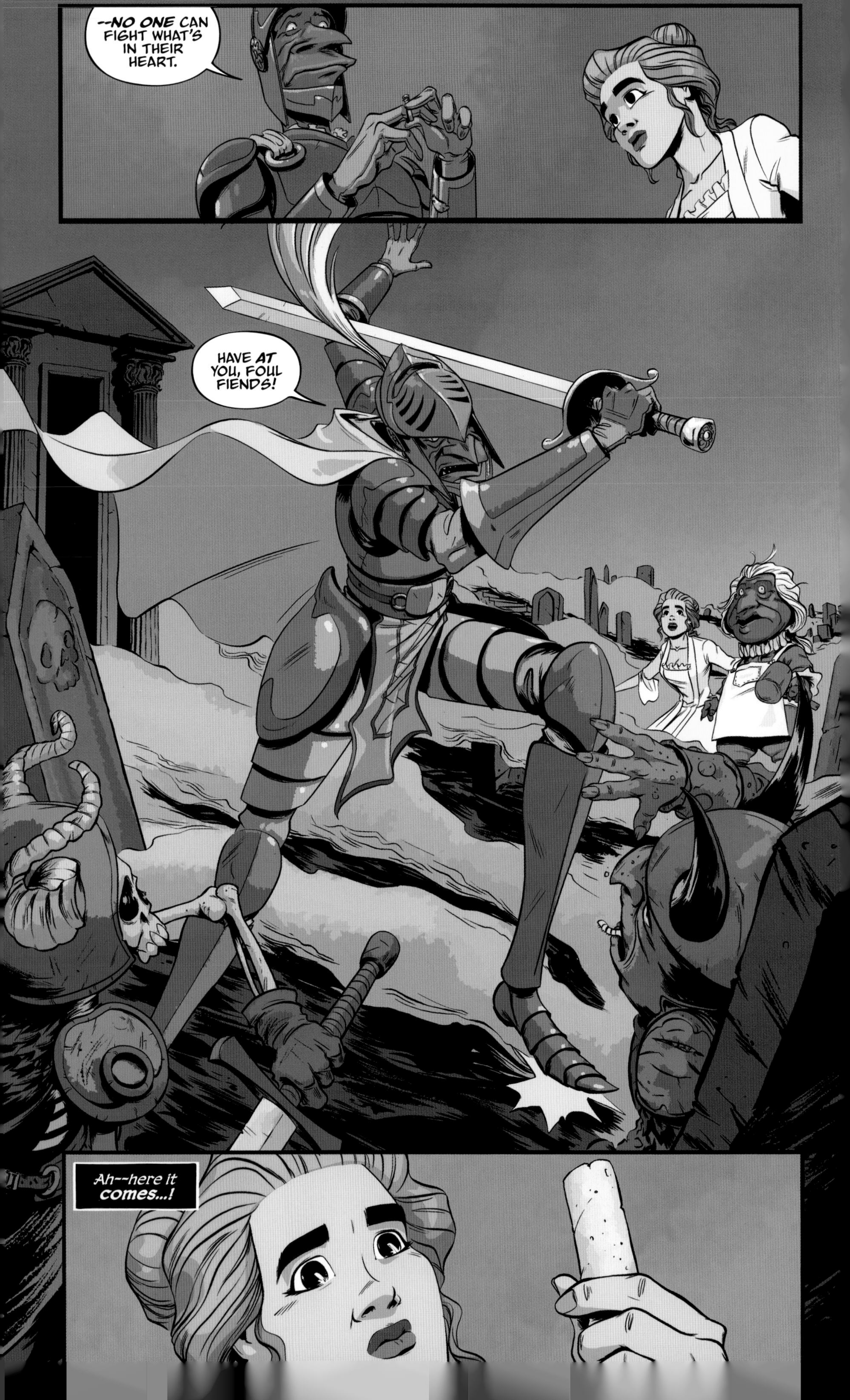
--NO ONE CAN FIGHT WHAT'S IN THEIR HEART.
HAVE AT YOU, FOUL FIENDS!
Ah--here it comes...!

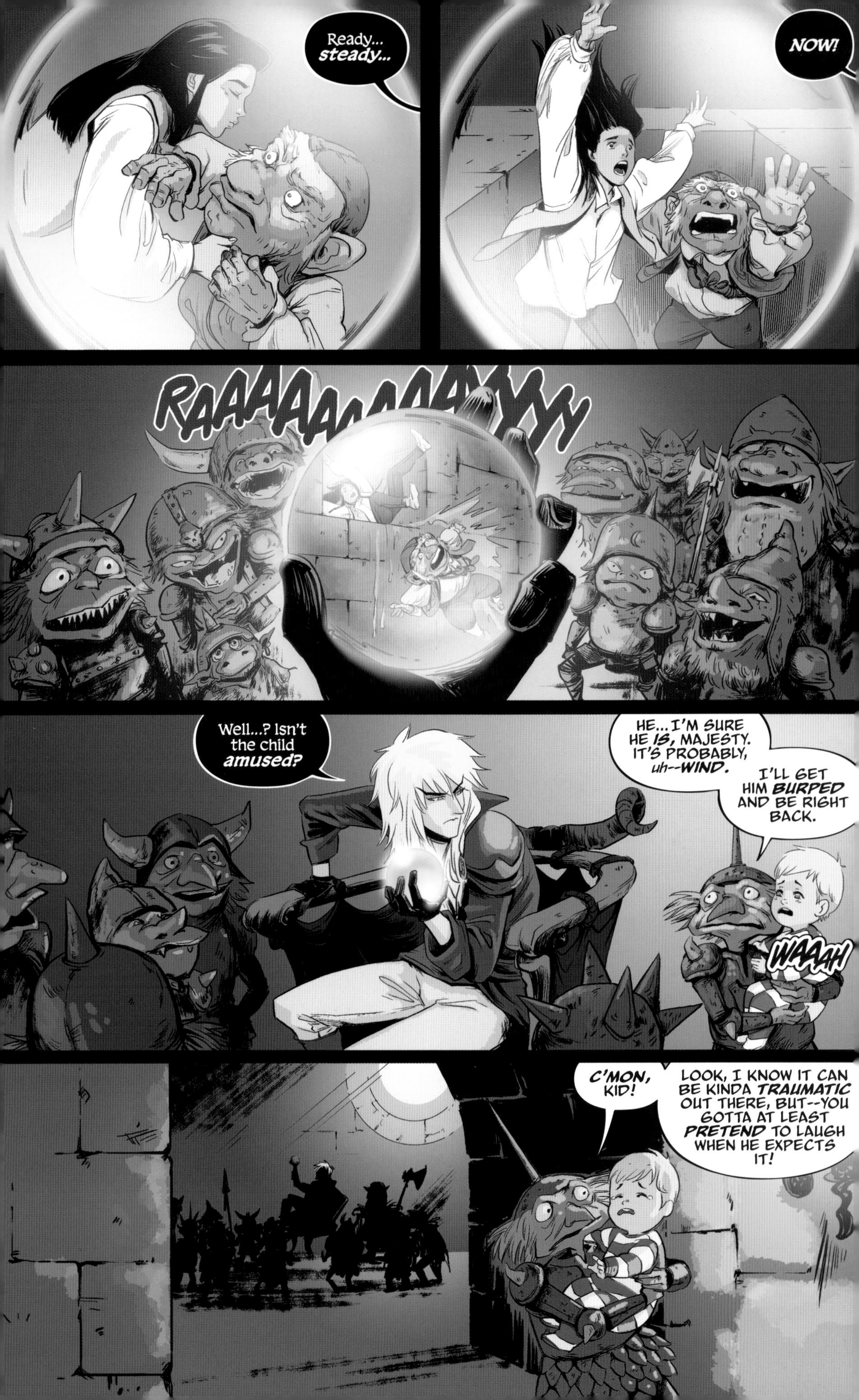
Ready... steady...
NOW!
RAAAAAAAAAYYY
Well...? Isn't the child amused?
HE... I'M SURE HE IS, MAJESTY. IT'S PROBABLY, uh--WIND.
I'LL GET HIM BURPED AND BE RIGHT BACK.
WAAAH
C'MON, KID!
LOOK, I KNOW IT CAN BE KINDA TRAUMATIC OUT THERE, BUT--YOU GOTTA AT LEAST PRETEND TO LAUGH WHEN HE EXPECTS IT!

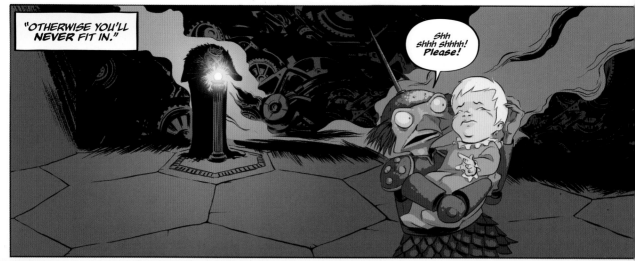

"OTHERWISE YOU'LL NEVER FIT IN."

Shh shhh shhhh! Please!

PRIDE... BITTERNESS... ANGER....

SHE *GNAWS* AT HER LOWLY STATION... SHE CANNOT THINK *STRAIGHT* WHEN SHE FEELS CONDESCENDED... SHE HAS SUCH *LOFTY* DREAMS...

Oh-- THAT POOR, *DOOMED* LITTLE MENIAL.

I THINK SHE STILL *LOVES* ME.

‡TT‡ LOVE.

Blp. Nnnp. Ww... wwww...

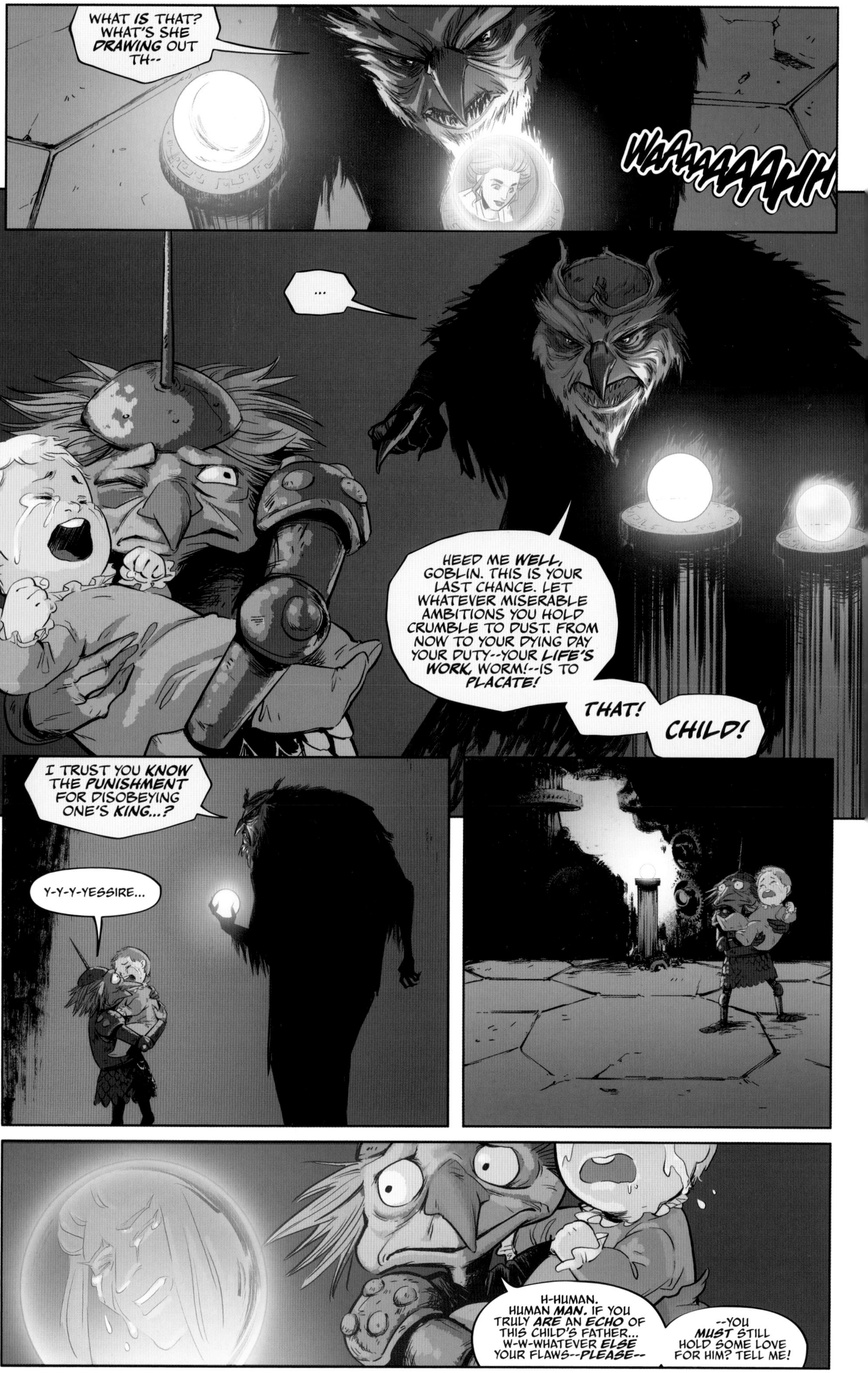

WHAT IS THAT? WHAT'S SHE DRAWING OUT TH--
WAAAAAAAAHH
...
HEED ME WELL, GOBLIN. THIS IS YOUR LAST CHANCE. LET WHATEVER MISERABLE AMBITIONS YOU HOLD CRUMBLE TO DUST. FROM NOW TO YOUR DYING DAY YOUR DUTY--YOUR LIFE'S WORK, WORM!--IS TO PLACATE!
THAT!
CHILD!
I TRUST YOU KNOW THE PUNISHMENT FOR DISOBEYING ONE'S KING...?
Y-Y-Y-YESSIRE...
H-HUMAN. HUMAN MAN. IF YOU TRULY ARE AN ECHO OF THIS CHILD'S FATHER... W-W-WHATEVER ELSE YOUR FLAWS--PLEASE--
--YOU MUST STILL HOLD SOME LOVE FOR HIM? TELL ME!

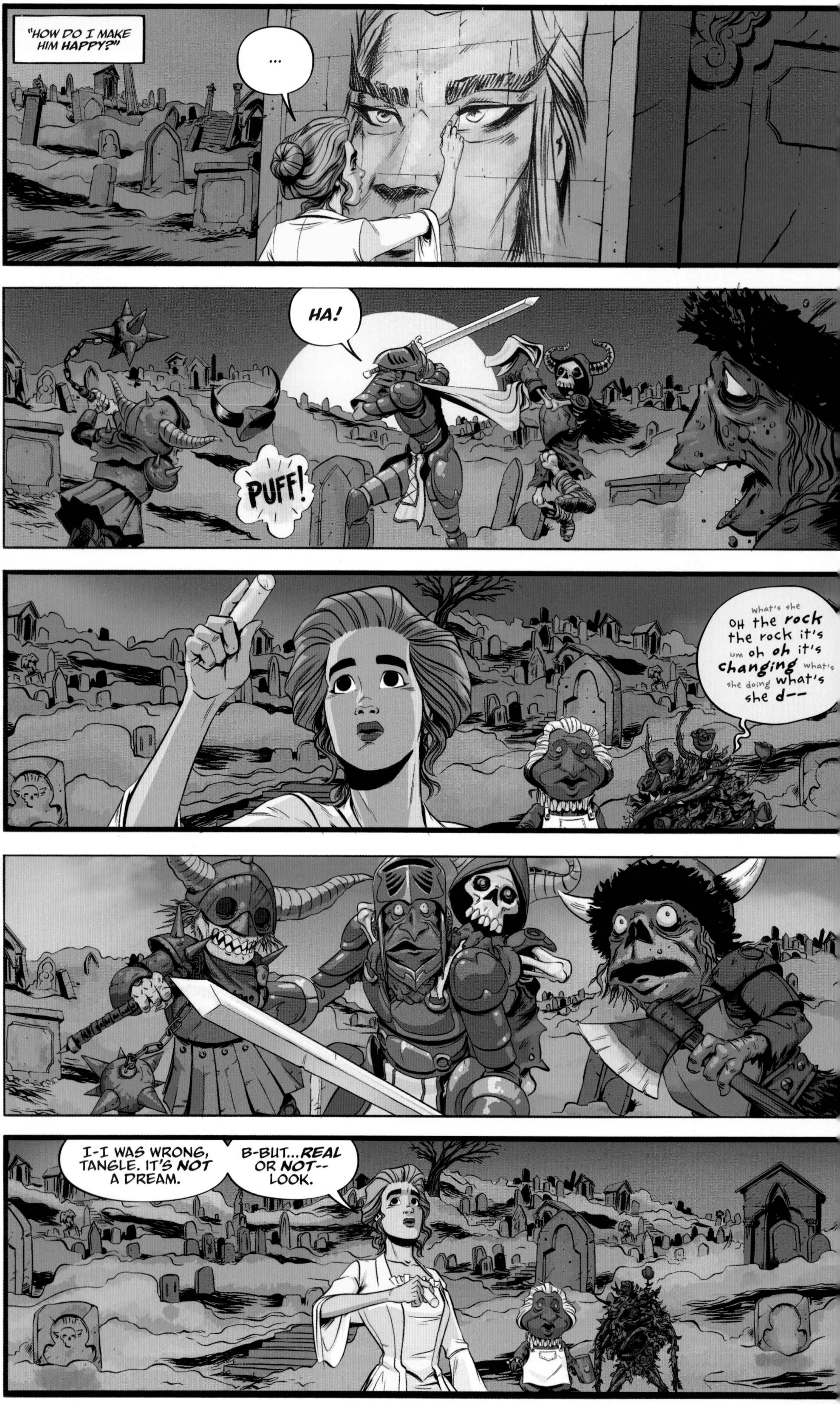
"HOW DO I MAKE HIM HAPPY?"
...
HA!
PUFF!
what's she oH the rock the rock it's um oh oh it's changing what's she doing what's she d--
I-I WAS WRONG, TANGLE. IT'S NOT A DREAM.
B-BUT...REAL OR NOT-- LOOK.

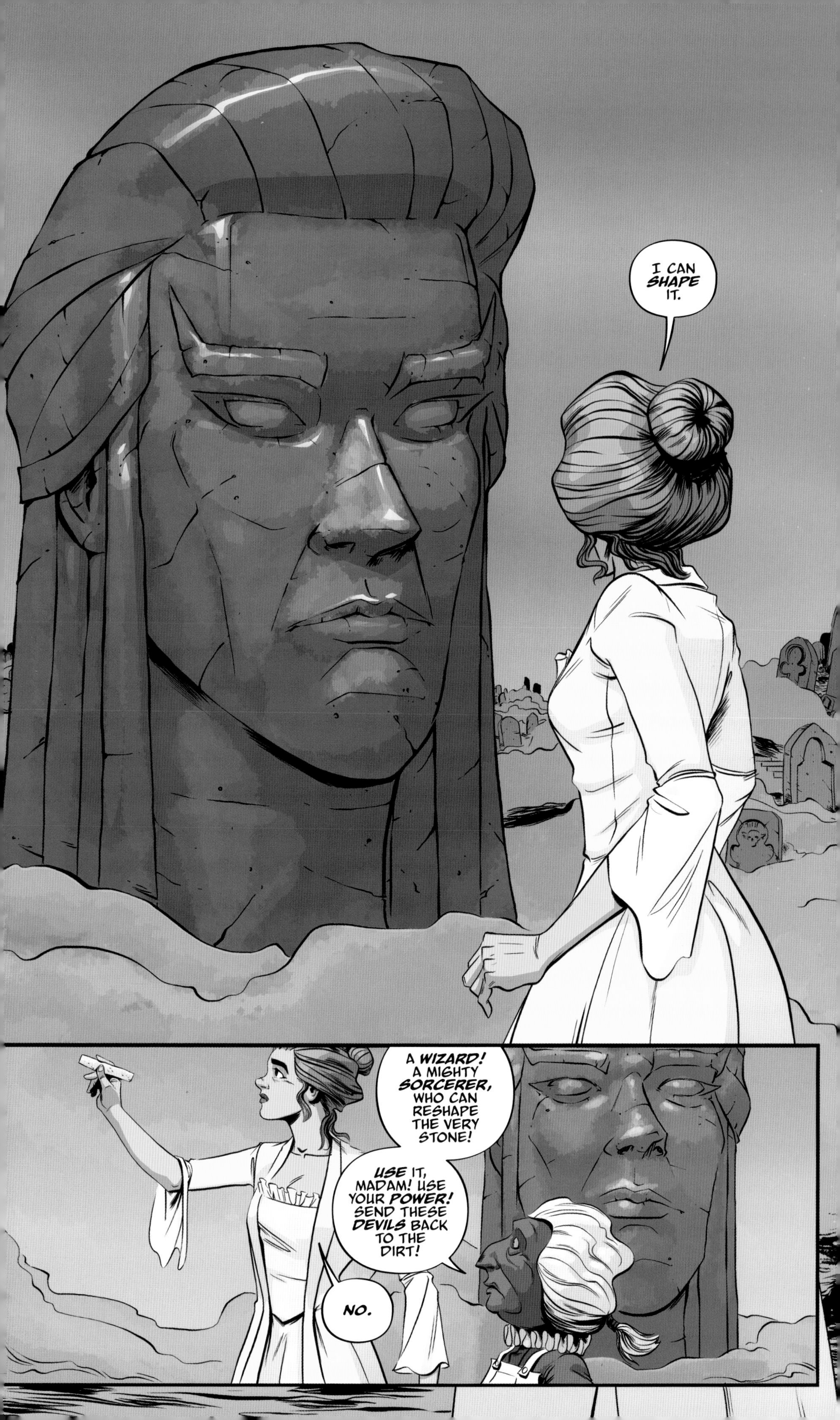
I CAN SHAPE IT.
A WIZARD! A MIGHTY SORCERER, WHO CAN RESHAPE THE VERY STONE!
USE IT, MADAM! USE YOUR POWER! SEND THESE DEVILS BACK TO THE DIRT!
NO.

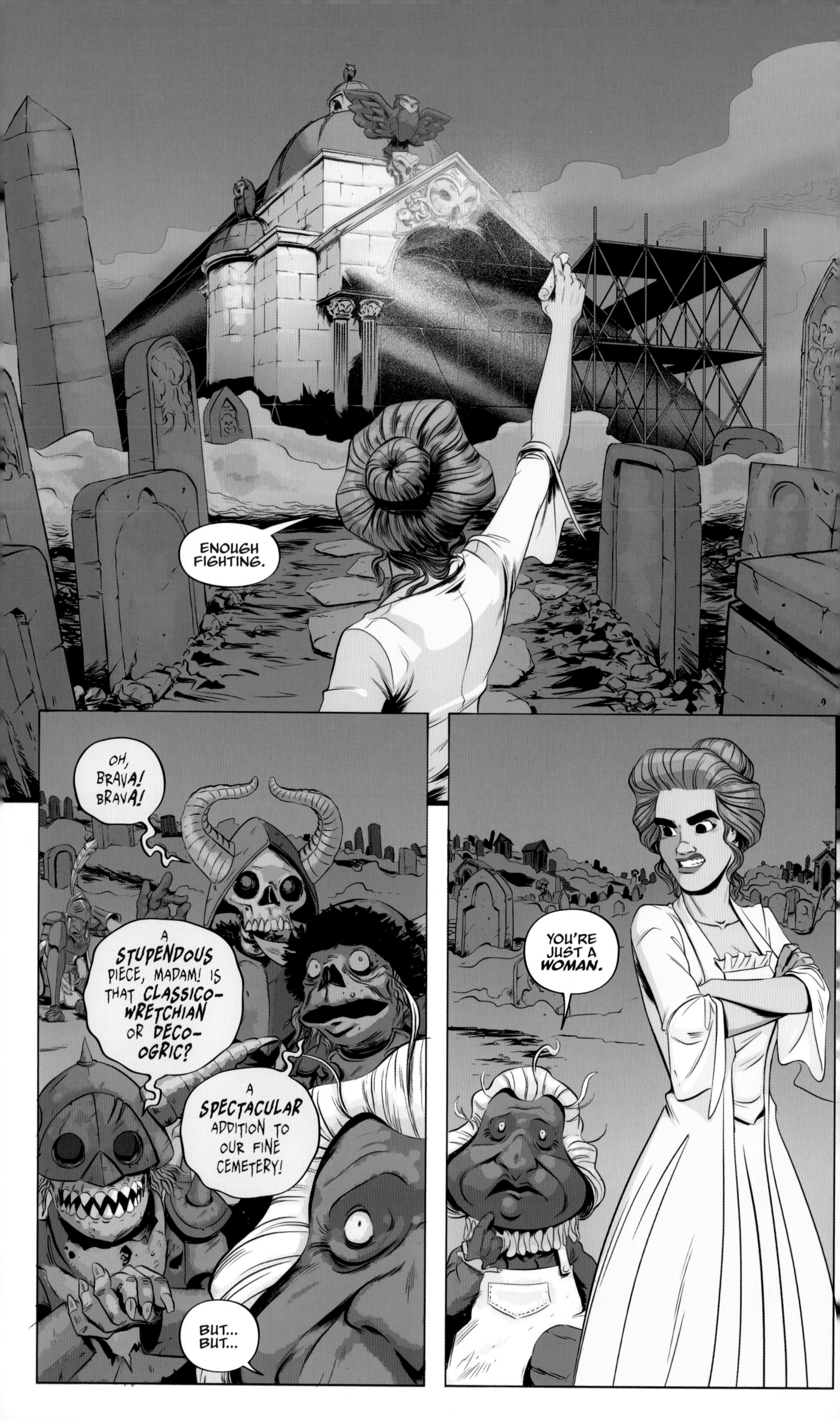

ENOUGH FIGHTING.
OH, BRAVA! BRAVA!
A STUPENDOUS PIECE, MADAM! IS THAT CLASSICO-WRETCHIAN OR DECO-OGRIC?
A SPECTACULAR ADDITION TO OUR FINE CEMETERY!
BUT... BUT...
YOU'RE JUST A WOMAN.

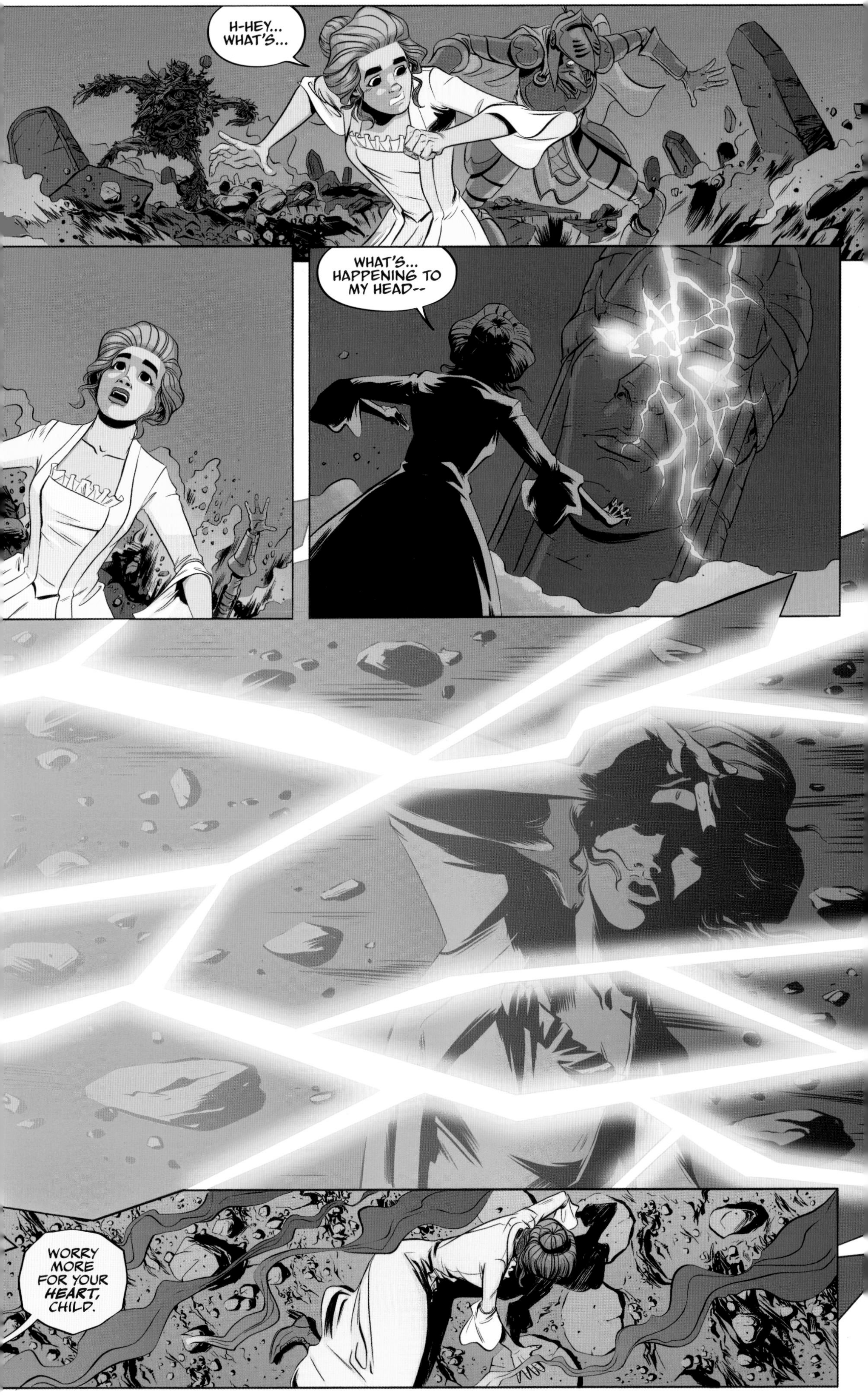
H-HEY... WHAT'S...
WHAT'S... HAPPENING TO MY HEAD--
WORRY MORE FOR YOUR HEART, CHILD.

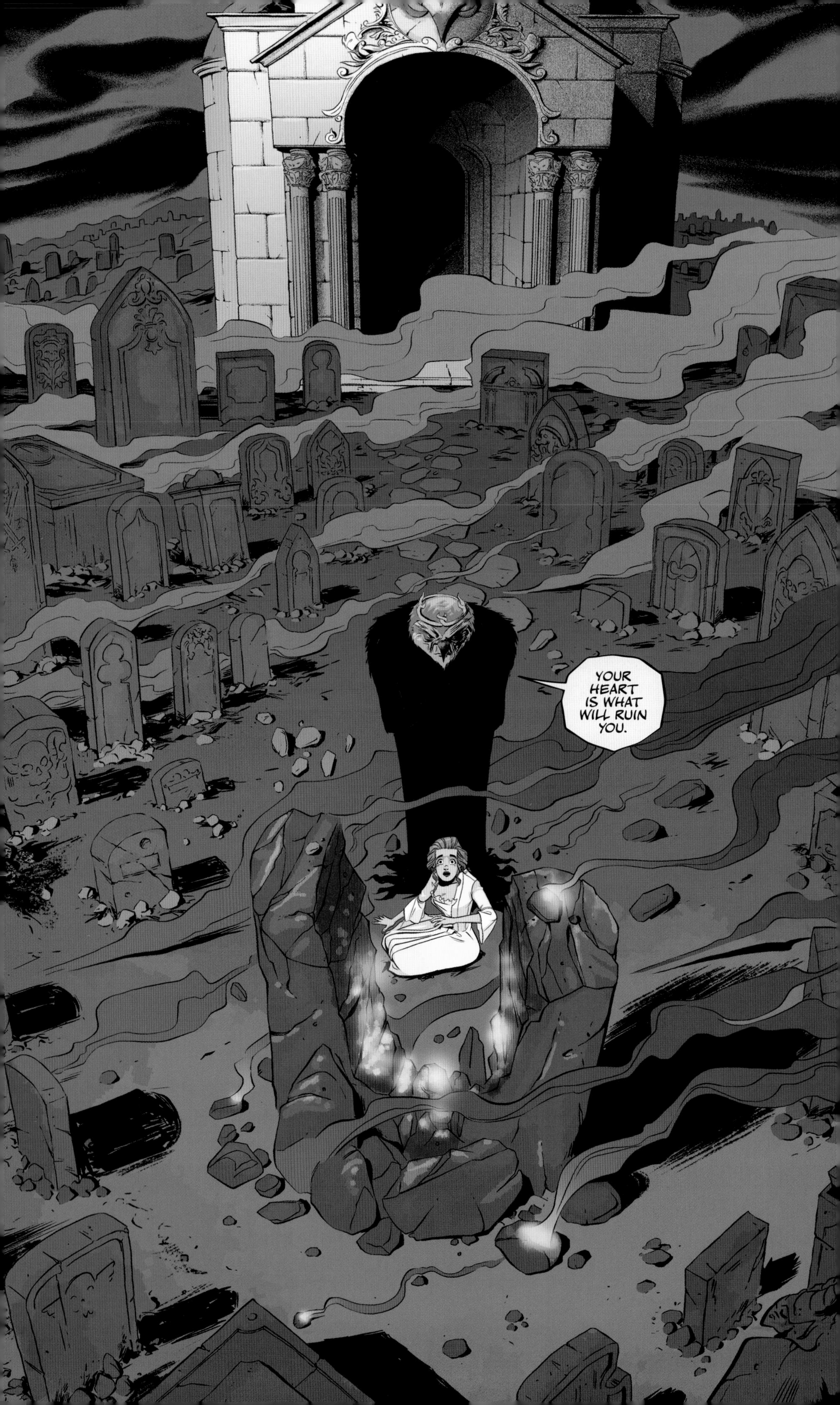
YOUR HEART IS WHAT WILL RUIN YOU.

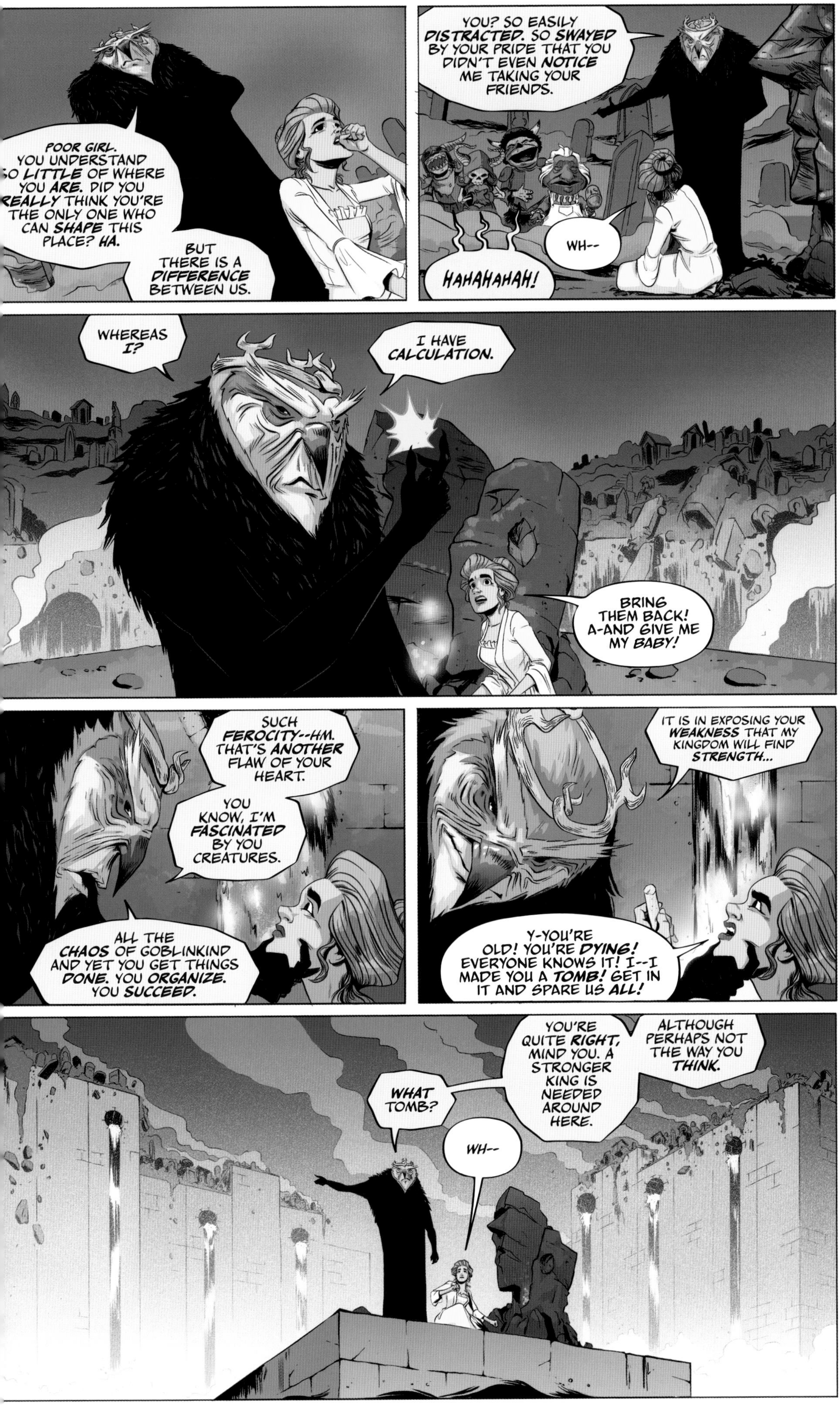

POOR GIRL. YOU UNDERSTAND SO LITTLE OF WHERE YOU ARE. DID YOU REALLY THINK YOU'RE THE ONLY ONE WHO CAN SHAPE THIS PLACE? HA.
BUT THERE IS A DIFFERENCE BETWEEN US.
YOU? SO EASILY DISTRACTED. SO SWAYED BY YOUR PRIDE THAT YOU DIDN'T EVEN NOTICE ME TAKING YOUR FRIENDS.
WH--
HAHAHAHAH!
WHEREAS I?
I HAVE CALCULATION.
BRING THEM BACK! A-AND GIVE ME MY BABY!
SUCH FEROCITY--HM. THAT'S ANOTHER FLAW OF YOUR HEART.
YOU KNOW, I'M FASCINATED BY YOU CREATURES.
ALL THE CHAOS OF GOBLINKIND AND YET YOU GET THINGS DONE. YOU ORGANIZE. YOU SUCCEED.
IT IS IN EXPOSING YOUR WEAKNESS THAT MY KINGDOM WILL FIND STRENGTH...
Y-YOU'RE OLD! YOU'RE DYING! EVERYONE KNOWS IT! I--I MADE YOU A TOMB! GET IN IT AND SPARE US ALL!
WHAT TOMB?
YOU'RE QUITE RIGHT, MIND YOU. A STRONGER KING IS NEEDED AROUND HERE.
ALTHOUGH PERHAPS NOT THE WAY YOU THINK.
WH--

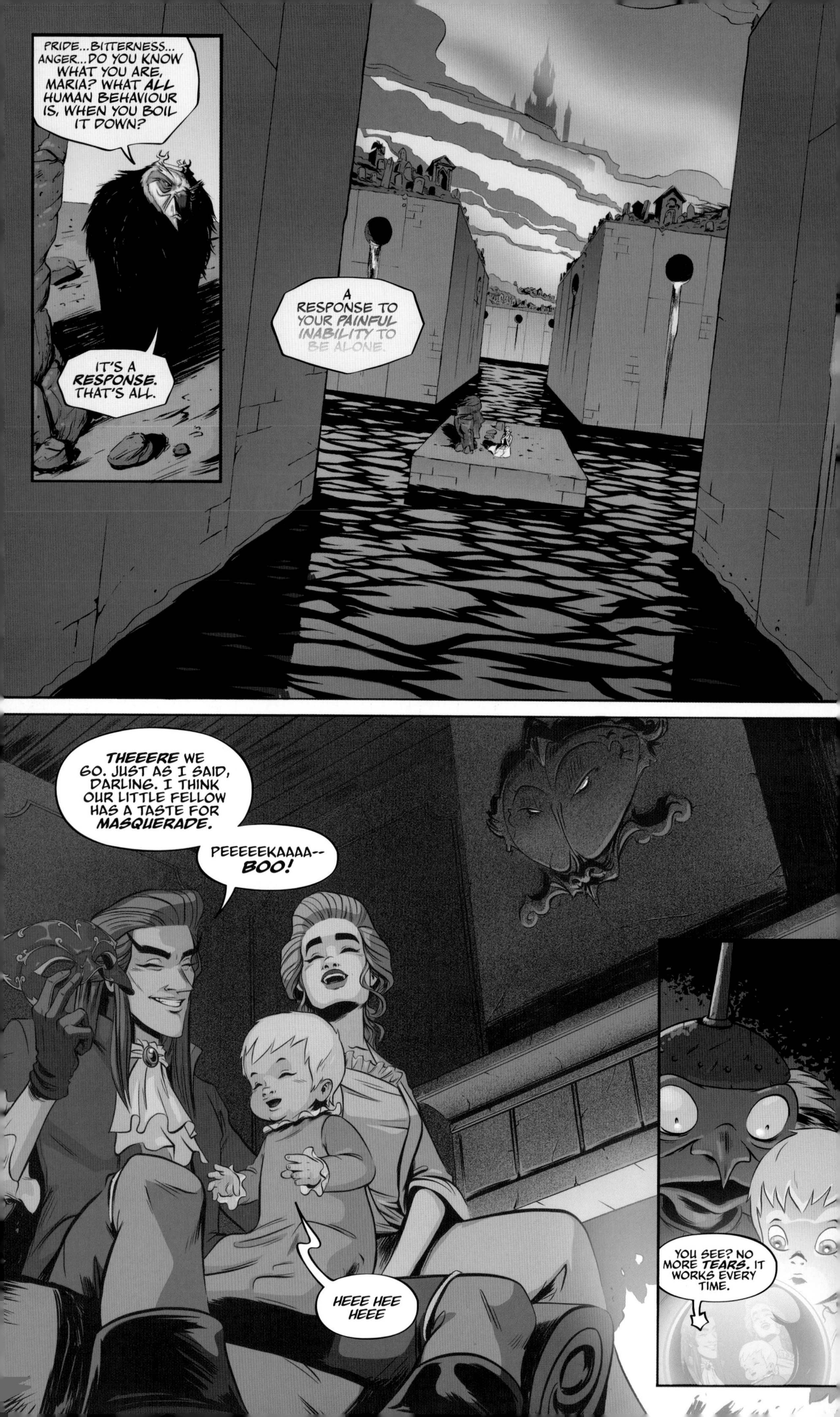
PRIDE...BITTERNESS... ANGER...DO YOU KNOW WHAT YOU ARE, MARIA? WHAT ALL HUMAN BEHAVIOUR IS, WHEN YOU BOIL IT DOWN?
IT'S A RESPONSE. THAT'S ALL.
A RESPONSE TO YOUR PAINFUL INABILITY TO BE ALONE.
THEEERE WE GO. JUST AS I SAID, DARLING. I THINK OUR LITTLE FELLOW HAS A TASTE FOR MASQUERADE.
PEEEEEKAAAA-- BOO!
HEEE HEE HEEE
YOU SEE? NO MORE TEARS. IT WORKS EVERY TIME.

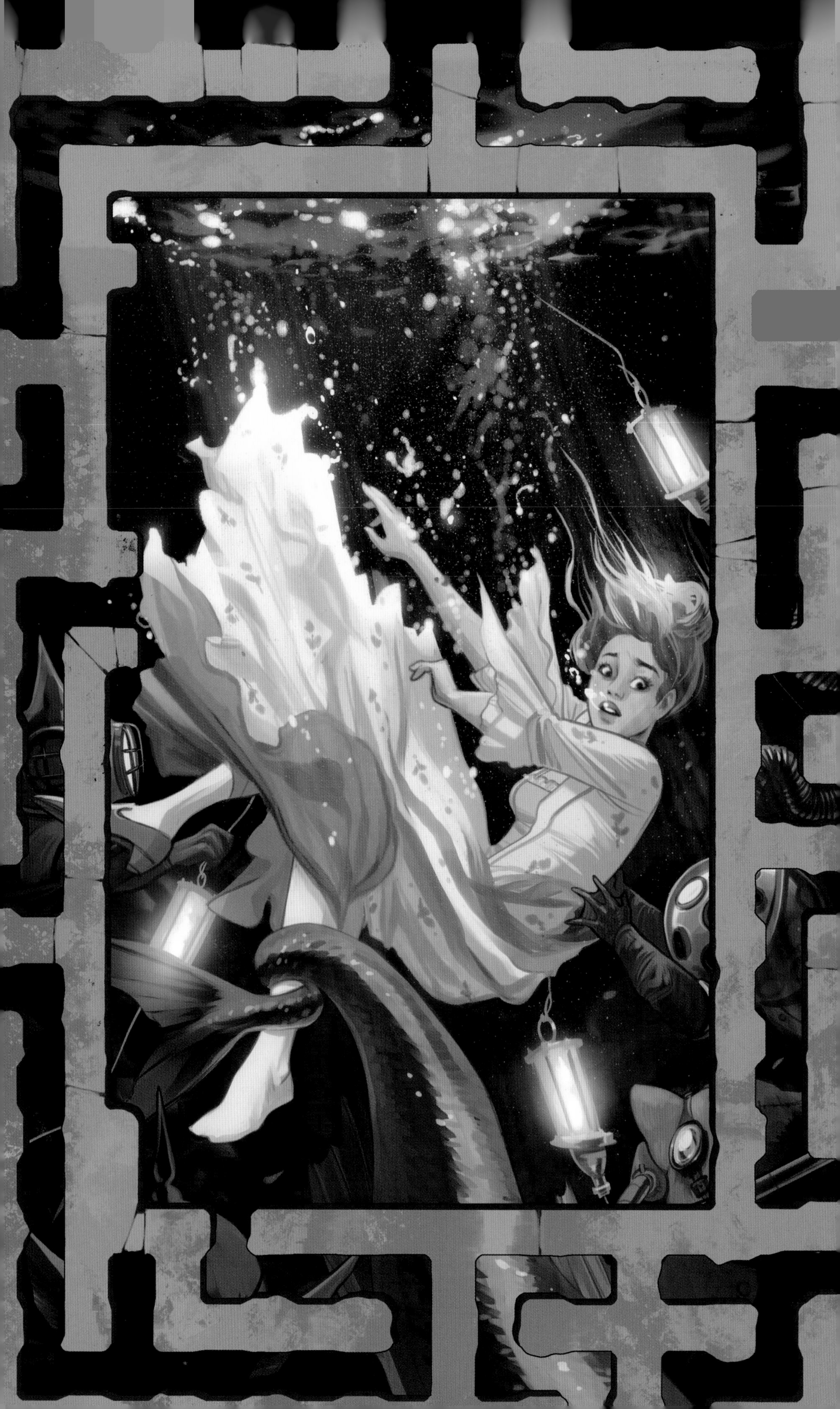

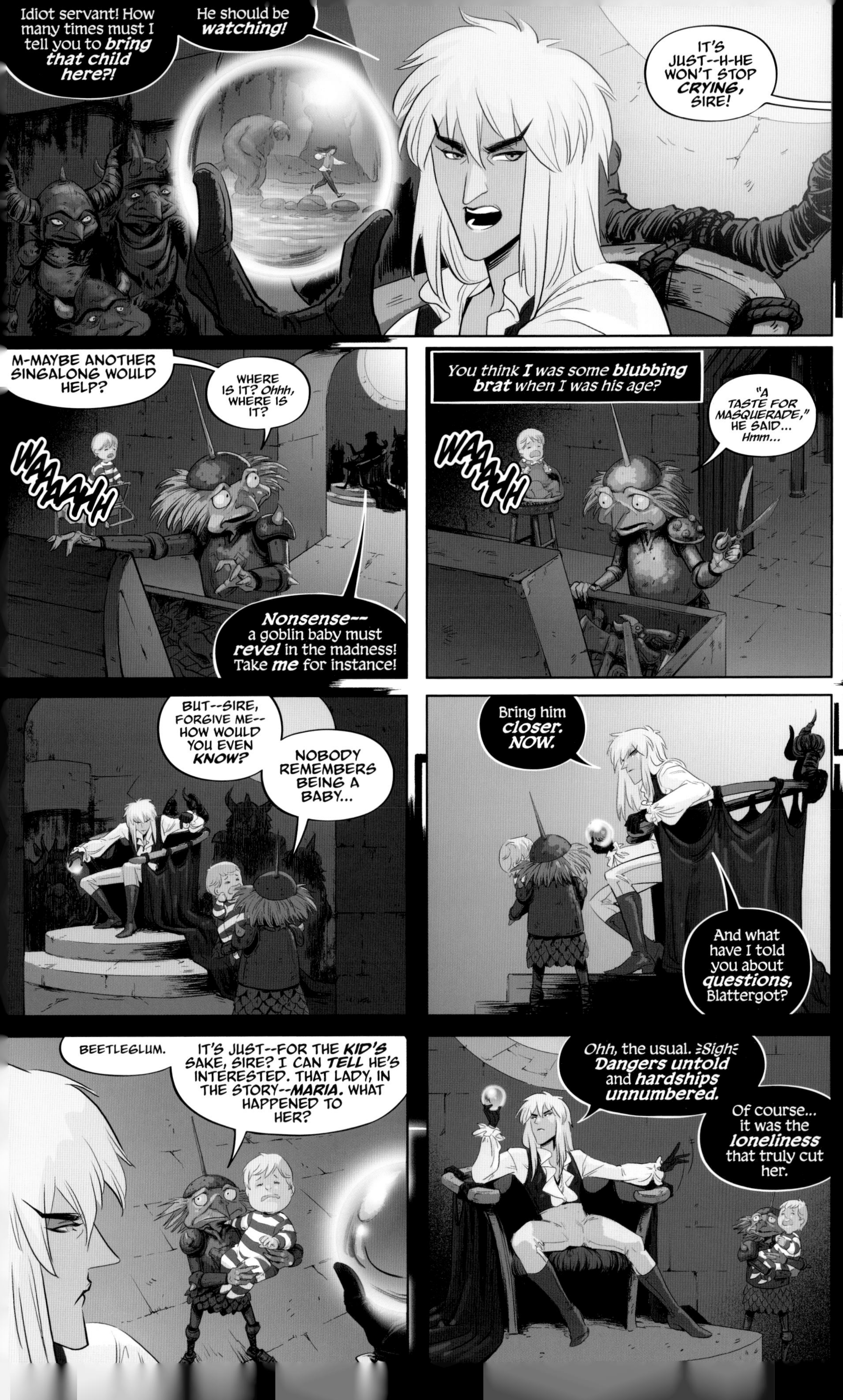

Idiot servant! How many times must I tell you to bring that child here?!
He should be watching!
IT'S JUST--H-HE WON'T STOP CRYING, SIRE!
M-MAYBE ANOTHER SINGALONG WOULD HELP?
WHERE IS IT? Ohhh, WHERE IS IT?
WAAAAHH
Nonsense-- a goblin baby must revel in the madness! Take me for instance!
You think I was some blubbing brat when I was his age?
WAAAAHH
"A TASTE FOR MASQUERADE," HE SAID... Hmm...
BUT--SIRE, FORGIVE ME-- HOW WOULD YOU EVEN KNOW?
NOBODY REMEMBERS BEING A BABY...
Bring him closer. NOW.
And what have I told you about questions, Blattergot?
BEETLEGLUM.
IT'S JUST--FOR THE KID'S SAKE, SIRE? I CAN TELL HE'S INTERESTED. THAT LADY, IN THE STORY--MARIA. WHAT HAPPENED TO HER?
Ohh, the usual. Sigh Dangers untold and hardships unnumbered.
Of course... it was the loneliness that truly cut her.

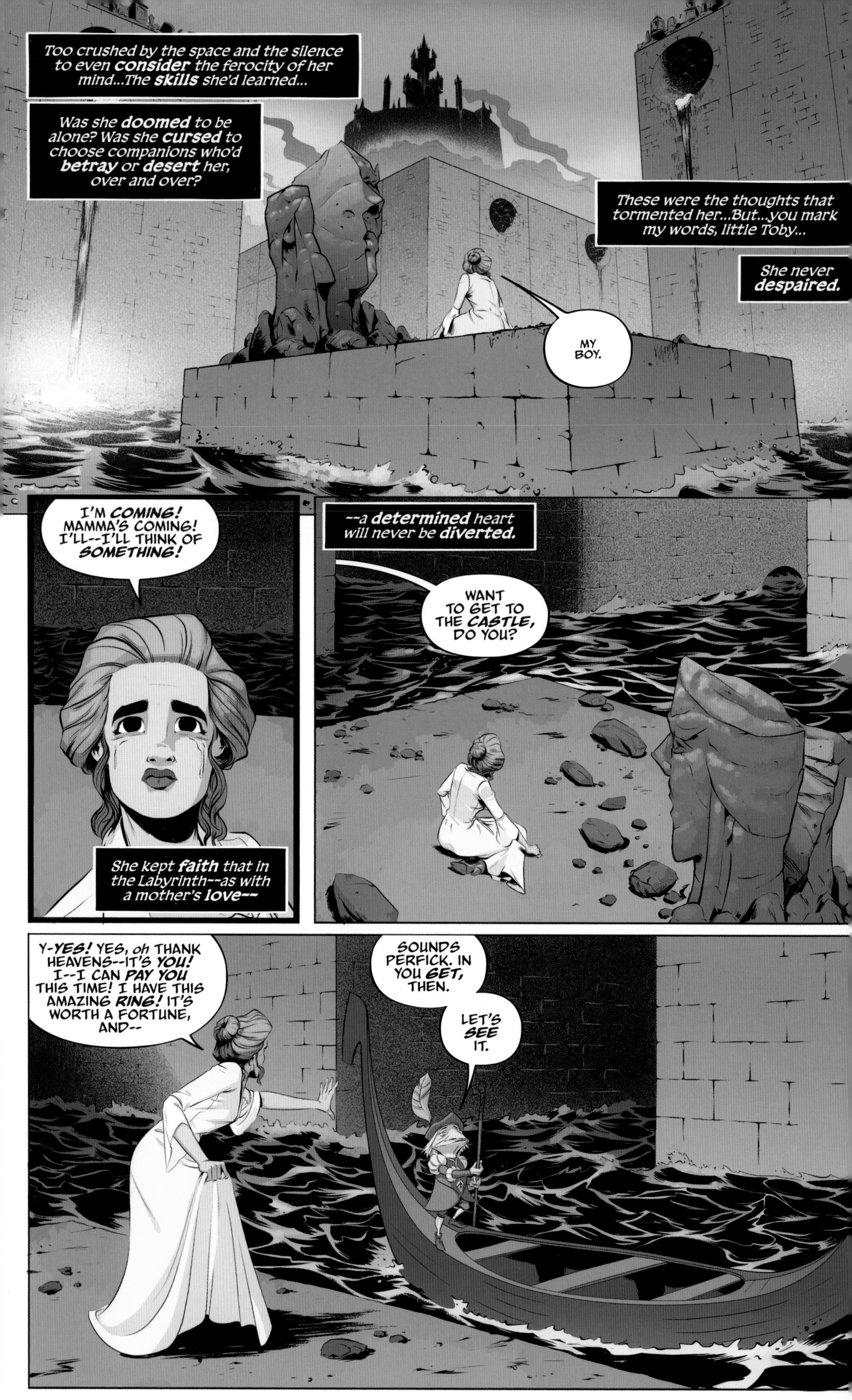

Too crushed by the space and the silence to even **consider** the ferocity of her mind...The **skills** she'd learned...
Was she **doomed** to be alone? Was she **cursed** to choose companions who'd **betray** or **desert** her, over and over?
These were the thoughts that tormented her...But...you mark my words, little Toby...
She never **despaired.**
MY BOY.
I'M **COMING!** MAMMA'S COMING! I'LL--I'LL THINK OF **SOMETHING!**
She kept **faith** that in the Labyrinth--as with a mother's **love**--
--a **determined** heart will never be **diverted.**
WANT TO GET TO THE **CASTLE,** DO YOU?
Y-**YES!** YES, *oh* THANK HEAVENS--IT'S **YOU!** I--I CAN **PAY YOU** THIS TIME! I HAVE THIS AMAZING **RING!** IT'S WORTH A FORTUNE, AND--
SOUNDS PERFICK. IN YOU **GET,** THEN.
LET'S **SEE** IT.

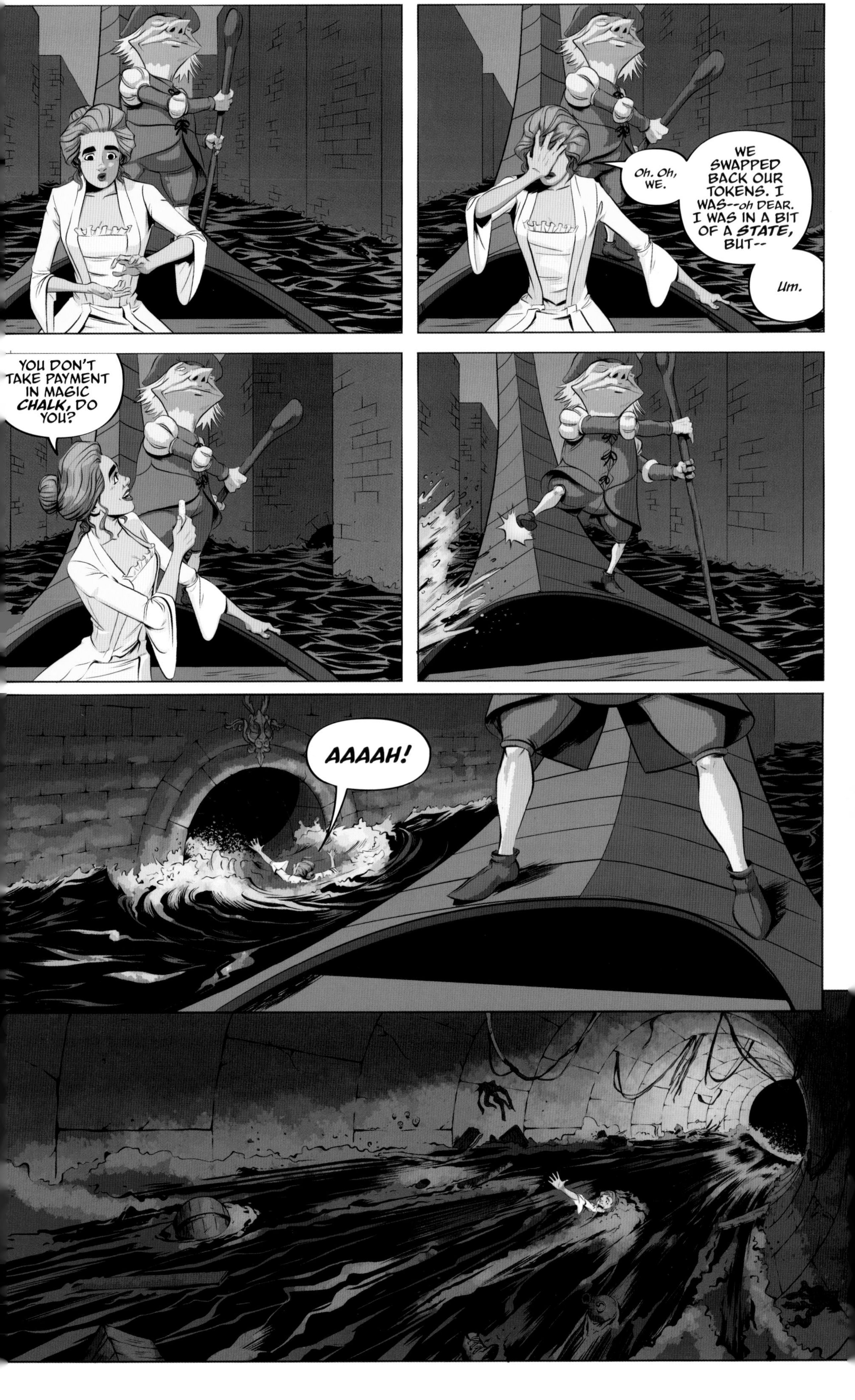
Oh. Oh, WE.
WE SWAPPED BACK OUR TOKENS. I WAS--oh DEAR. I WAS IN A BIT OF A STATE, BUT--
Um.
YOU DON'T TAKE PAYMENT IN MAGIC CHALK, DO YOU?
AAAAH!

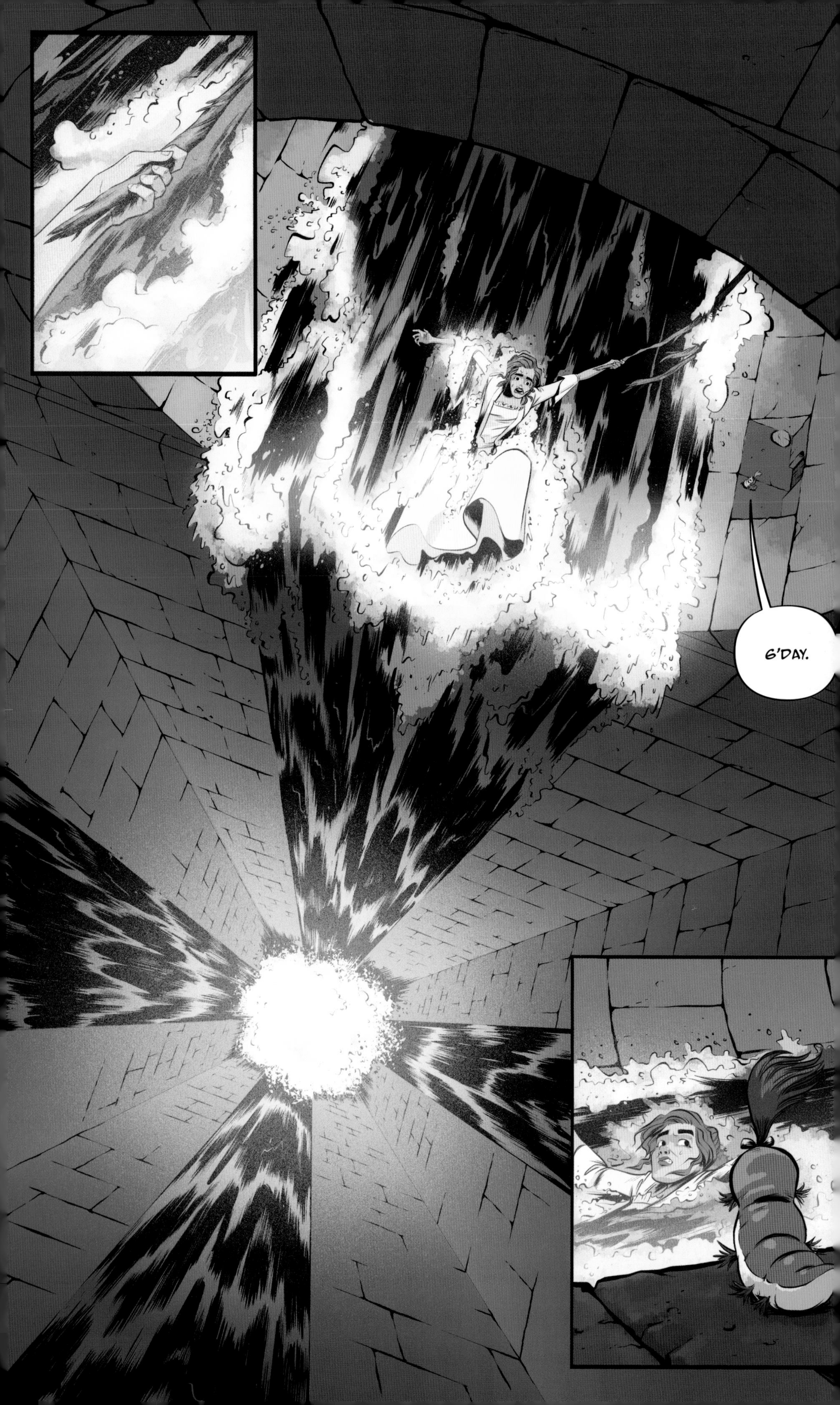
G'DAY.

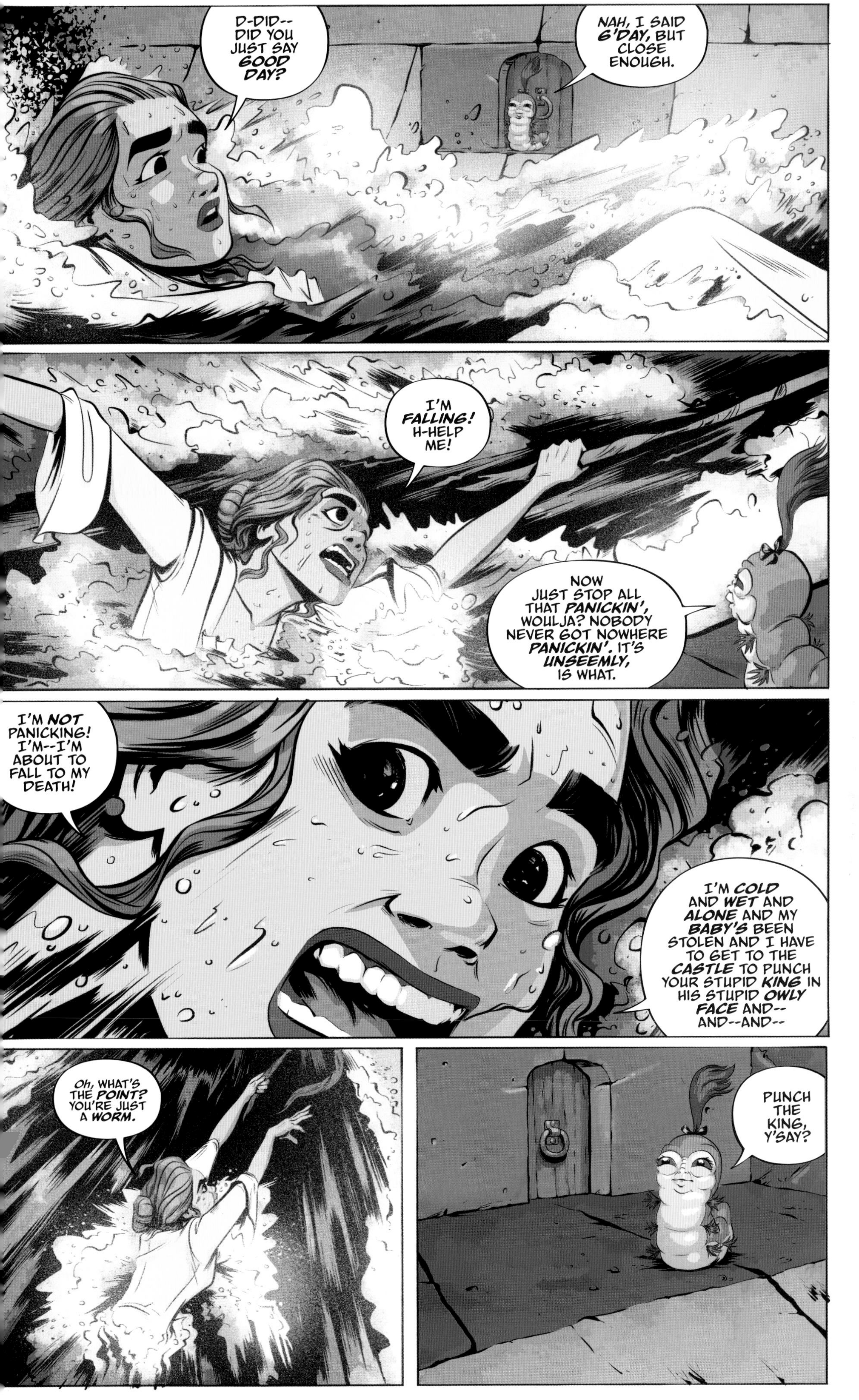
D-DID-- DID YOU JUST SAY GOOD DAY?
NAH, I SAID G'DAY, BUT CLOSE ENOUGH.
I'M FALLING! H-HELP ME!
NOW JUST STOP ALL THAT PANICKIN', WOULJA? NOBODY NEVER GOT NOWHERE PANICKIN'. IT'S UNSEEMLY, IS WHAT.
I'M NOT PANICKING! I'M--I'M ABOUT TO FALL TO MY DEATH!
I'M COLD AND WET AND ALONE AND MY BABY'S BEEN STOLEN AND I HAVE TO GET TO THE CASTLE TO PUNCH YOUR STUPID KING IN HIS STUPID OWLY FACE AND-- AND--AND--
Oh, WHAT'S THE POINT? YOU'RE JUST A WORM.
PUNCH THE KING, Y'SAY?

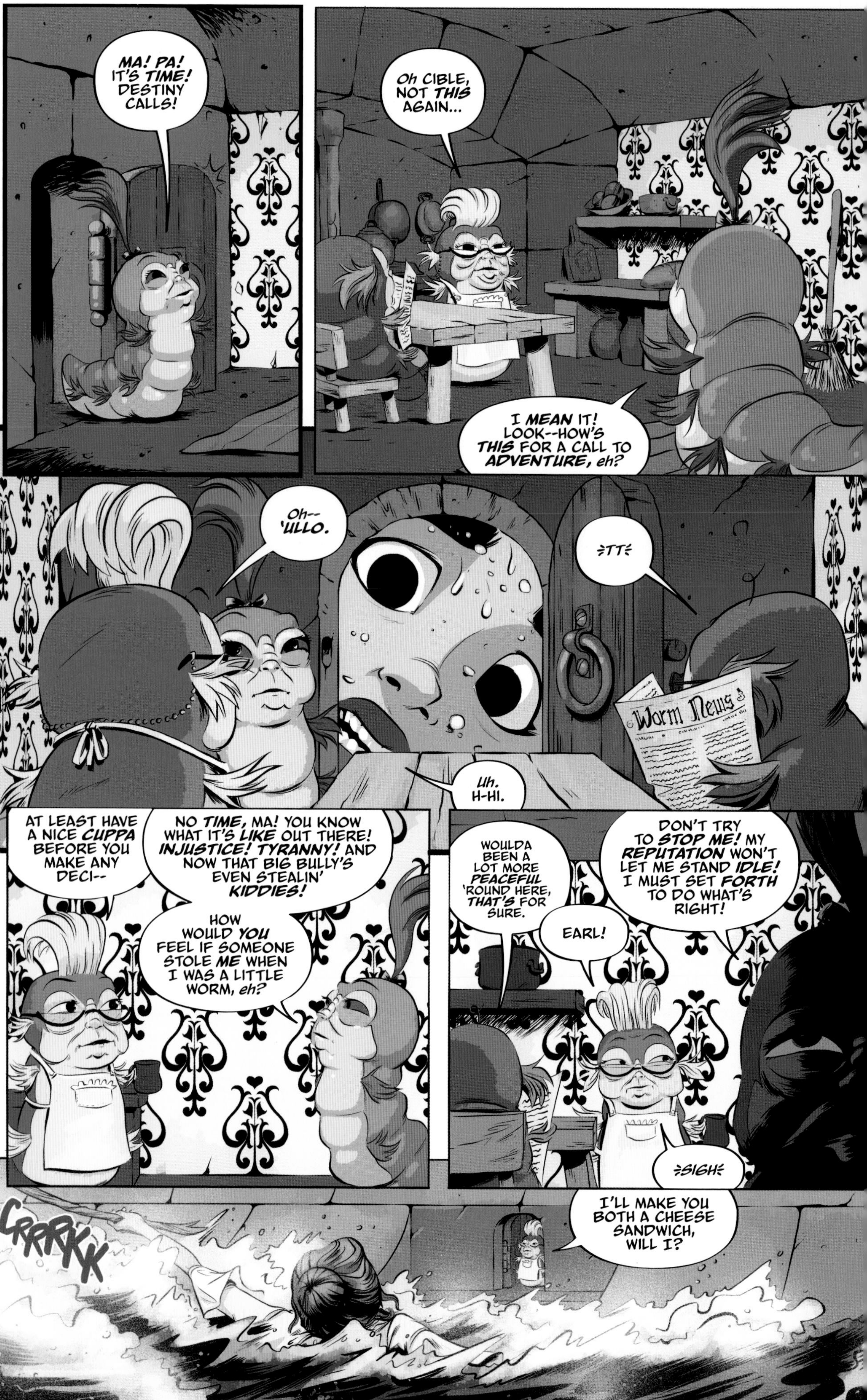
MA! PA! IT'S TIME! DESTINY CALLS!
Oh CIBLE, NOT THIS AGAIN...
I MEAN IT! LOOK--HOW'S THIS FOR A CALL TO ADVENTURE, eh?
Oh-- 'ULLO.
TT
Worm News
UH. H-HI.
AT LEAST HAVE A NICE CUPPA BEFORE YOU MAKE ANY DECI--
NO TIME, MA! YOU KNOW WHAT IT'S LIKE OUT THERE! INJUSTICE! TYRANNY! AND NOW THAT BIG BULLY'S EVEN STEALIN' KIDDIES!
HOW WOULD YOU FEEL IF SOMEONE STOLE ME WHEN I WAS A LITTLE WORM, eh?
WOULDA BEEN A LOT MORE PEACEFUL 'ROUND HERE, THAT'S FOR SURE.
DON'T TRY TO STOP ME! MY REPUTATION WON'T LET ME STAND IDLE! I MUST SET FORTH TO DO WHAT'S RIGHT!
EARL!
SIGH
CRRRKKK
I'LL MAKE YOU BOTH A CHEESE SANDWICH, WILL I?

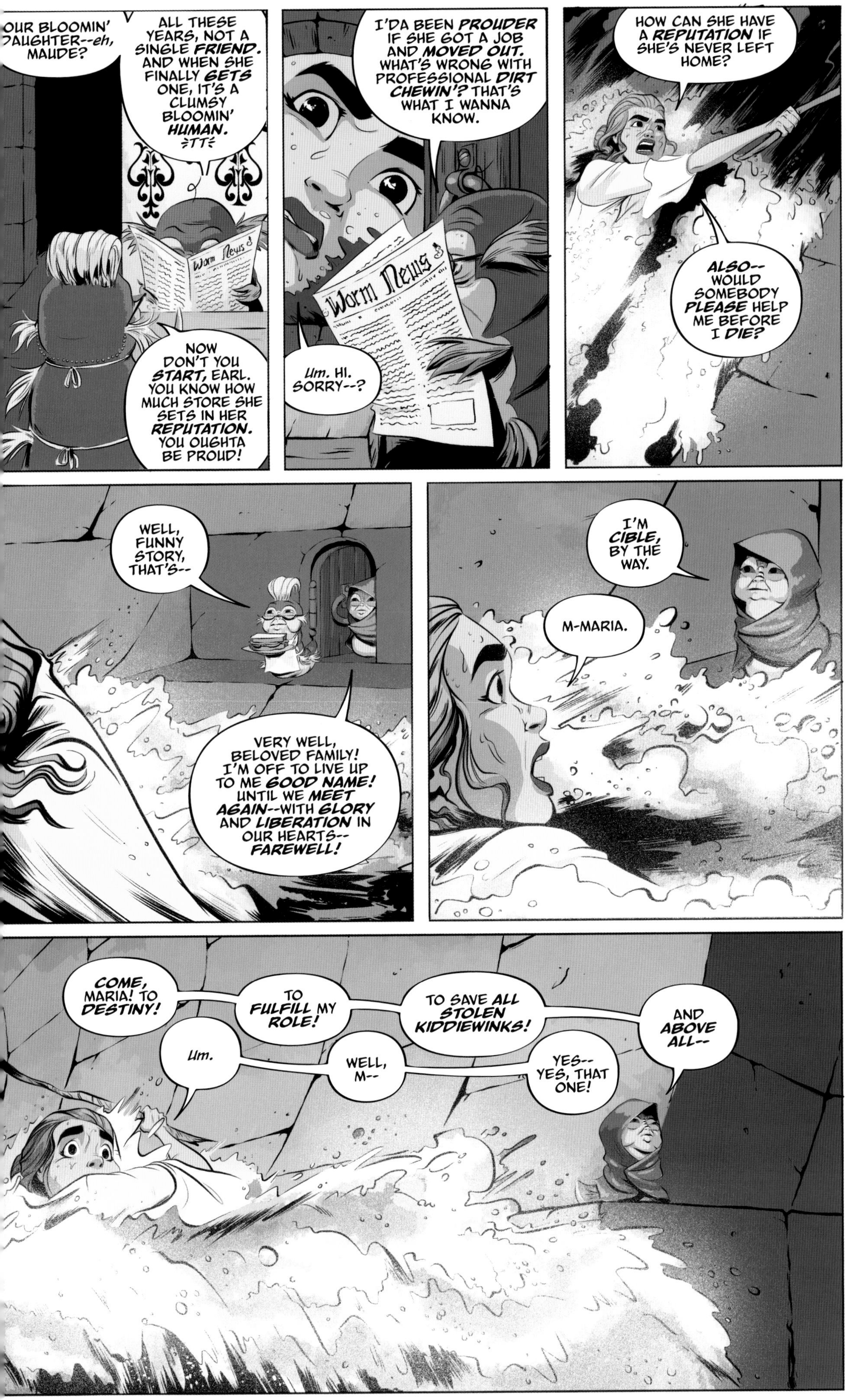

OUR BLOOMIN' DAUGHTER--eh, MAUDE?
ALL THESE YEARS, NOT A SINGLE FRIEND. AND WHEN SHE FINALLY GETS ONE, IT'S A CLUMSY BLOOMIN' HUMAN. TT
Worm News
NOW DON'T YOU START, EARL. YOU KNOW HOW MUCH STORE SHE SETS IN HER REPUTATION. YOU OUGHTA BE PROUD!
I'DA BEEN PROUDER IF SHE GOT A JOB AND MOVED OUT. WHAT'S WRONG WITH PROFESSIONAL DIRT CHEWIN'? THAT'S WHAT I WANNA KNOW.
Worm News
Um. HI. SORRY--?
HOW CAN SHE HAVE A REPUTATION IF SHE'S NEVER LEFT HOME?
ALSO-- WOULD SOMEBODY PLEASE HELP ME BEFORE I DIE?
WELL, FUNNY STORY, THAT'S--
VERY WELL, BELOVED FAMILY! I'M OFF TO LIVE UP TO ME GOOD NAME! UNTIL WE MEET AGAIN--WITH GLORY AND LIBERATION IN OUR HEARTS-- FAREWELL!
I'M CIBLE, BY THE WAY.
M-MARIA.
COME, MARIA! TO DESTINY!
Um.
TO FULFILL MY ROLE!
WELL, M--
TO SAVE ALL STOLEN KIDDIEWINKS!
YES-- YES, THAT ONE!
AND ABOVE ALL--

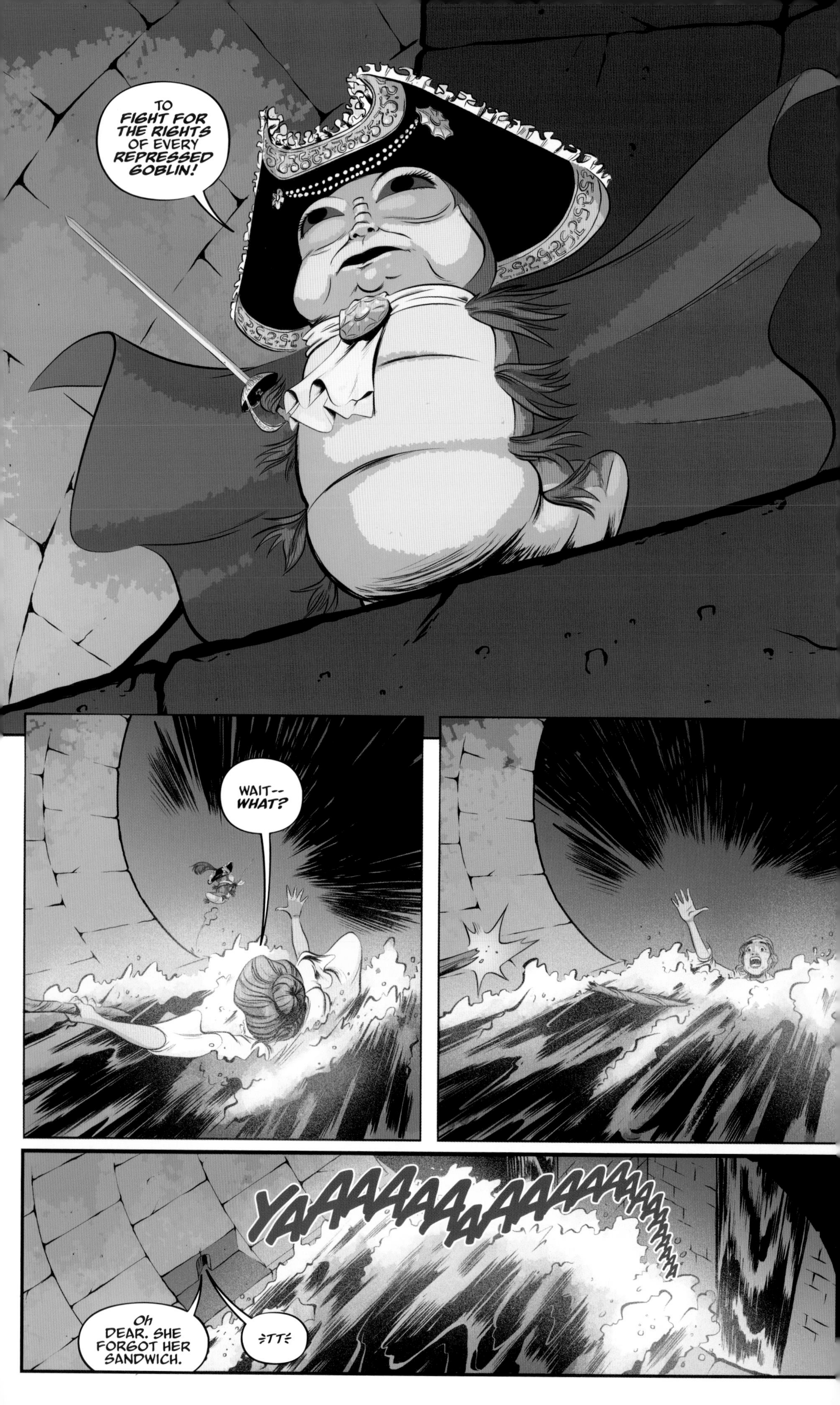
TO FIGHT FOR THE RIGHTS OF EVERY REPRESSED GOBLIN!
WAIT-- WHAT?
YAAAAAAAAAAAAAAAAAAAAA
Oh DEAR. SHE FORGOT HER SANDWICH.
TT

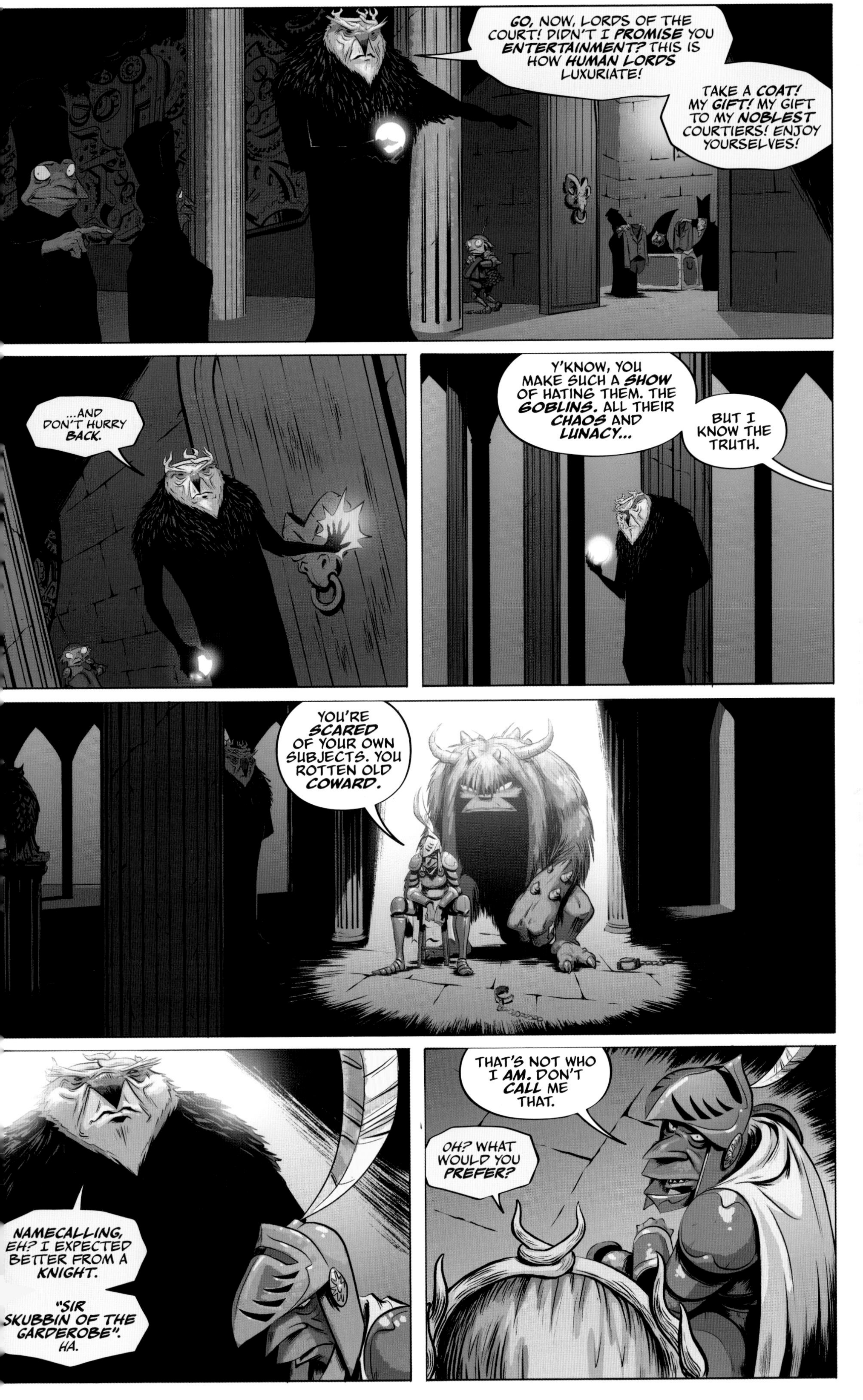

GO, NOW, LORDS OF THE COURT! DIDN'T I PROMISE YOU ENTERTAINMENT? THIS IS HOW HUMAN LORDS LUXURIATE!
TAKE A COAT! MY GIFT! MY GIFT TO MY NOBLEST COURTIERS! ENJOY YOURSELVES!
...AND DON'T HURRY BACK.
Y'KNOW, YOU MAKE SUCH A SHOW OF HATING THEM. THE GOBLINS. ALL THEIR CHAOS AND LUNACY...
BUT I KNOW THE TRUTH.
YOU'RE SCARED OF YOUR OWN SUBJECTS. YOU ROTTEN OLD COWARD.
NAMECALLING, EH? I EXPECTED BETTER FROM A KNIGHT.
"SIR SKUBBIN OF THE GARDEROBE". HA.
THAT'S NOT WHO I AM. DON'T CALL ME THAT.
OH? WHAT WOULD YOU PREFER?

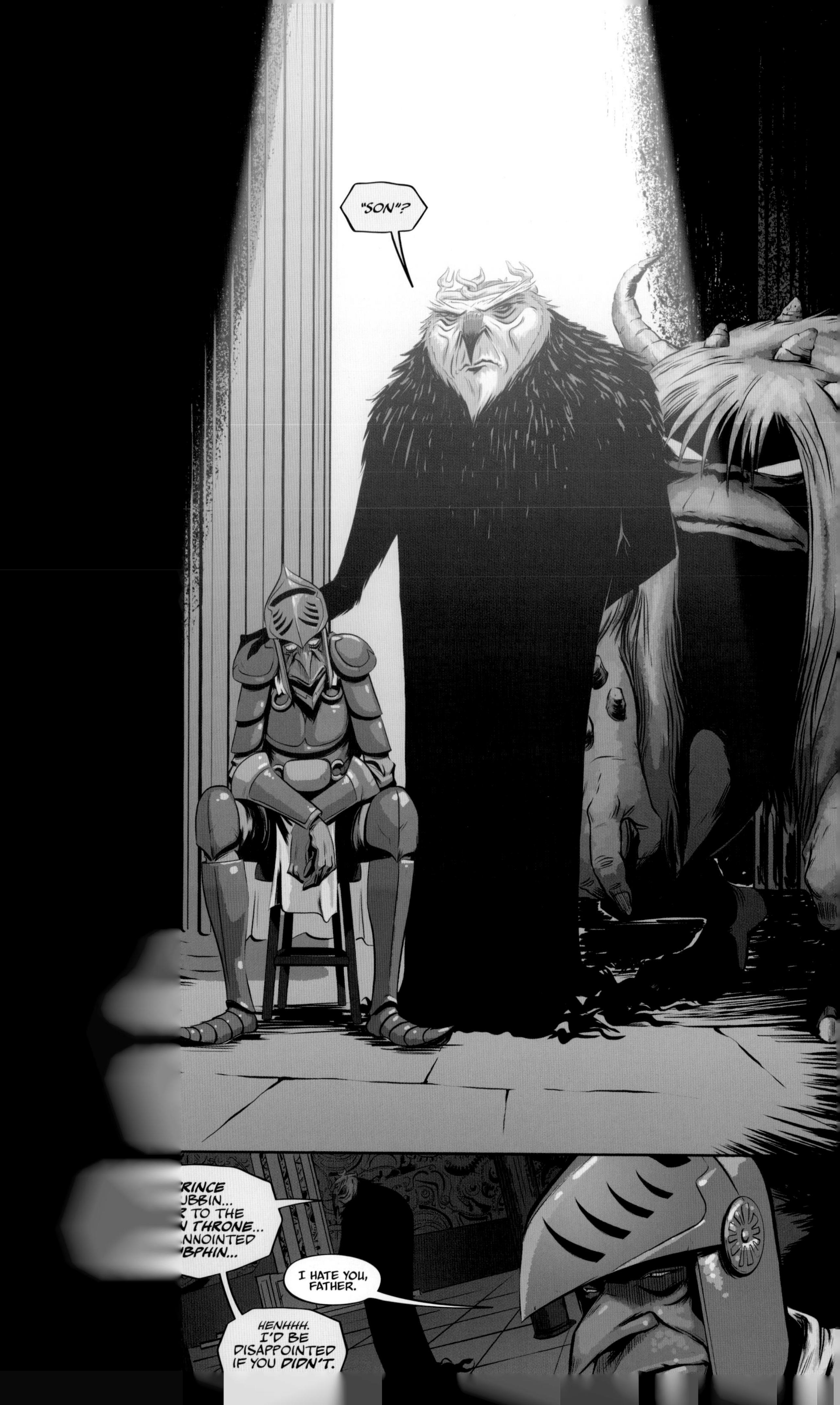
"SON"?
I HATE YOU, FATHER.
HENHHH. I'D BE DISAPPOINTED IF YOU DIDN'T.

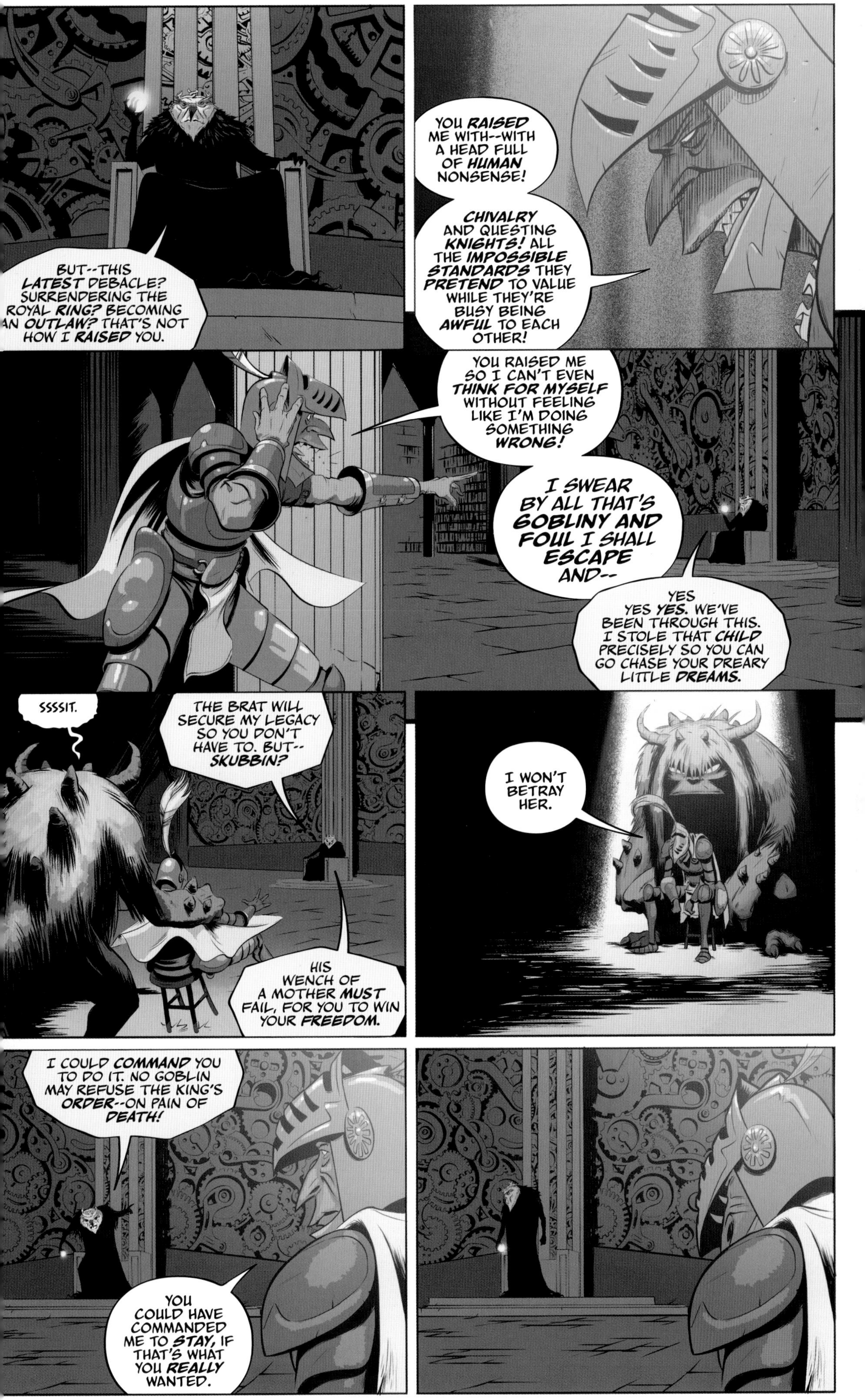

BUT--THIS LATEST DEBACLE? SURRENDERING THE ROYAL RING? BECOMING AN OUTLAW? THAT'S NOT HOW I RAISED YOU.
YOU RAISED ME WITH--WITH A HEAD FULL OF HUMAN NONSENSE!
CHIVALRY AND QUESTING KNIGHTS! ALL THE IMPOSSIBLE STANDARDS THEY PRETEND TO VALUE WHILE THEY'RE BUSY BEING AWFUL TO EACH OTHER!
YOU RAISED ME SO I CAN'T EVEN THINK FOR MYSELF WITHOUT FEELING LIKE I'M DOING SOMETHING WRONG!
I SWEAR BY ALL THAT'S GOBLINY AND FOUL I SHALL ESCAPE AND--
YES YES YES. WE'VE BEEN THROUGH THIS. I STOLE THAT CHILD PRECISELY SO YOU CAN GO CHASE YOUR DREARY LITTLE DREAMS.
SSSSIT.
THE BRAT WILL SECURE MY LEGACY SO YOU DON'T HAVE TO. BUT-- SKUBBIN?
HIS WENCH OF A MOTHER MUST FAIL, FOR YOU TO WIN YOUR FREEDOM.
I WON'T BETRAY HER.
I COULD COMMAND YOU TO DO IT. NO GOBLIN MAY REFUSE THE KING'S ORDER--ON PAIN OF DEATH!
YOU COULD HAVE COMMANDED ME TO STAY, IF THAT'S WHAT YOU REALLY WANTED.

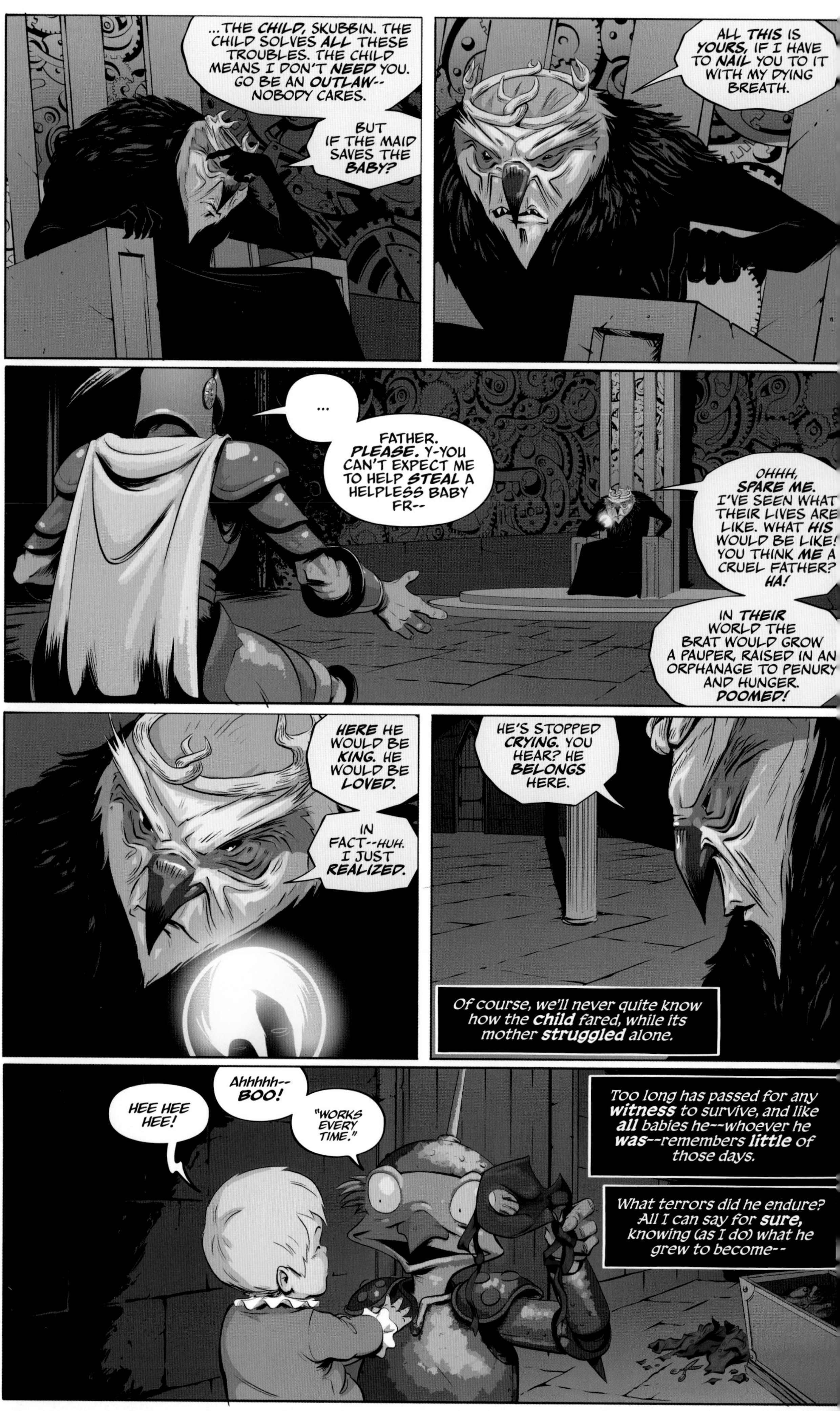
...THE CHILD, SKUBBIN. THE CHILD SOLVES ALL THESE TROUBLES. THE CHILD MEANS I DON'T NEED YOU. GO BE AN OUTLAW--NOBODY CARES.
BUT IF THE MAID SAVES THE BABY?
ALL THIS IS YOURS, IF I HAVE TO NAIL YOU TO IT WITH MY DYING BREATH.
...
FATHER. PLEASE. Y-YOU CAN'T EXPECT ME TO HELP STEAL A HELPLESS BABY FR--
OHHH, SPARE ME. I'VE SEEN WHAT THEIR LIVES ARE LIKE. WHAT HIS WOULD BE LIKE! YOU THINK ME A CRUEL FATHER? HA!
IN THEIR WORLD THE BRAT WOULD GROW A PAUPER, RAISED IN AN ORPHANAGE TO PENURY AND HUNGER. DOOMED!
HERE HE WOULD BE KING. HE WOULD BE LOVED.
IN FACT--HUH. I JUST REALIZED.
HE'S STOPPED CRYING. YOU HEAR? HE BELONGS HERE.
Of course, we'll never quite know how the child fared, while its mother struggled alone.
HEE HEE HEE!
Ahhhhh--BOO!
"WORKS EVERY TIME."
Too long has passed for any witness to survive, and like all babies he--whoever he was--remembers little of those days.
What terrors did he endure? All I can say for sure, knowing (as I do) what he grew to become--

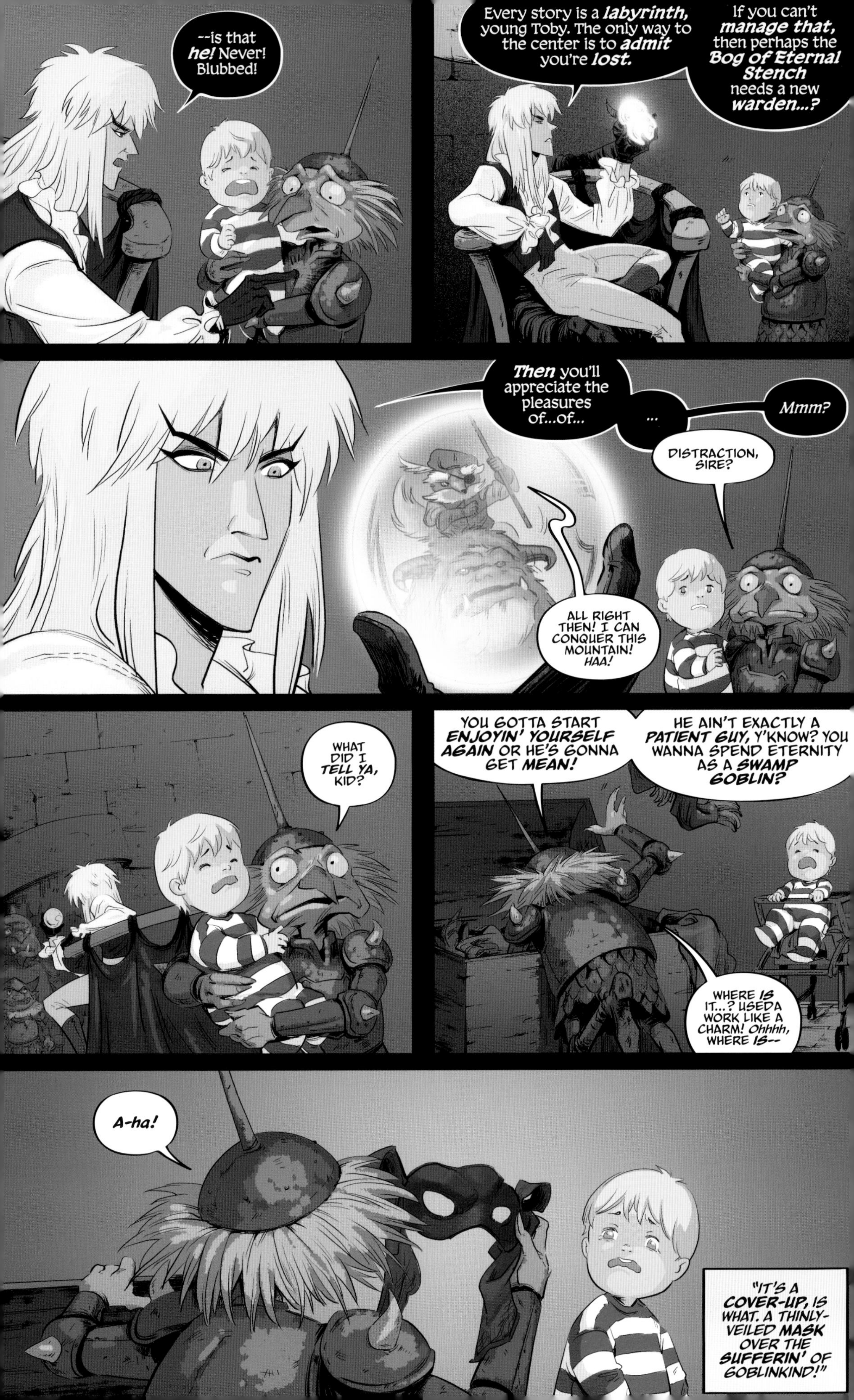
--is that *he!* Never! Blubbed!
Every story is a ***labyrinth,*** young Toby. The only way to the center is to ***admit*** you're ***lost.***
If you can't ***manage that,*** then perhaps the ***Bog of Eternal Stench*** needs a new ***warden...?***
Then you'll appreciate the pleasures of...of...
...
Mmm?
DISTRACTION, SIRE?
ALL RIGHT THEN! I CAN CONQUER THIS MOUNTAIN! *HAA!*
WHAT DID I ***TELL YA,*** KID?
YOU GOTTA START ***ENJOYIN' YOURSELF AGAIN*** OR HE'S GONNA GET ***MEAN!***
HE AIN'T EXACTLY A ***PATIENT GUY,*** Y'KNOW? YOU WANNA SPEND ETERNITY AS A ***SWAMP GOBLIN?***
WHERE ***IS*** IT...? USEDA WORK LIKE A CHARM! *Ohhhh,* WHERE ***IS***--
A-ha!
*"IT'S A **COVER-UP,** IS WHAT. A THINLY-VEILED **MASK** OVER THE **SUFFERIN'** OF GOBLINKIND!"*

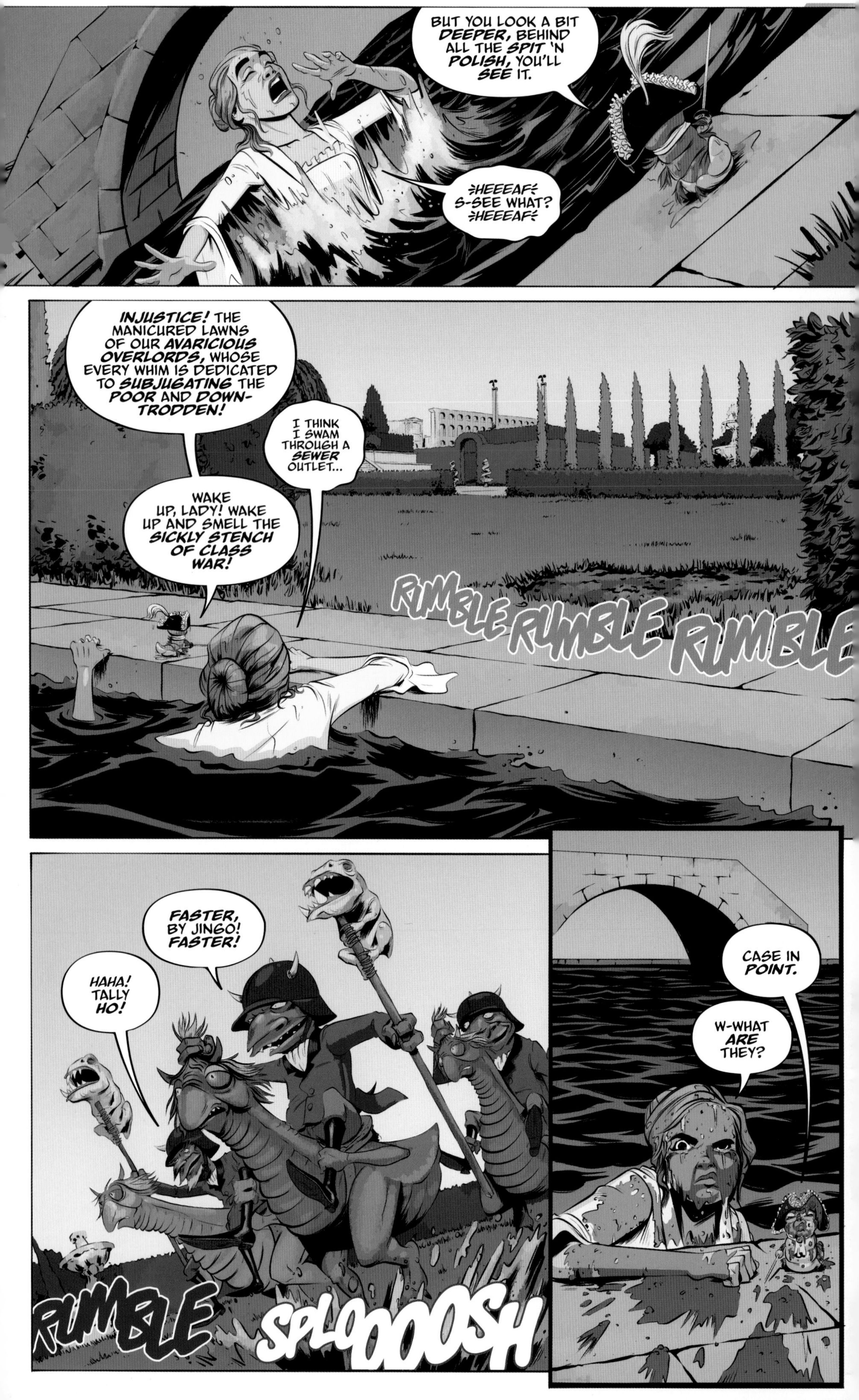
BUT YOU LOOK A BIT DEEPER, BEHIND ALL THE SPIT 'N POLISH, YOU'LL SEE IT.
≠HEEEAF≠ S-SEE WHAT? ≠HEEEAF≠
INJUSTICE! THE MANICURED LAWNS OF OUR AVARICIOUS OVERLORDS, WHOSE EVERY WHIM IS DEDICATED TO SUBJUGATING THE POOR AND DOWN-TRODDEN!
I THINK I SWAM THROUGH A SEWER OUTLET...
WAKE UP, LADY! WAKE UP AND SMELL THE SICKLY STENCH OF CLASS WAR!
RUMBLE RUMBLE RUMBLE
FASTER, BY JINGO! FASTER!
HAHA! TALLY HO!
RUMBLE
SPLOOOOSH
CASE IN POINT.
W-WHAT ARE THEY?

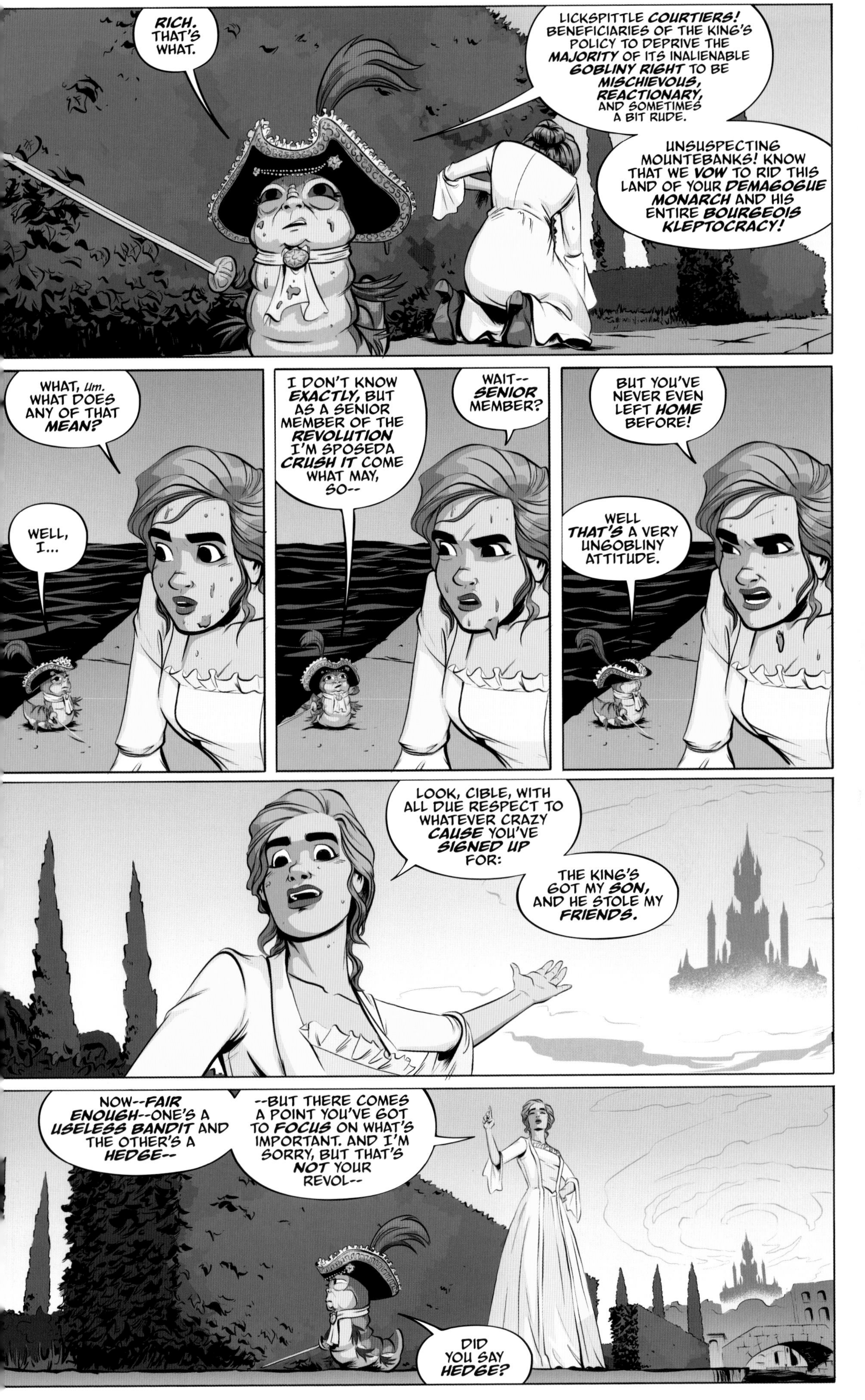

RICH. THAT'S WHAT.
LICKSPITTLE COURTIERS! BENEFICIARIES OF THE KING'S POLICY TO DEPRIVE THE MAJORITY OF ITS INALIENABLE GOBLINY RIGHT TO BE MISCHIEVOUS, REACTIONARY, AND SOMETIMES A BIT RUDE.
UNSUSPECTING MOUNTEBANKS! KNOW THAT WE VOW TO RID THIS LAND OF YOUR DEMAGOGUE MONARCH AND HIS ENTIRE BOURGEOIS KLEPTOCRACY!
WHAT, Um. WHAT DOES ANY OF THAT MEAN?
WELL, I...
I DON'T KNOW EXACTLY, BUT AS A SENIOR MEMBER OF THE REVOLUTION I'M SPOSEDA CRUSH IT COME WHAT MAY, SO--
WAIT-- SENIOR MEMBER?
BUT YOU'VE NEVER EVEN LEFT HOME BEFORE!
WELL THAT'S A VERY UNGOBLINY ATTITUDE.
LOOK, CIBLE, WITH ALL DUE RESPECT TO WHATEVER CRAZY CAUSE YOU'VE SIGNED UP FOR:
THE KING'S GOT MY SON, AND HE STOLE MY FRIENDS.
NOW--FAIR ENOUGH--ONE'S A USELESS BANDIT AND THE OTHER'S A HEDGE--
--BUT THERE COMES A POINT YOU'VE GOT TO FOCUS ON WHAT'S IMPORTANT. AND I'M SORRY, BUT THAT'S NOT YOUR REVOL--
DID YOU SAY HEDGE?

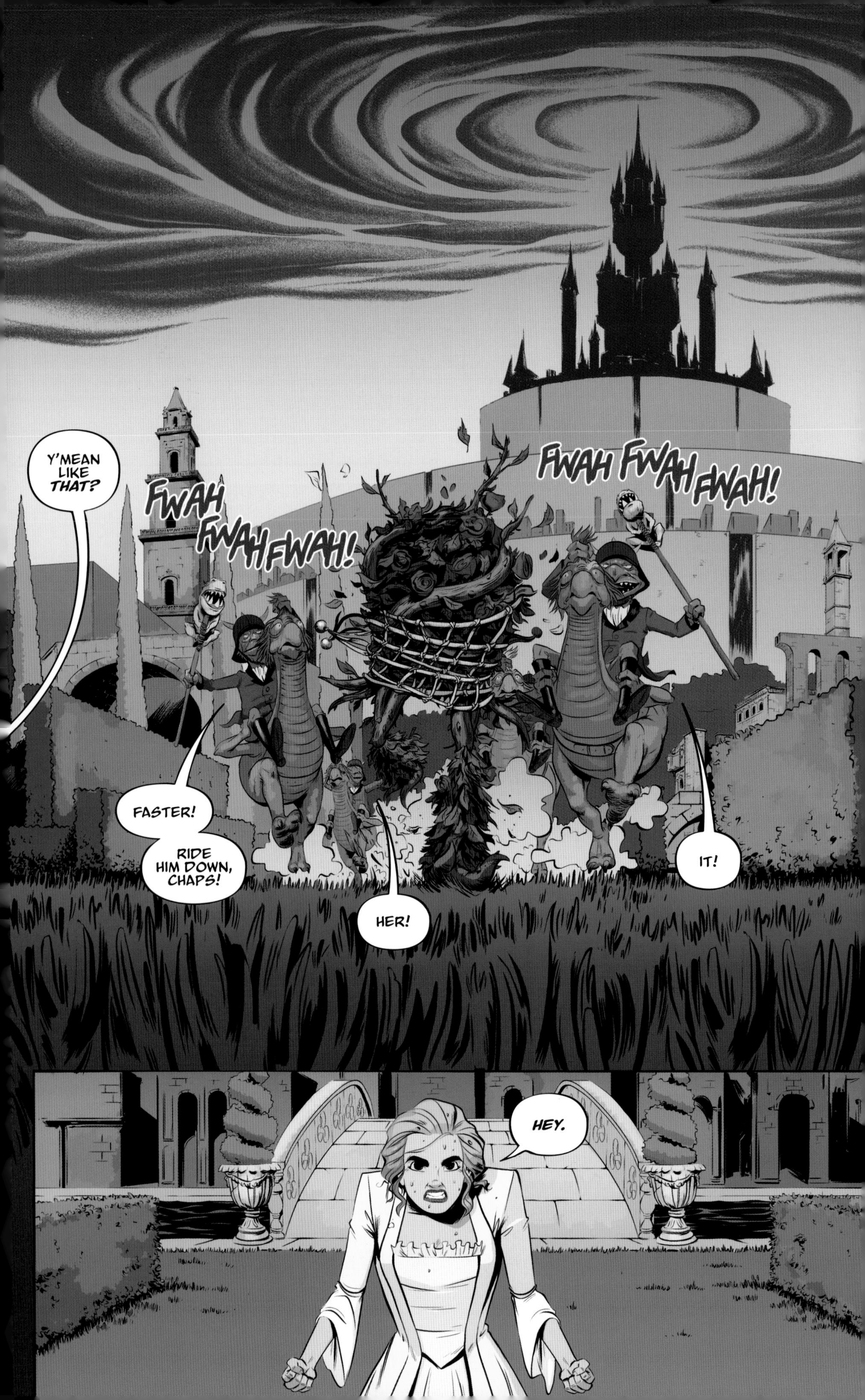
Y'MEAN LIKE THAT?
FWAH FWAH FWAH!
FWAH FWAH FWAH!
FASTER!
RIDE HIM DOWN, CHAPS!
HER!
IT!
HEY.

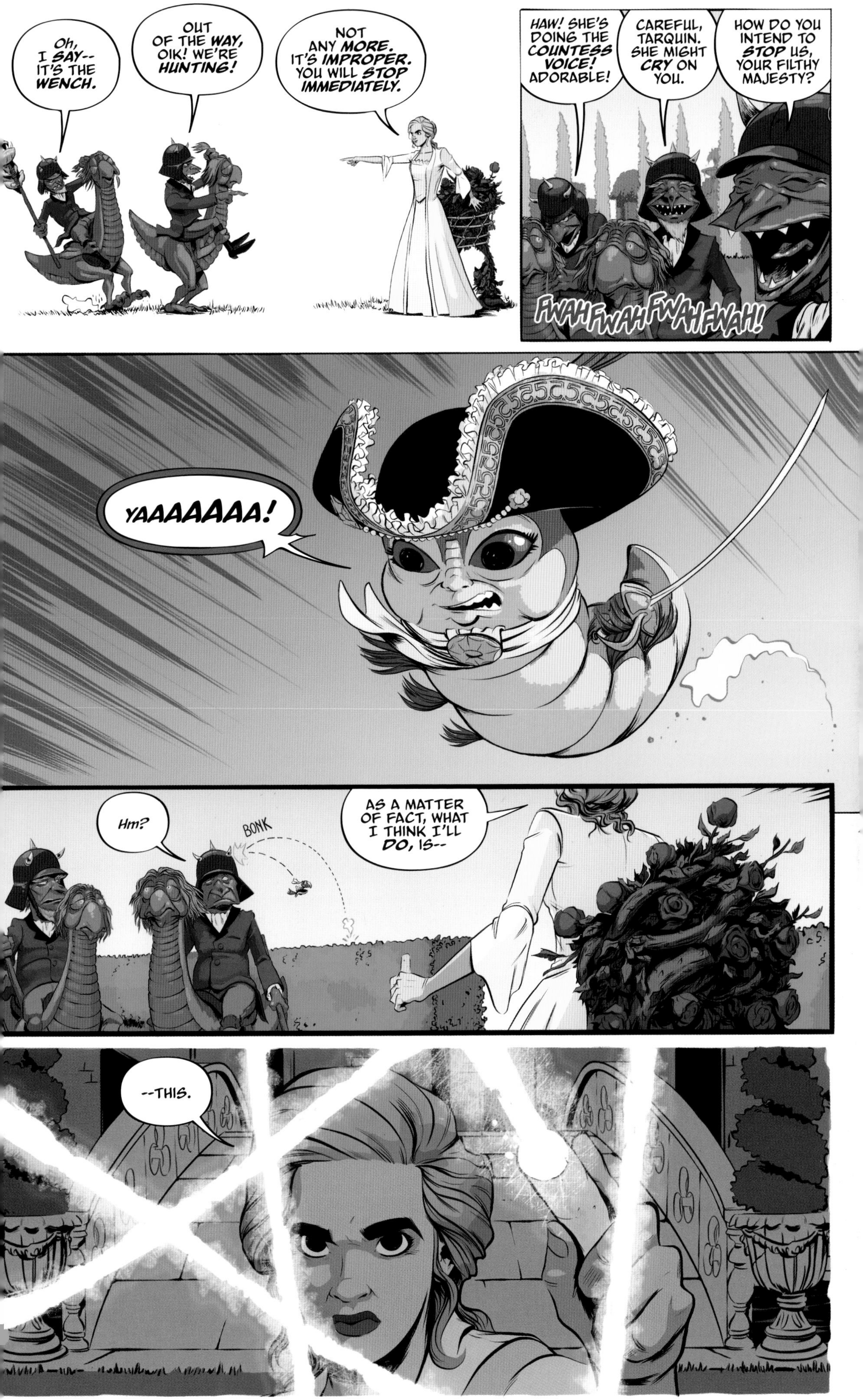
Oh, I SAY-- IT'S THE WENCH.
OUT OF THE WAY, OIK! WE'RE HUNTING!
NOT ANY MORE. IT'S IMPROPER. YOU WILL STOP IMMEDIATELY.
HAW! SHE'S DOING THE COUNTESS VOICE! ADORABLE!
CAREFUL, TARQUIN. SHE MIGHT CRY ON YOU.
HOW DO YOU INTEND TO STOP US, YOUR FILTHY MAJESTY?
FWAH FWAH FWAH FWAH!
YAAAAAAA!
Hm?
BONK
AS A MATTER OF FACT, WHAT I THINK I'LL DO, IS--
--THIS.

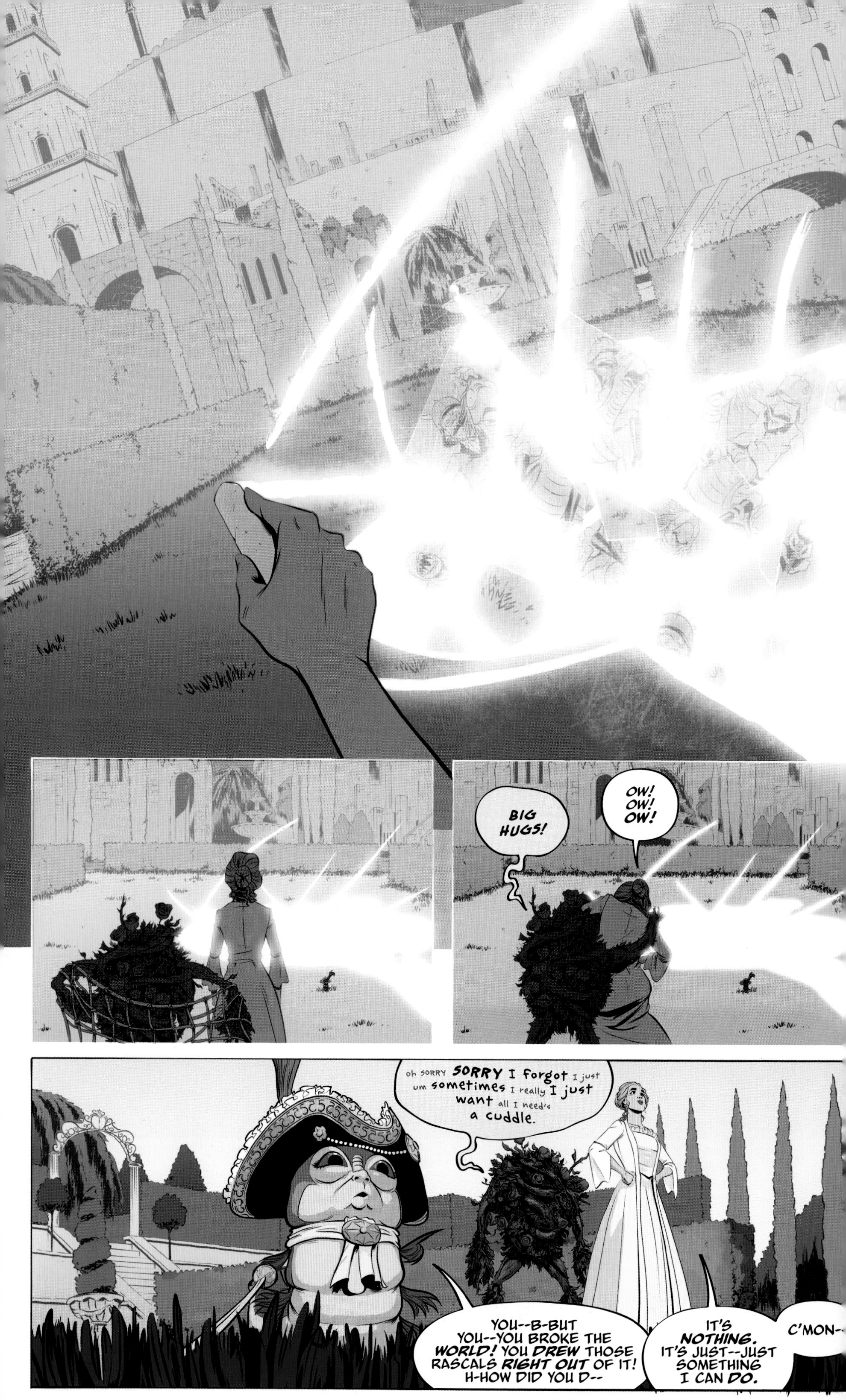

BIG HUGS!
OW! OW! OW!
oh SORRY SORRY I forgot I just um sometimes I really I just want all I need's a cuddle.
YOU--B-BUT YOU--YOU BROKE THE WORLD! YOU DREW THOSE RASCALS RIGHT OUT OF IT! H-HOW DID YOU D--
IT'S NOTHING. IT'S JUST--JUST SOMETHING I CAN DO.
C'MON--

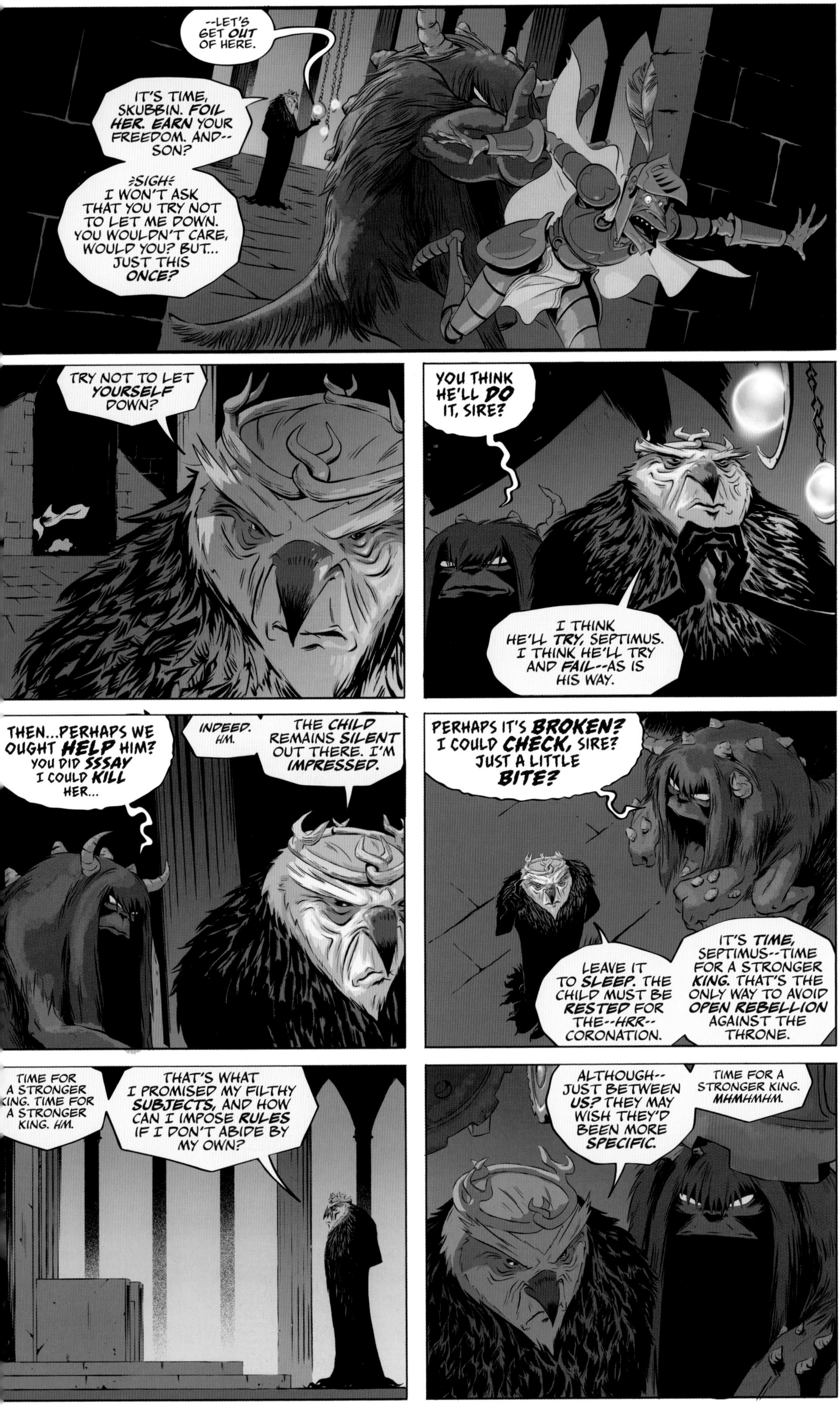
--LET'S GET OUT OF HERE.
IT'S TIME, SKUBBIN. FOIL HER. EARN YOUR FREEDOM. AND--SON?
SIGH I WON'T ASK THAT YOU TRY NOT TO LET ME DOWN. YOU WOULDN'T CARE, WOULD YOU? BUT... JUST THIS ONCE?
TRY NOT TO LET YOURSELF DOWN?
YOU THINK HE'LL DO IT, SIRE?
I THINK HE'LL TRY, SEPTIMUS. I THINK HE'LL TRY AND FAIL--AS IS HIS WAY.
THEN...PERHAPS WE OUGHT HELP HIM? YOU DID SSSAY I COULD KILL HER...
INDEED. HM.
THE CHILD REMAINS SILENT OUT THERE. I'M IMPRESSED.
PERHAPS IT'S BROKEN? I COULD CHECK, SIRE? JUST A LITTLE BITE?
LEAVE IT TO SLEEP. THE CHILD MUST BE RESTED FOR THE--HRR--CORONATION.
IT'S TIME, SEPTIMUS--TIME FOR A STRONGER KING. THAT'S THE ONLY WAY TO AVOID OPEN REBELLION AGAINST THE THRONE.
TIME FOR A STRONGER KING. TIME FOR A STRONGER KING. HM.
THAT'S WHAT I PROMISED MY FILTHY SUBJECTS, AND HOW CAN I IMPOSE RULES IF I DON'T ABIDE BY MY OWN?
ALTHOUGH--JUST BETWEEN US? THEY MAY WISH THEY'D BEEN MORE SPECIFIC.
TIME FOR A STRONGER KING. MHMHMHM.

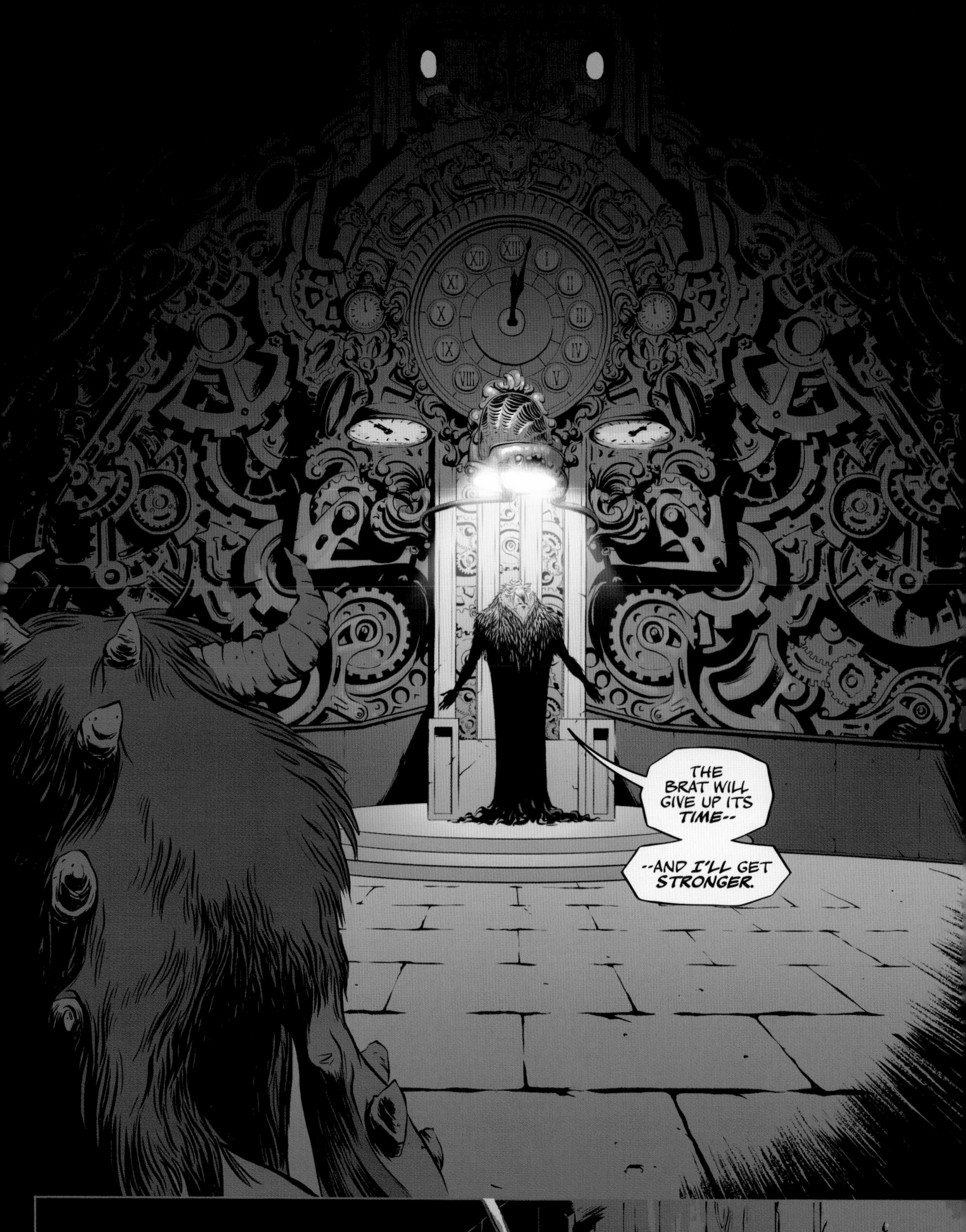
THE BRAT WILL GIVE UP ITS *TIME*--
--AND *I'LL* GET **STRONGER.**

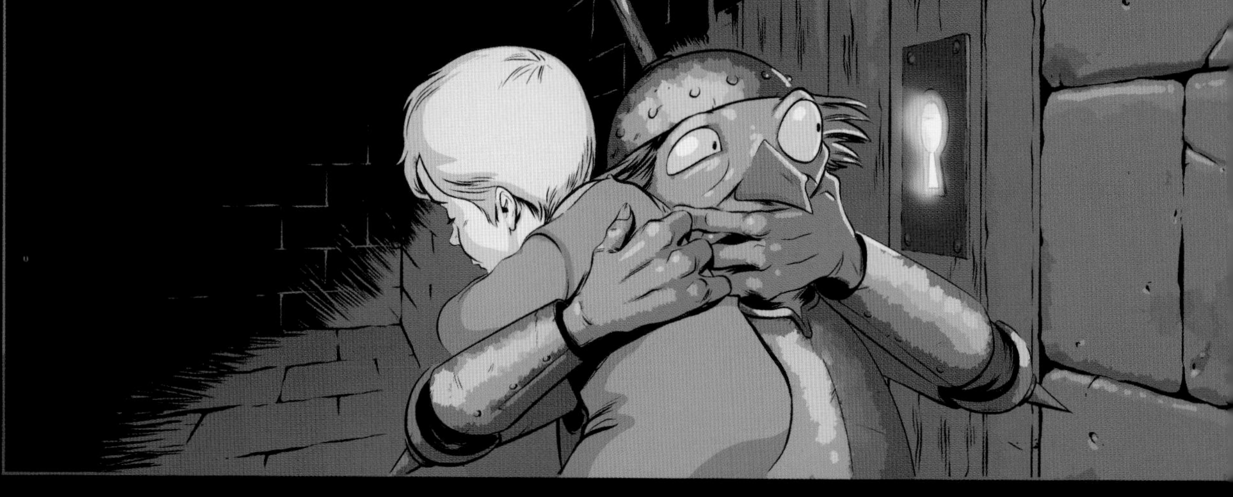

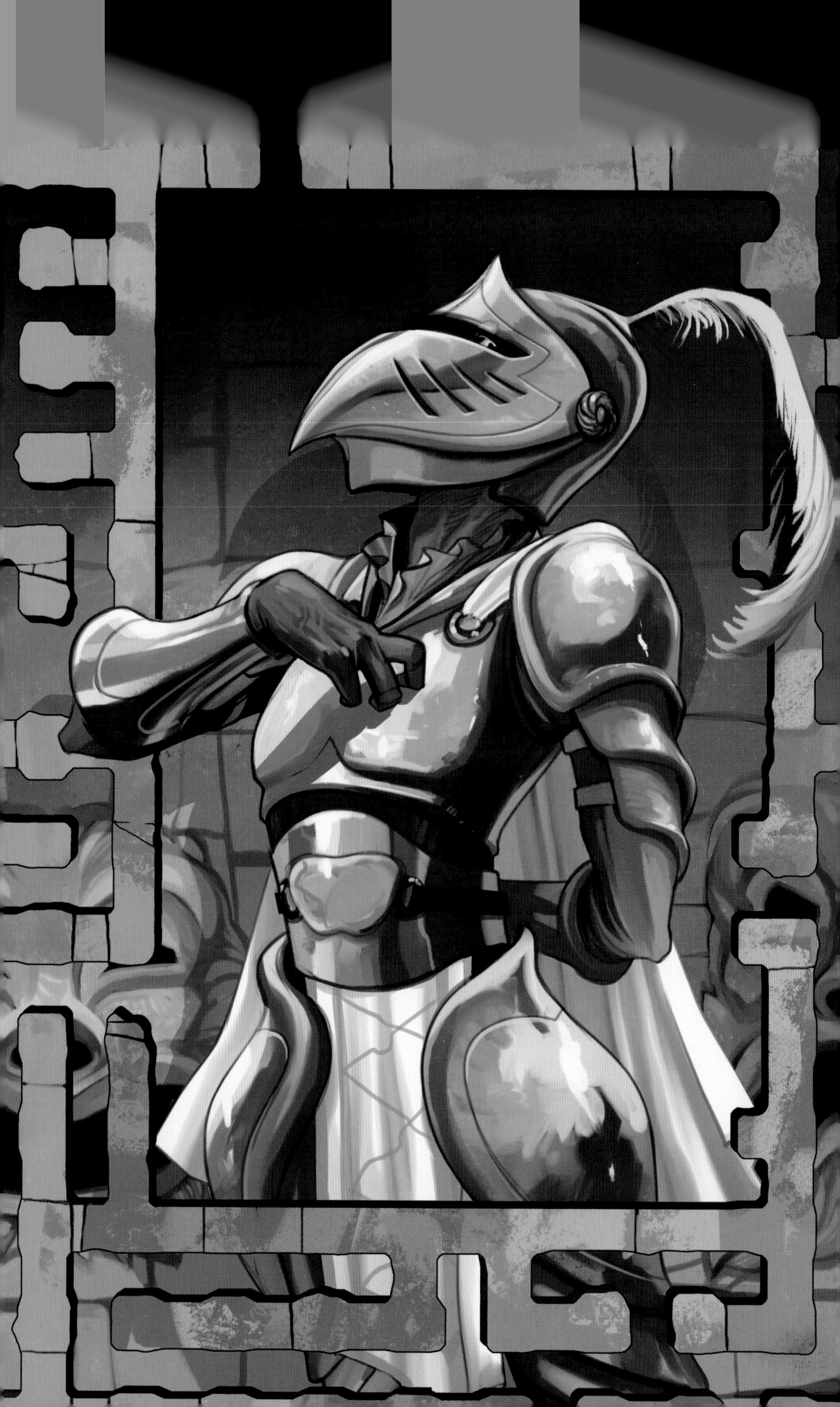

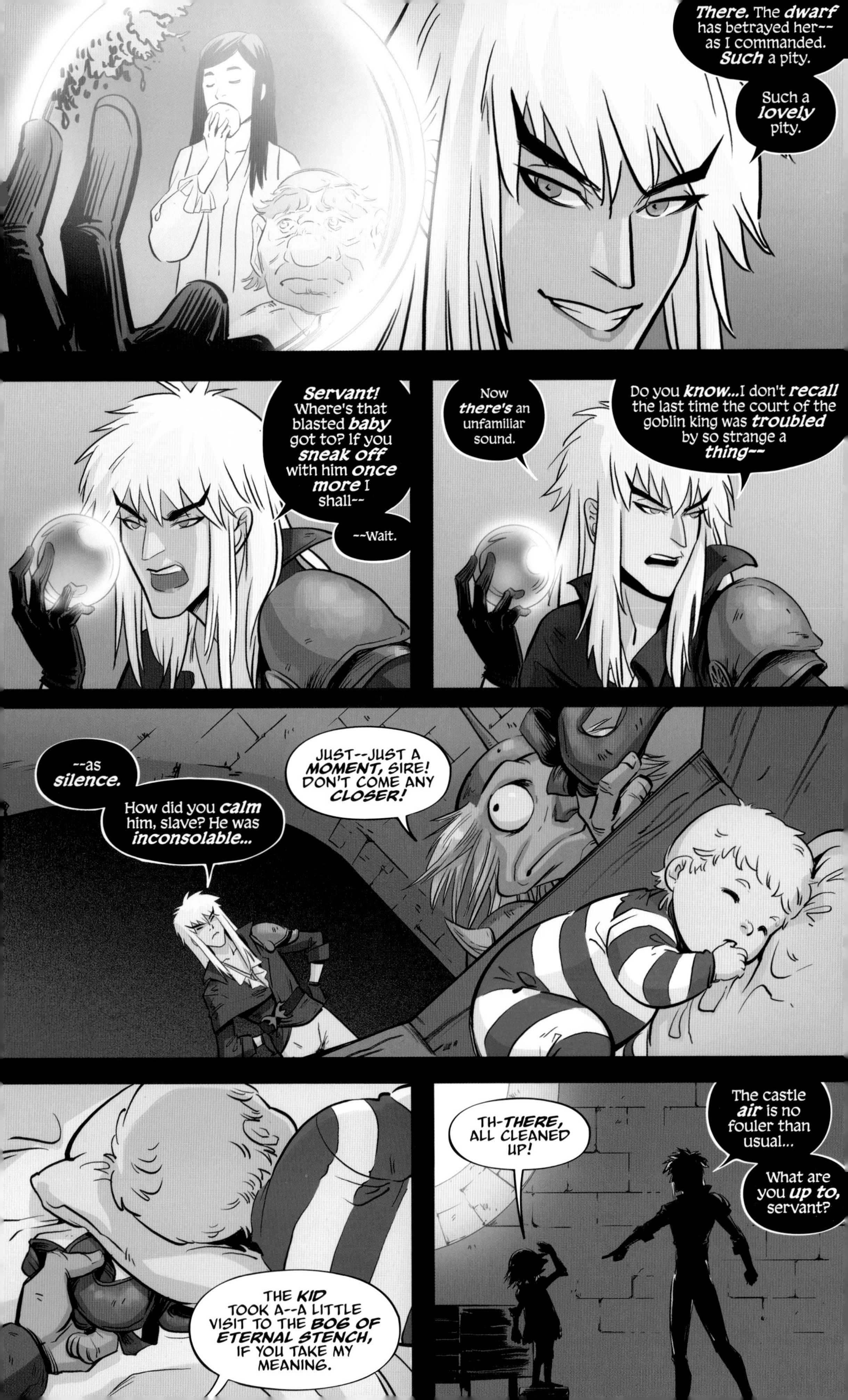
There. The dwarf has betrayed her-- as I commanded. Such a pity.
Such a lovely pity.
Servant! Where's that blasted baby got to? If you sneak off with him once more I shall--
--Wait.
Now there's an unfamiliar sound.
Do you know...I don't recall the last time the court of the goblin king was troubled by so strange a thing--
--as silence.
How did you calm him, slave? He was inconsolable...
JUST--JUST A MOMENT, SIRE! DON'T COME ANY CLOSER!
THE KID TOOK A--A LITTLE VISIT TO THE BOG OF ETERNAL STENCH, IF YOU TAKE MY MEANING.
TH-THERE, ALL CLEANED UP!
The castle air is no fouler than usual...
What are you up to, servant?

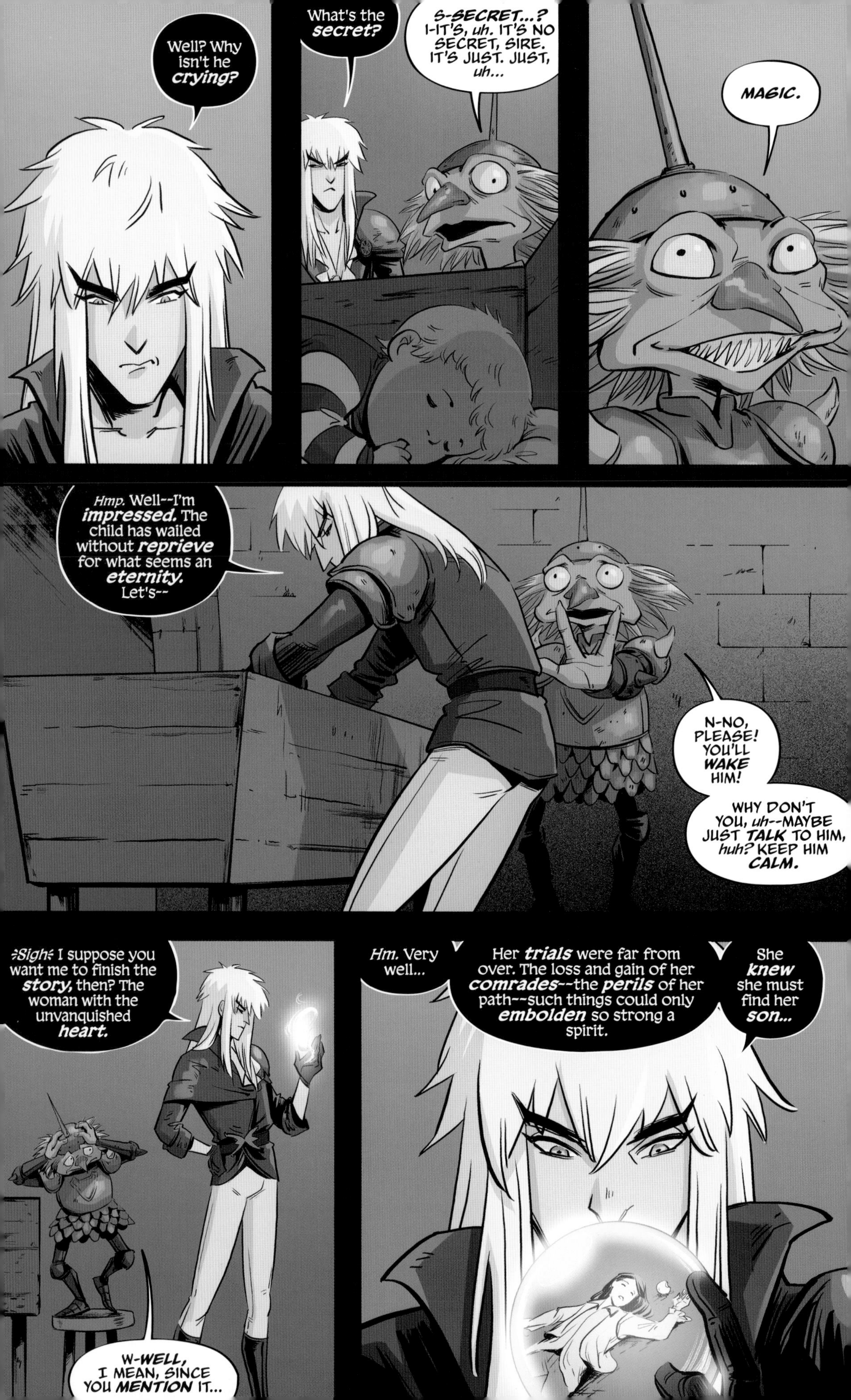
Well? Why isn't he *crying?*
What's the *secret?*
S-SECRET...? I-IT'S, *uh.* IT'S NO SECRET, SIRE. IT'S JUST. JUST, *uh...*
MAGIC.
Hmp. Well--I'm ***impressed.*** The child has wailed without ***reprieve*** for what seems an ***eternity.*** Let's--
N-NO, PLEASE! YOU'LL ***WAKE*** HIM!
WHY DON'T YOU, *uh*--MAYBE JUST ***TALK*** TO HIM, *huh?* KEEP HIM ***CALM.***
Sigh I suppose you want me to finish the ***story,*** then? The woman with the unvanquished ***heart.***
W-***WELL,*** I MEAN, SINCE YOU ***MENTION*** IT...
Hm. Very well...
Her ***trials*** were far from over. The loss and gain of her ***comrades***--the ***perils*** of her path--such things could only ***embolden*** so strong a spirit.
She ***knew*** she must find her ***son...***

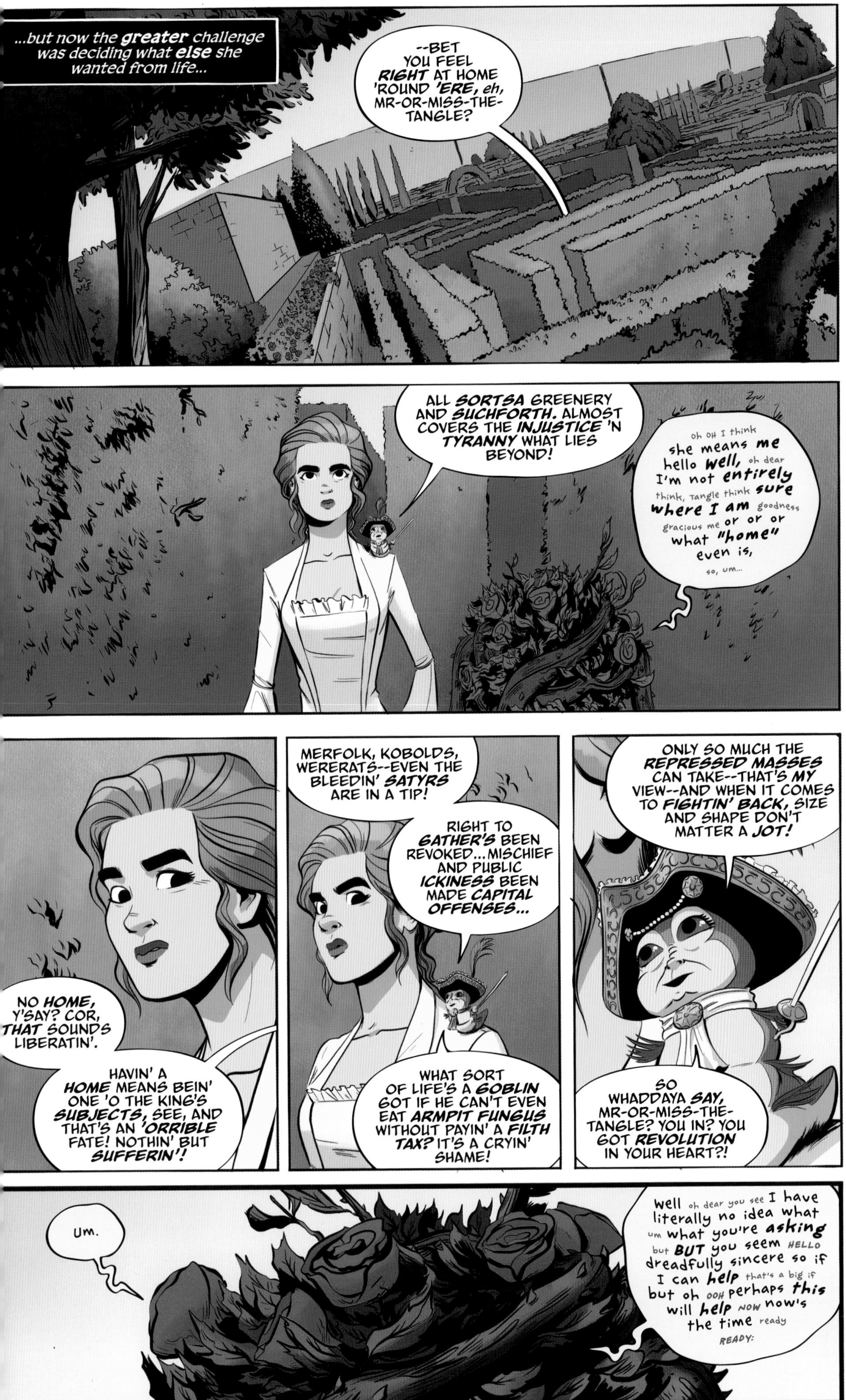
...but now the greater challenge was deciding what else she wanted from life...
--BET YOU FEEL RIGHT AT HOME 'ROUND 'ERE, eh, MR-OR-MISS-THE-TANGLE?
ALL SORTSA GREENERY AND SUCHFORTH. ALMOST COVERS THE INJUSTICE 'N TYRANNY WHAT LIES BEYOND!
oh OH I think she means me hello well, oh dear I'm not entirely think, Tangle think sure where I am goodness gracious me or or or what "home" even is, so, um...
NO HOME, Y'SAY? COR, THAT SOUNDS LIBERATIN'.
HAVIN' A HOME MEANS BEIN' ONE 'O THE KING'S SUBJECTS, SEE, AND THAT'S AN 'ORRIBLE FATE! NOTHIN' BUT SUFFERIN'!
MERFOLK, KOBOLDS, WERERATS--EVEN THE BLEEDIN' SATYRS ARE IN A TIP!
RIGHT TO GATHER'S BEEN REVOKED...MISCHIEF AND PUBLIC ICKINESS BEEN MADE CAPITAL OFFENSES...
WHAT SORT OF LIFE'S A GOBLIN GOT IF HE CAN'T EVEN EAT ARMPIT FUNGUS WITHOUT PAYIN' A FILTH TAX? IT'S A CRYIN' SHAME!
ONLY SO MUCH THE REPRESSED MASSES CAN TAKE--THAT'S MY VIEW--AND WHEN IT COMES TO FIGHTIN' BACK, SIZE AND SHAPE DON'T MATTER A JOT!
SO WHADDAYA SAY, MR-OR-MISS-THE-TANGLE? YOU IN? YOU GOT REVOLUTION IN YOUR HEART?!
Um.
well oh dear you see I have literally no idea what um what you're asking but BUT you seem HELLO dreadfully sincere so if I can help that's a big if but oh OOH perhaps this will help NOW now's the time ready READY:

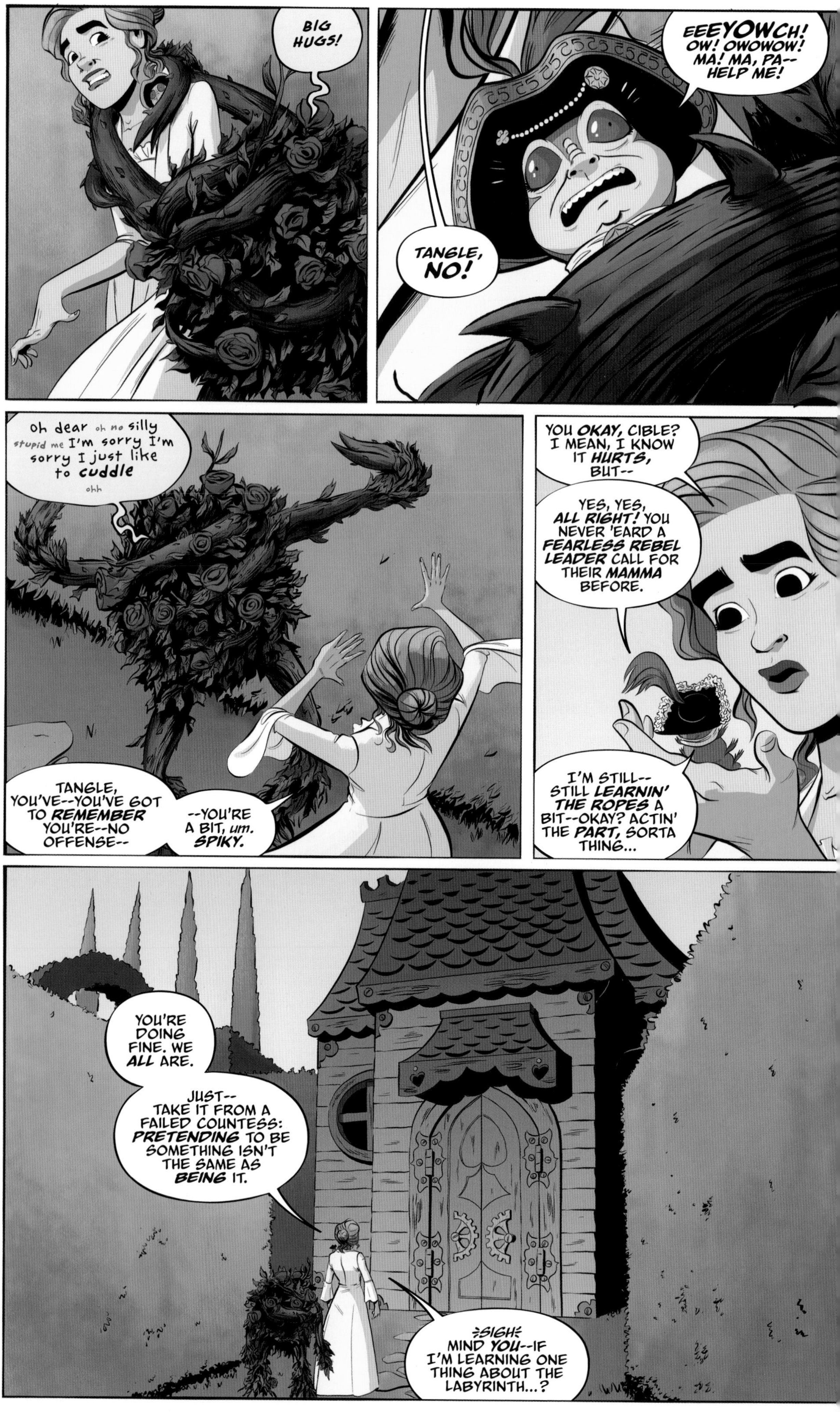
BIG HUGS!
EEEYOWCH! OW! OWOWOW! MA! MA, PA-- HELP ME!
TANGLE, NO!
oh dear oh no silly stupid me I'm sorry I'm sorry I just like to cuddle ohh
TANGLE, YOU'VE--YOU'VE GOT TO REMEMBER YOU'RE--NO OFFENSE--
--YOU'RE A BIT, um. SPIKY.
YOU OKAY, CIBLE? I MEAN, I KNOW IT HURTS, BUT--
YES, YES, ALL RIGHT! YOU NEVER 'EARD A FEARLESS REBEL LEADER CALL FOR THEIR MAMMA BEFORE.
I'M STILL-- STILL LEARNIN' THE ROPES A BIT--OKAY? ACTIN' THE PART, SORTA THING...
YOU'RE DOING FINE. WE ALL ARE.
JUST-- TAKE IT FROM A FAILED COUNTESS: PRETENDING TO BE SOMETHING ISN'T THE SAME AS BEING IT.
SIGH MIND YOU--IF I'M LEARNING ONE THING ABOUT THE LABYRINTH...?

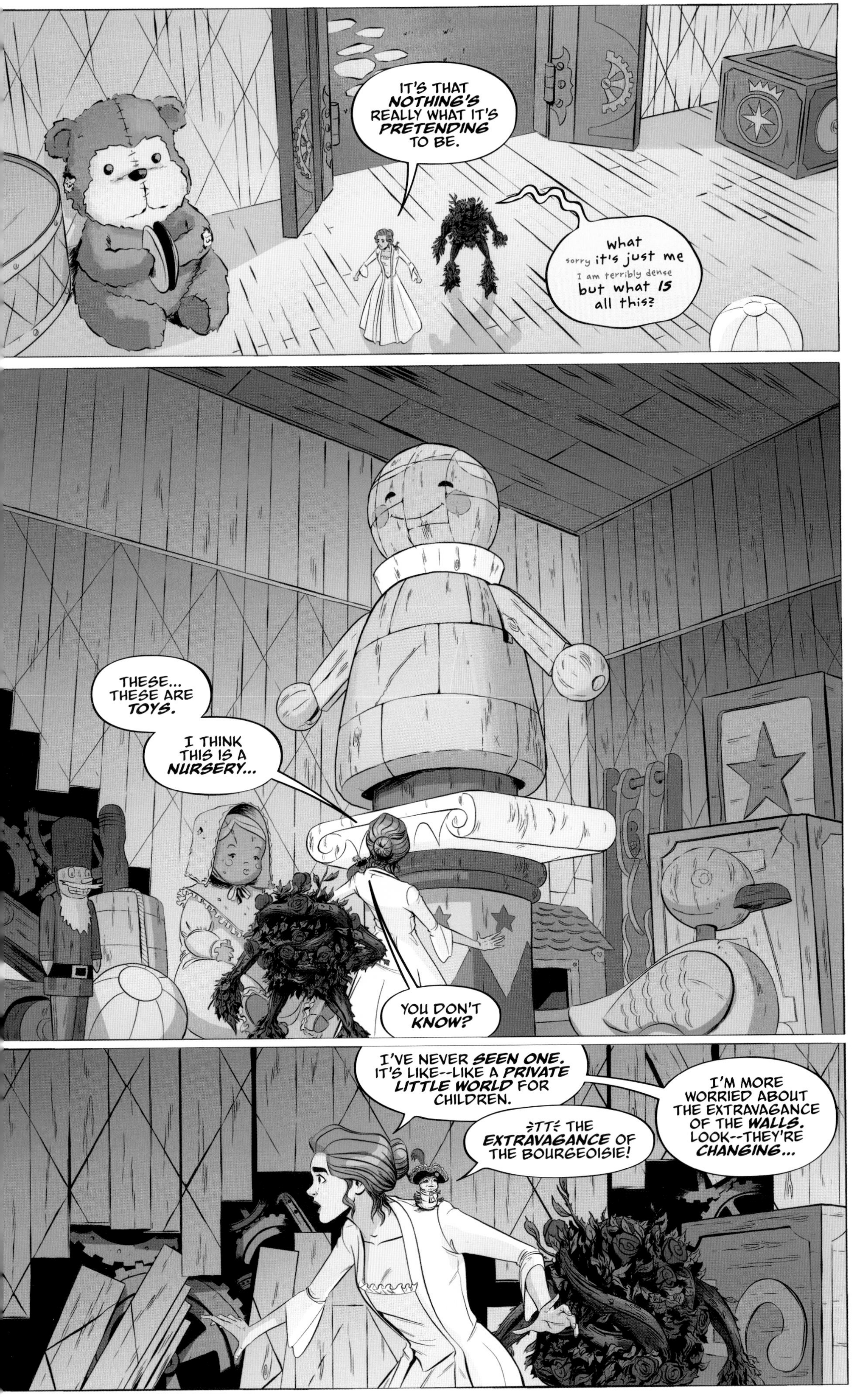
IT'S THAT NOTHING'S REALLY WHAT IT'S PRETENDING TO BE.
what sorry it's just me I am terribly dense but what IS all this?
THESE... THESE ARE TOYS.
I THINK THIS IS A NURSERY...
YOU DON'T KNOW?
I'VE NEVER SEEN ONE. IT'S LIKE--LIKE A PRIVATE LITTLE WORLD FOR CHILDREN.
TT THE EXTRAVAGANCE OF THE BOURGEOISIE!
I'M MORE WORRIED ABOUT THE EXTRAVAGANCE OF THE WALLS. LOOK--THEY'RE CHANGING...

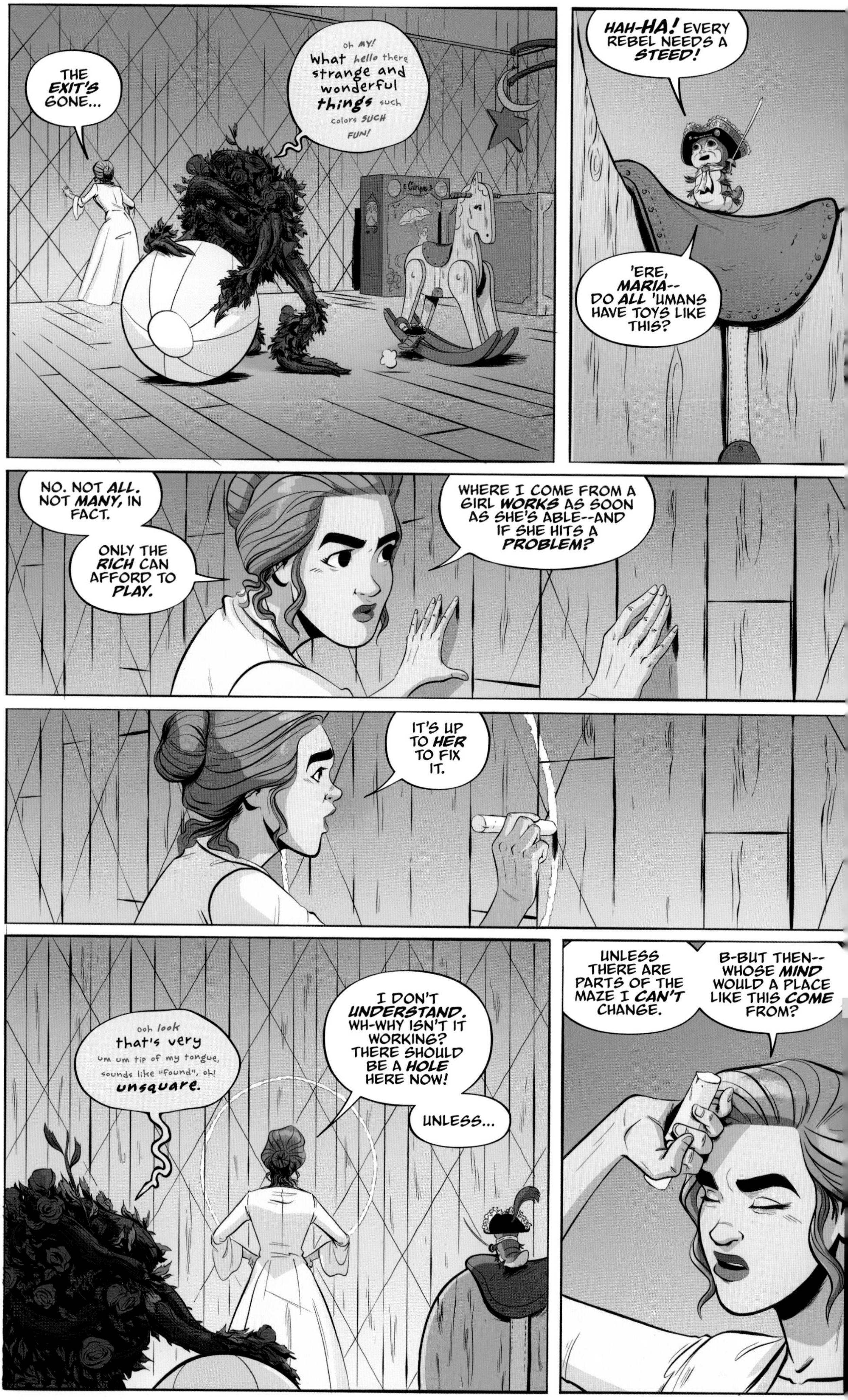
THE EXIT'S GONE...
oh MY! What hello there strange and wonderful things such colors SUCH FUN!
HAH-HA! EVERY REBEL NEEDS A STEED!
'ERE, MARIA-- DO ALL 'UMANS HAVE TOYS LIKE THIS?
NO. NOT ALL. NOT MANY, IN FACT.
ONLY THE RICH CAN AFFORD TO PLAY.
WHERE I COME FROM A GIRL WORKS AS SOON AS SHE'S ABLE--AND IF SHE HITS A PROBLEM?
IT'S UP TO HER TO FIX IT.
ooh look that's very um um tip of my tongue, sounds like "found", oh! unsquare.
I DON'T UNDERSTAND. WH-WHY ISN'T IT WORKING? THERE SHOULD BE A HOLE HERE NOW!
UNLESS...
UNLESS THERE ARE PARTS OF THE MAZE I CAN'T CHANGE.
B-BUT THEN-- WHOSE MIND WOULD A PLACE LIKE THIS COME FROM?

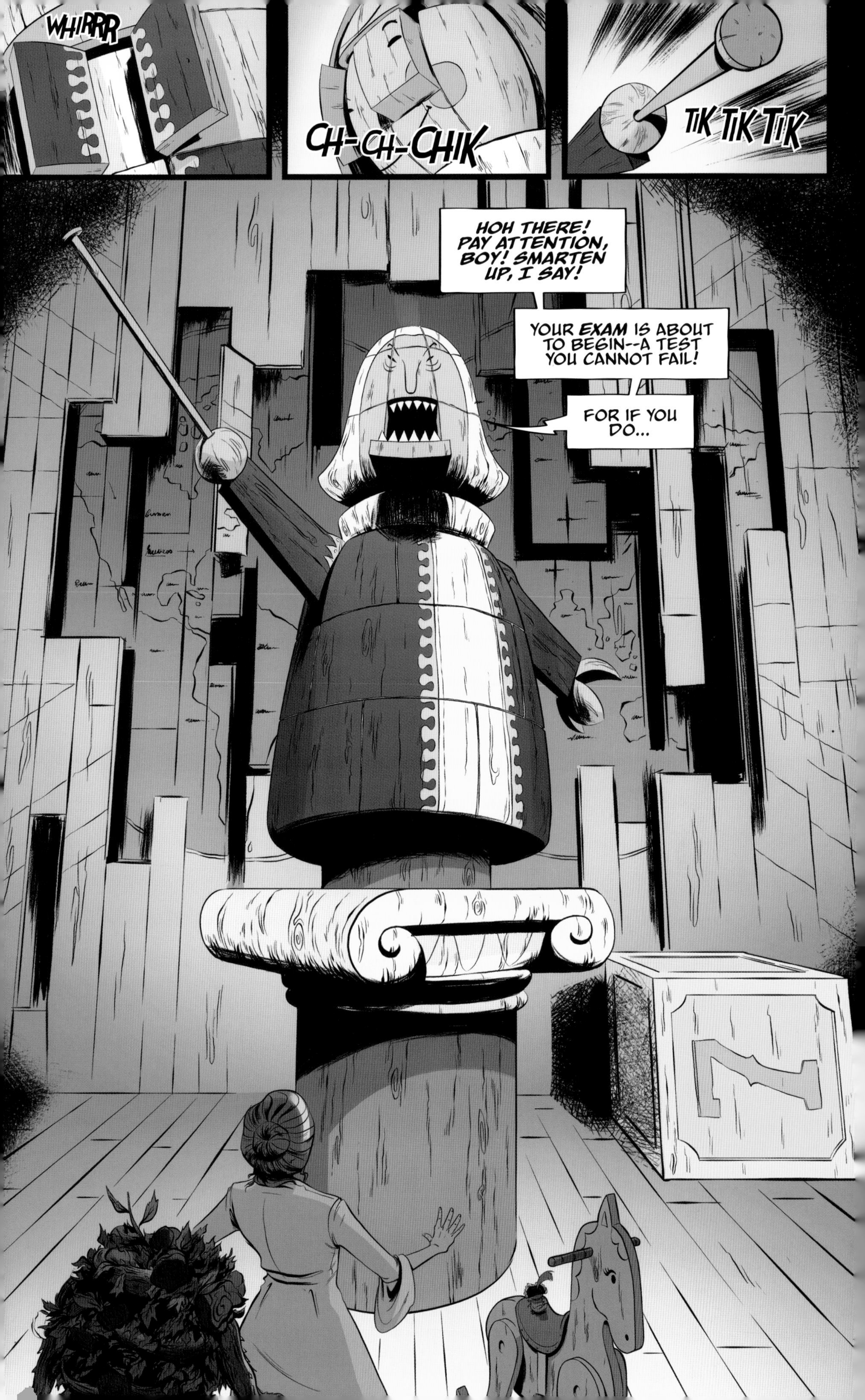
WHIRRR
CH-CH-CHIK
TIK TIK TIK
HOH THERE! PAY ATTENTION, BOY! SMARTEN UP, I SAY!
YOUR *EXAM* IS ABOUT TO BEGIN--A TEST YOU CANNOT FAIL!
FOR IF YOU DO...

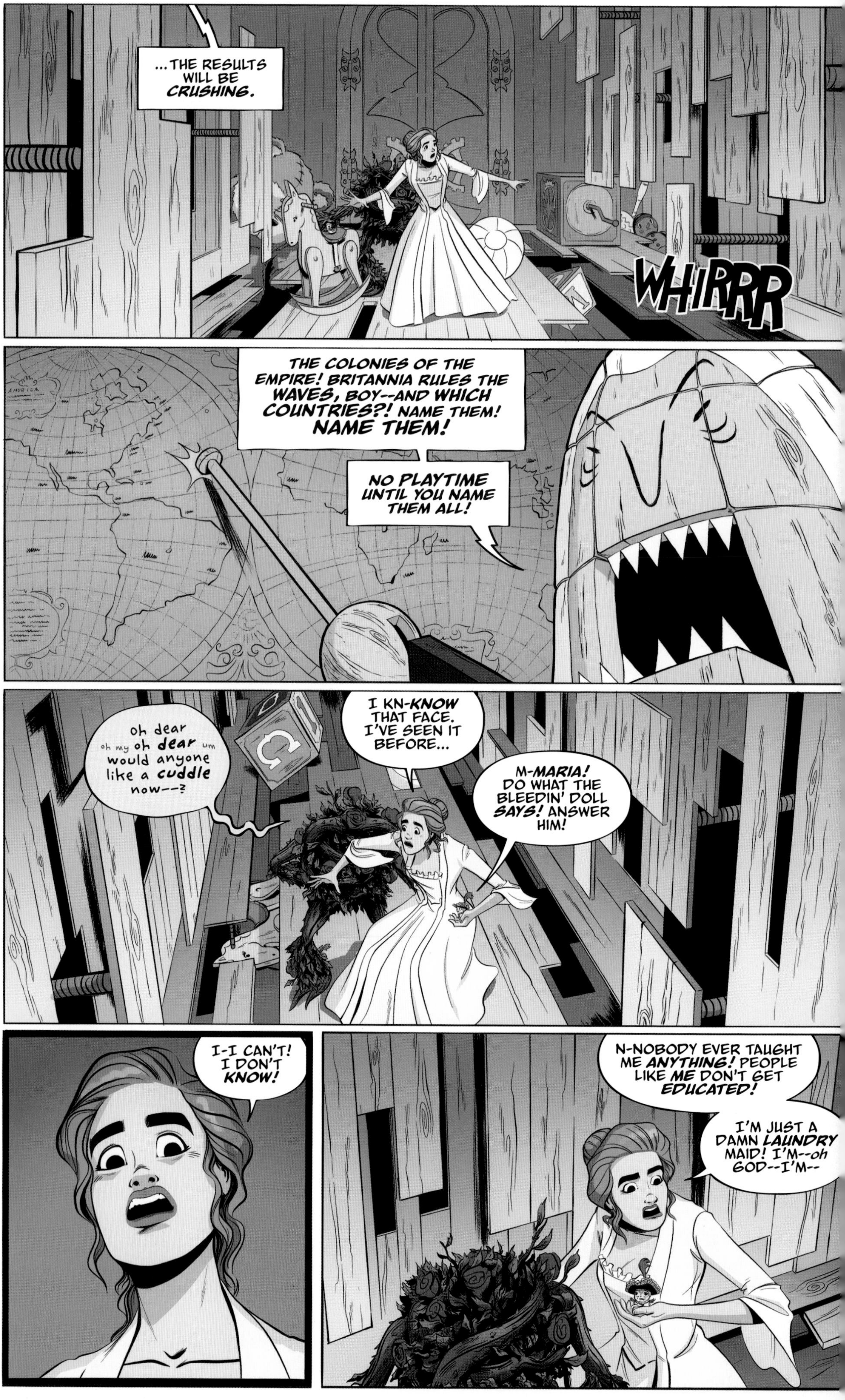

...THE RESULTS WILL BE CRUSHING.
WHIRRR
THE COLONIES OF THE EMPIRE! BRITANNIA RULES THE WAVES, BOY--AND WHICH COUNTRIES?! NAME THEM! NAME THEM!
NO PLAYTIME UNTIL YOU NAME THEM ALL!
oh dear oh my oh dear um would anyone like a cuddle now--?
I KN-KNOW THAT FACE. I'VE SEEN IT BEFORE...
M-MARIA! DO WHAT THE BLEEDIN' DOLL SAYS! ANSWER HIM!
I-I CAN'T! I DON'T KNOW!
N-NOBODY EVER TAUGHT ME ANYTHING! PEOPLE LIKE ME DON'T GET EDUCATED!
I'M JUST A DAMN LAUNDRY MAID! I'M--oh GOD--I'M--

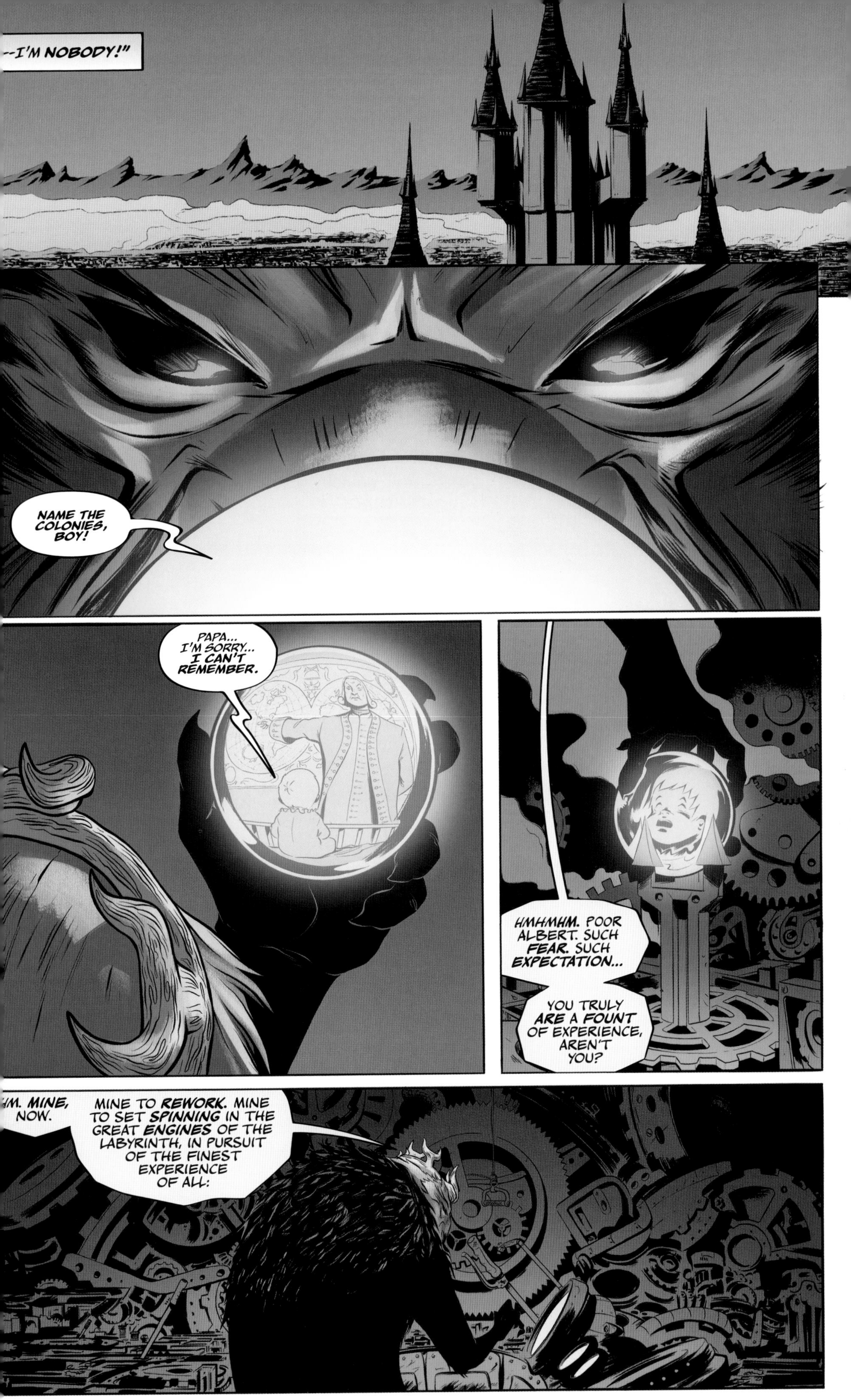
--I'M NOBODY!"
NAME THE COLONIES, BOY!
PAPA... I'M SORRY... I CAN'T REMEMBER.
HMHMHM. POOR ALBERT. SUCH FEAR. SUCH EXPECTATION...
YOU TRULY ARE A FOUNT OF EXPERIENCE, AREN'T YOU?
HM. MINE, NOW.
MINE TO REWORK. MINE TO SET SPINNING IN THE GREAT ENGINES OF THE LABYRINTH, IN PURSUIT OF THE FINEST EXPERIENCE OF ALL:

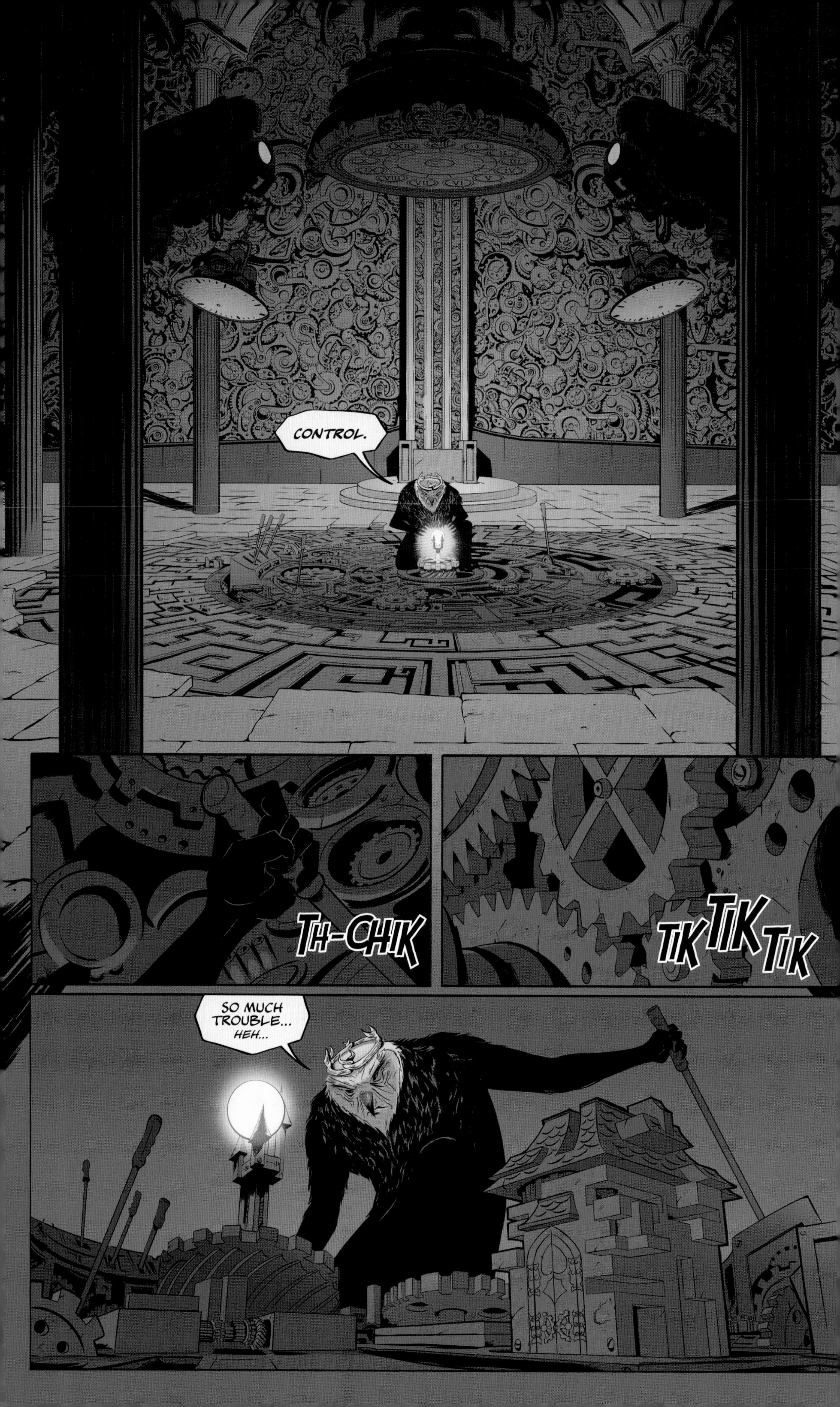
CONTROL.
TH-CHIK
TIK TIK TIK
SO MUCH TROUBLE... HEH...

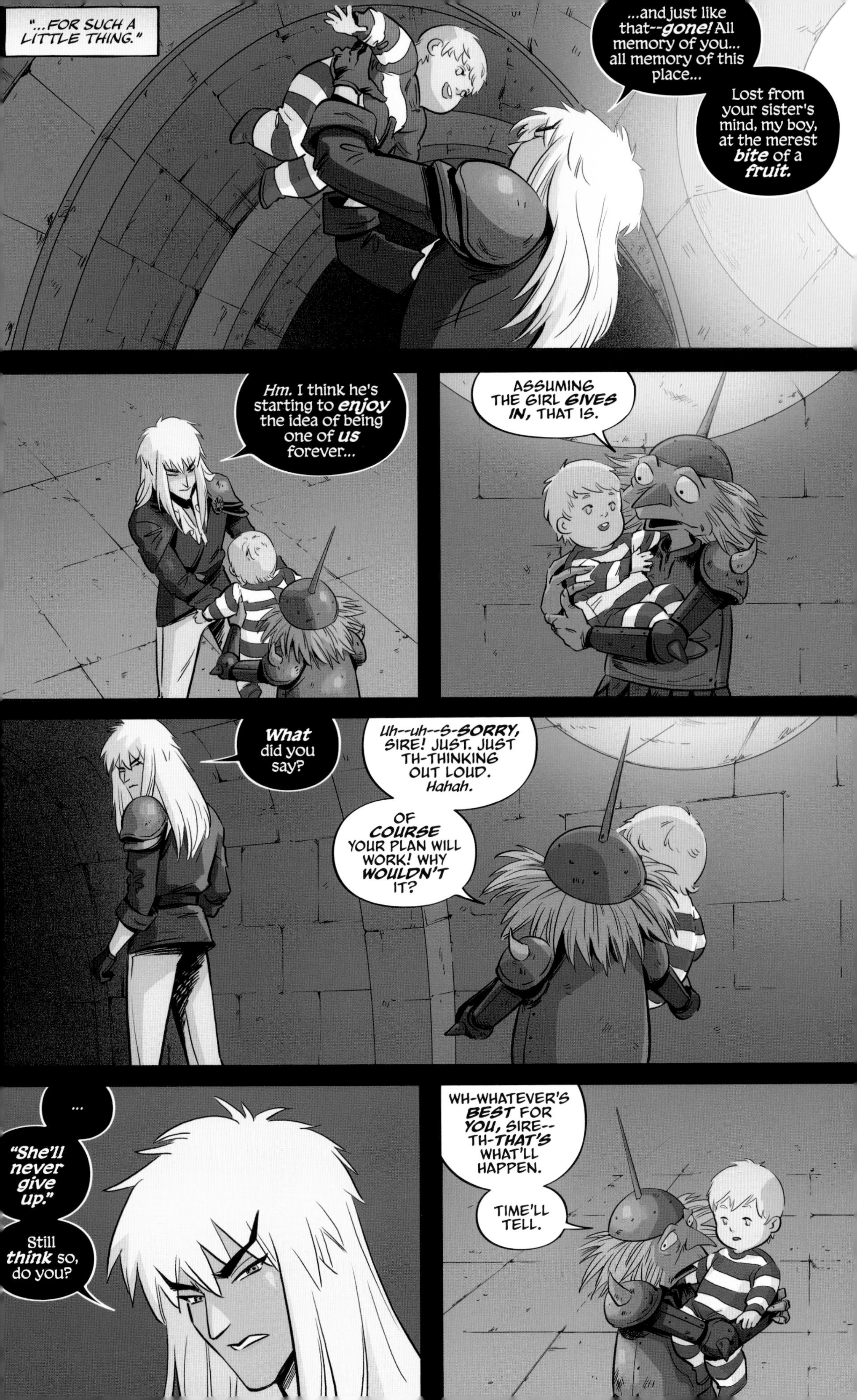
"...FOR SUCH A LITTLE THING."
...and just like that--gone! All memory of you... all memory of this place...
Lost from your sister's mind, my boy, at the merest bite of a fruit.
Hm. I think he's starting to enjoy the idea of being one of us forever...
ASSUMING THE GIRL GIVES IN, THAT IS.
What did you say?
Uh--uh--S-SORRY, SIRE! JUST. JUST TH-THINKING OUT LOUD. Hahah.
OF COURSE YOUR PLAN WILL WORK! WHY WOULDN'T IT?
...
"She'll never give up."
Still think so, do you?
WH-WHATEVER'S BEST FOR YOU, SIRE--TH-THAT'S WHAT'LL HAPPEN.
TIME'LL TELL.

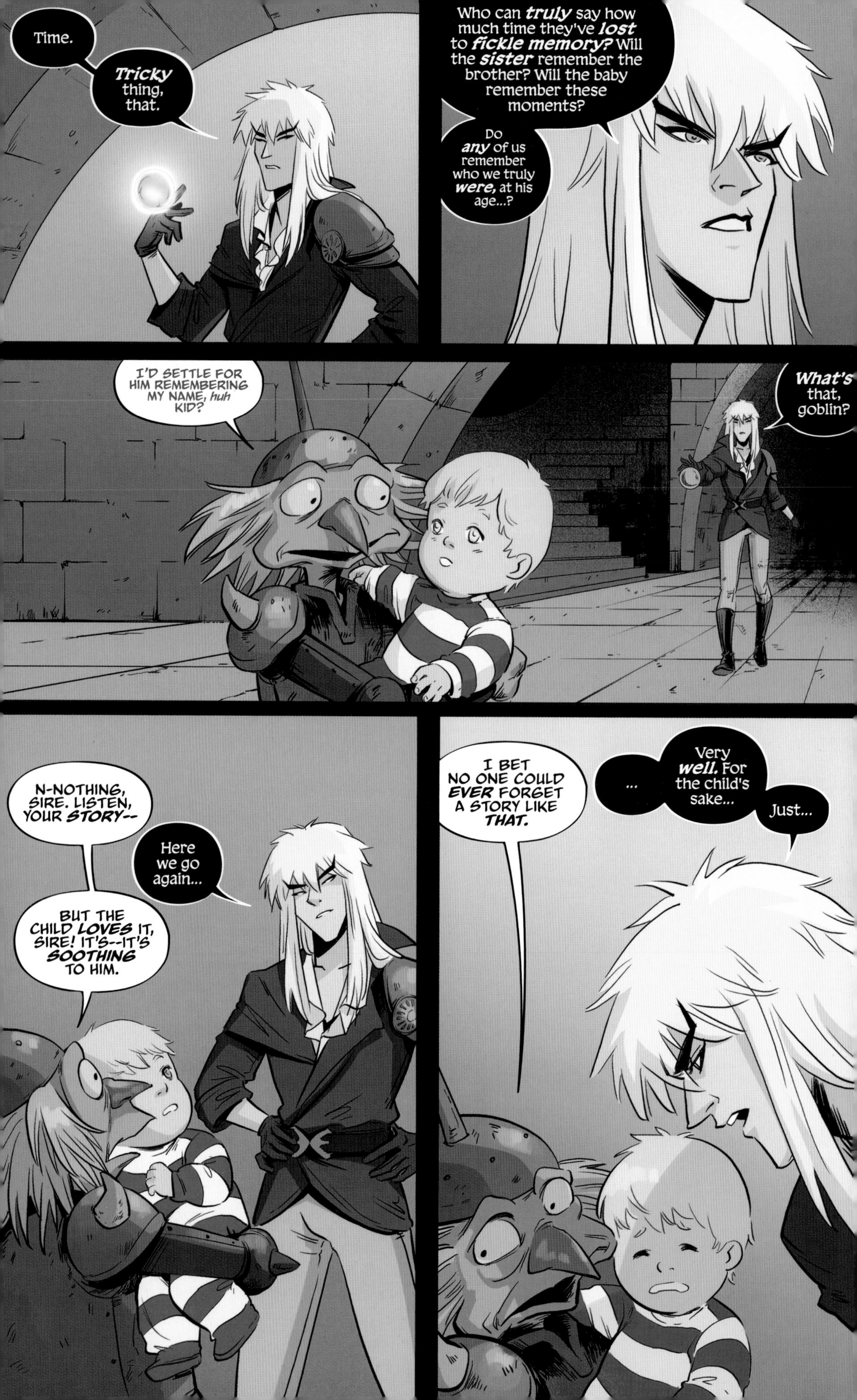
Time.
Tricky thing, that.
Who can truly say how much time they've lost to fickle memory? Will the sister remember the brother? Will the baby remember these moments?
Do any of us remember who we truly were, at his age...?
I'D SETTLE FOR HIM REMEMBERING MY NAME, huh KID?
What's that, goblin?
N-NOTHING, SIRE. LISTEN, YOUR STORY--
Here we go again...
BUT THE CHILD LOVES IT, SIRE! IT'S--IT'S SOOTHING TO HIM.
I BET NO ONE COULD EVER FORGET A STORY LIKE THAT.
...
Very well. For the child's sake...
Just...

...don't expect a cheerful *nursery rhyme.*

ANSWER! ANSWER! ANSWER!

oh dear this is bad oh my I think BIG HUGS? someone? Anyone?

COME ON! MAGIC CHALK--BE-- BE MORE MAGIC!

'ERE-- WHAT'S THAT THING?

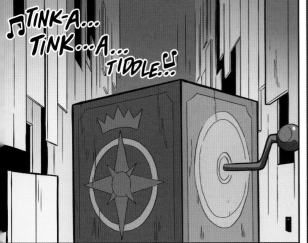

♪TINK-A... TINK...A... TIDDLE...♪

IT'S... uh...

≵hnnf≶

TINK-T-TINK ♪-A- DIDDLE- LINK♪

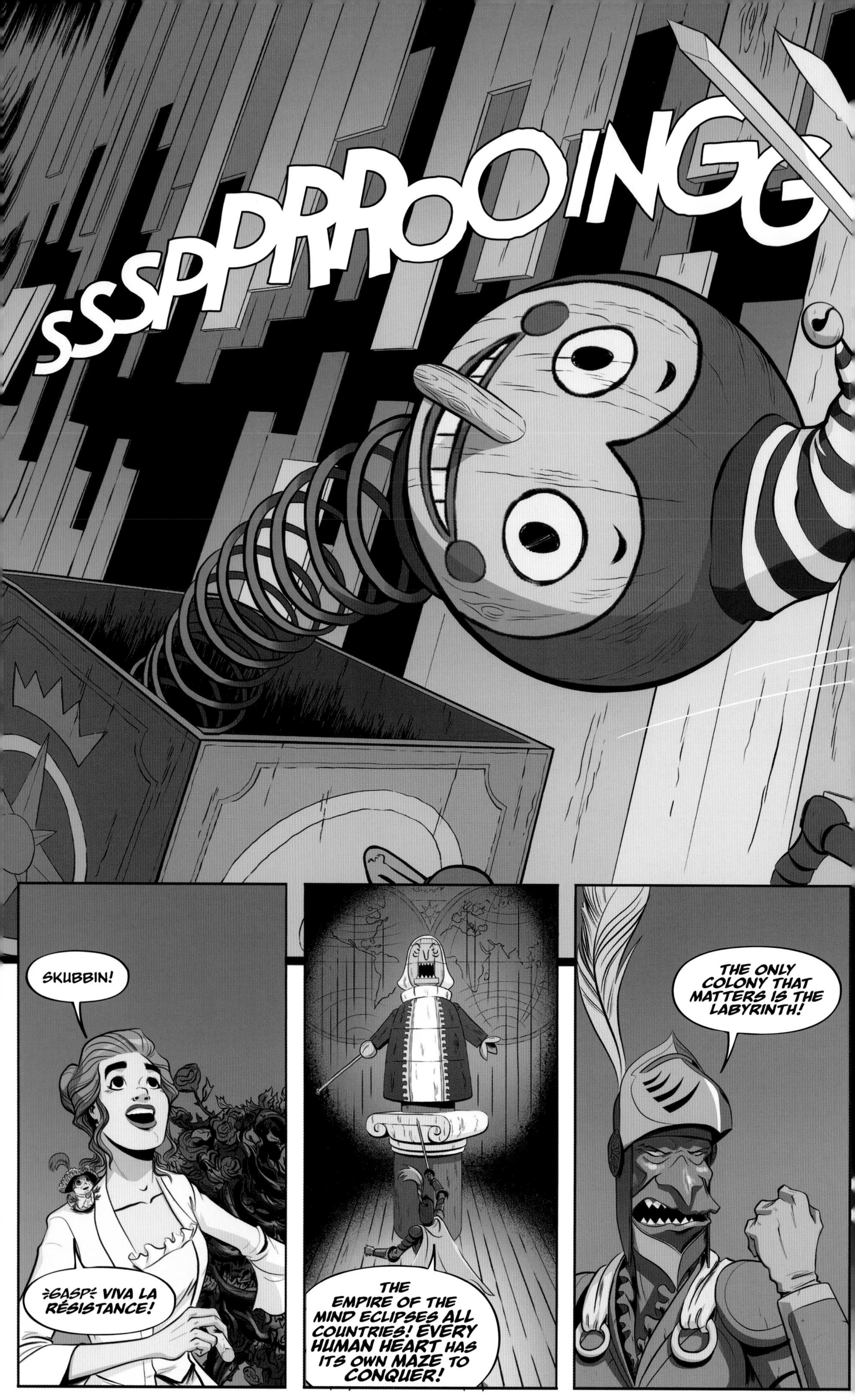
SSSPPRROOINGG
SKUBBIN!
≶GASP≶ VIVA LA RÉSISTANCE!
THE EMPIRE OF THE MIND ECLIPSES ALL COUNTRIES! EVERY HUMAN HEART HAS ITS OWN MAZE TO CONQUER!
THE ONLY COLONY THAT MATTERS IS THE LABYRINTH!

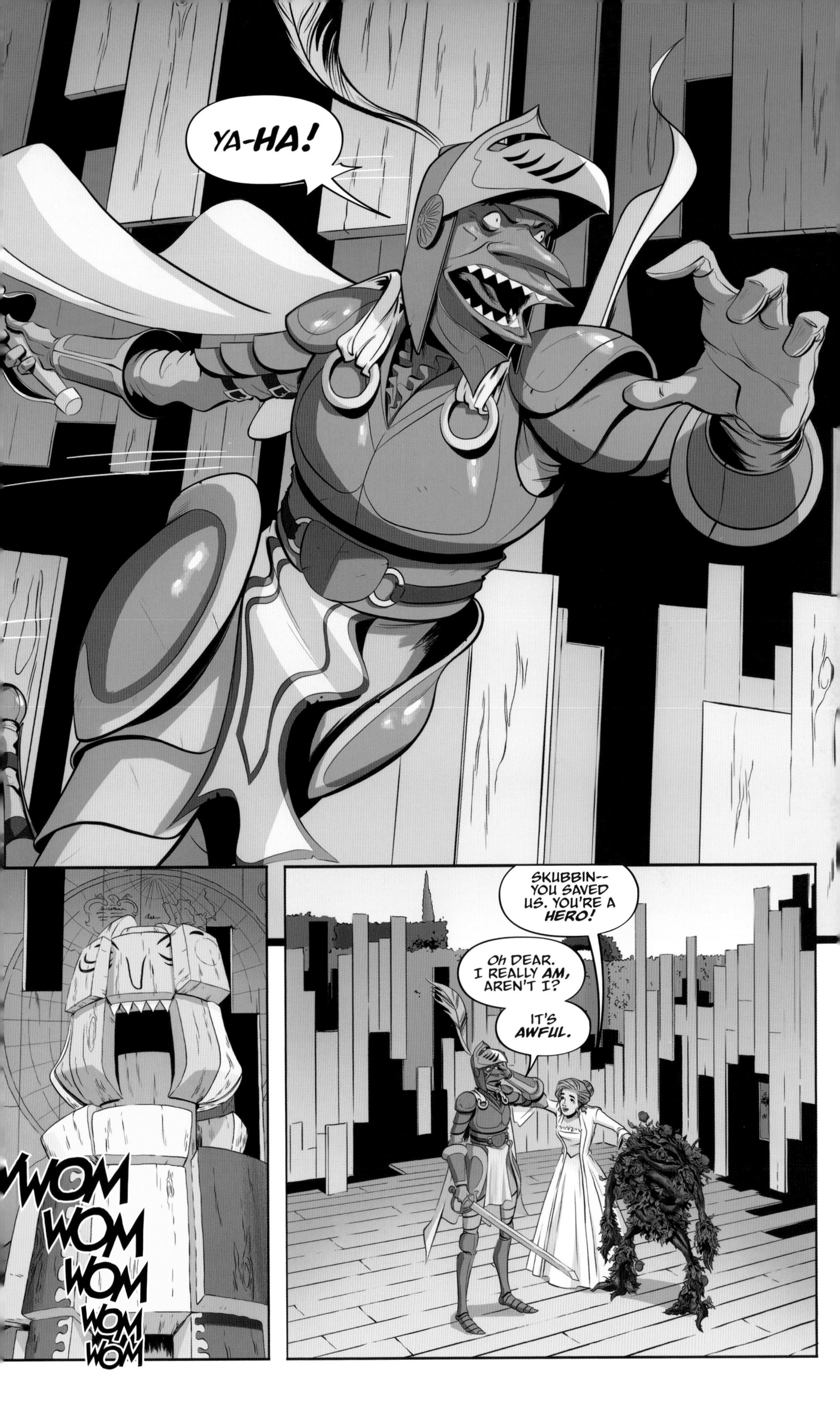
YA-HA!
WOM
WOM
WOM
WOM
WOM
SKUBBIN--
YOU SAVED
US. YOU'RE A
HERO!
Oh DEAR.
I REALLY AM,
AREN'T I?
IT'S
AWFUL.

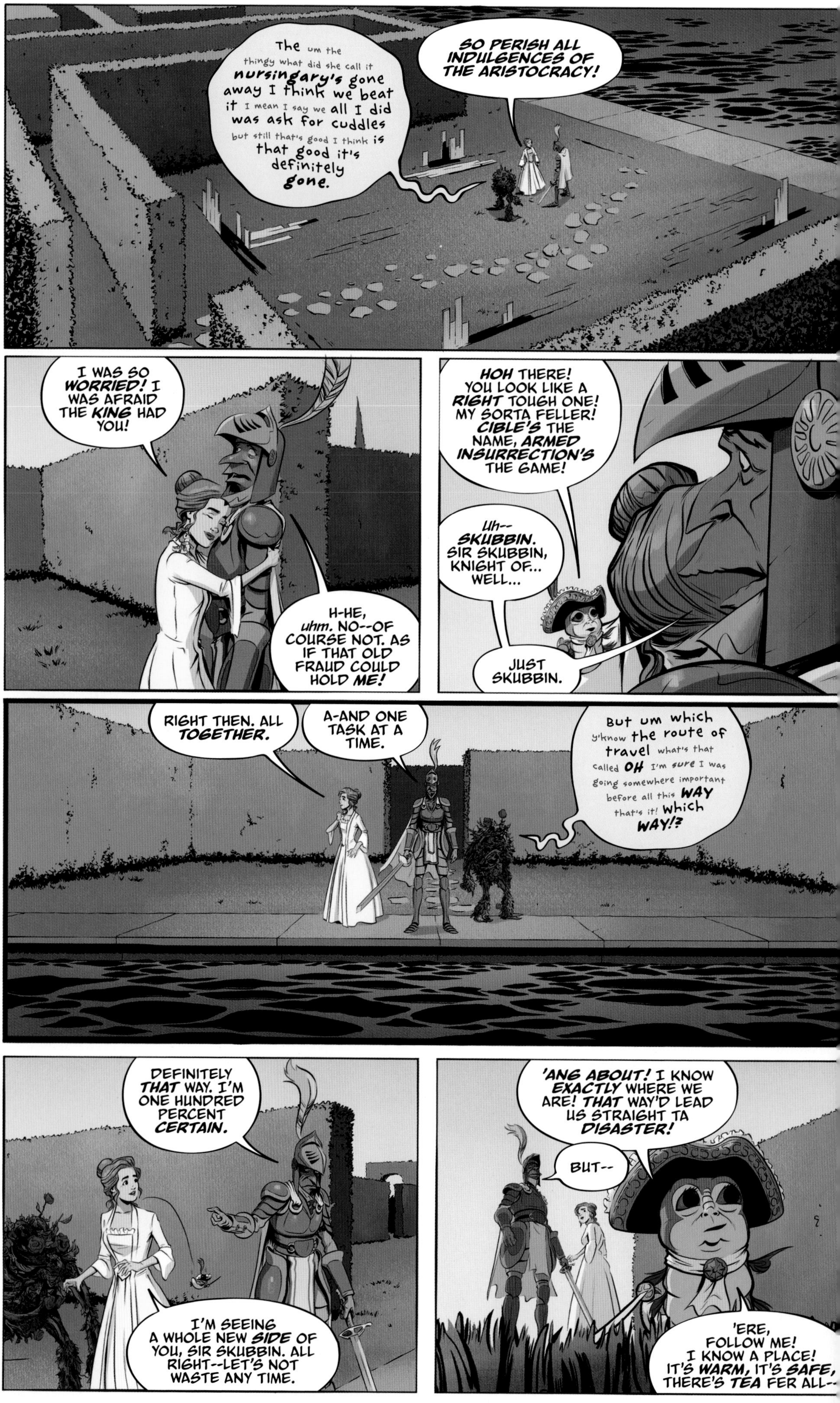

The um the thingy what did she call it nursingary's gone away I think we beat it I mean I say we all I did was ask for cuddles but still that's good I think is that good it's definitely gone.
SO PERISH ALL INDULGENCES OF THE ARISTOCRACY!
I WAS SO WORRIED! I WAS AFRAID THE KING HAD YOU!
H-HE, uhm. NO--OF COURSE NOT. AS IF THAT OLD FRAUD COULD HOLD ME!
HOH THERE! YOU LOOK LIKE A RIGHT TOUGH ONE! MY SORTA FELLER! CIBLE'S THE NAME, ARMED INSURRECTION'S THE GAME!
Uh-- SKUBBIN. SIR SKUBBIN, KNIGHT OF... WELL...
JUST SKUBBIN.
RIGHT THEN. ALL TOGETHER.
A-AND ONE TASK AT A TIME.
But um which y'know the route of travel what's that called OH I'm sure I was going somewhere important before all this WAY that's it! Which WAY!?
DEFINITELY THAT WAY. I'M ONE HUNDRED PERCENT CERTAIN.
I'M SEEING A WHOLE NEW SIDE OF YOU, SIR SKUBBIN. ALL RIGHT--LET'S NOT WASTE ANY TIME.
'ANG ABOUT! I KNOW EXACTLY WHERE WE ARE! THAT WAY'D LEAD US STRAIGHT TA DISASTER!
BUT--
'ERE, FOLLOW ME! I KNOW A PLACE! IT'S WARM, IT'S SAFE, THERE'S TEA FER ALL--

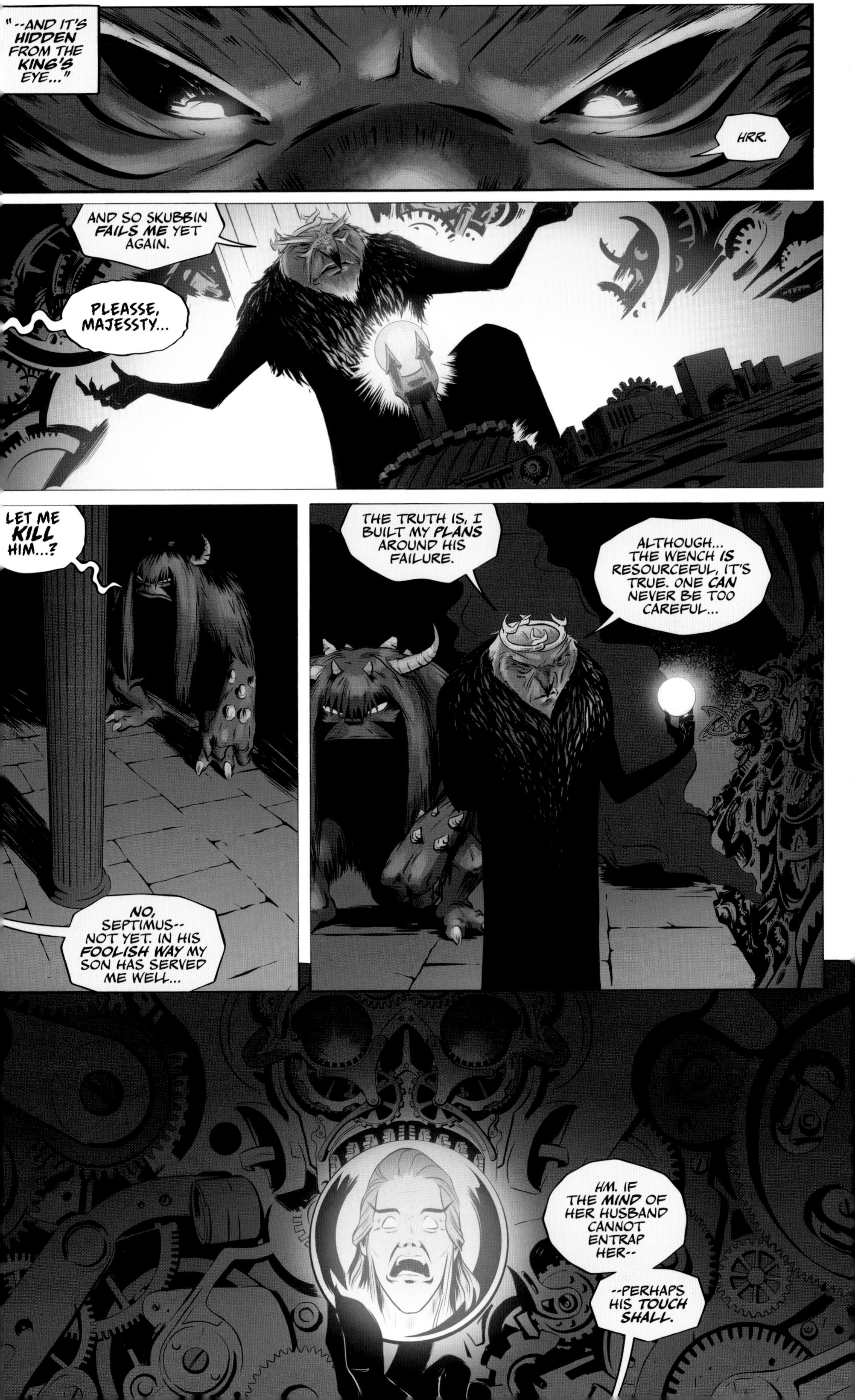
"--AND IT'S HIDDEN FROM THE KING'S EYE..."
HRR.
AND SO SKUBBIN FAILS ME YET AGAIN.
PLEASSE, MAJESSTY...
LET ME KILL HIM...?
NO, SEPTIMUS--NOT YET. IN HIS FOOLISH WAY MY SON HAS SERVED ME WELL...
THE TRUTH IS, I BUILT MY PLANS AROUND HIS FAILURE.
ALTHOUGH... THE WENCH IS RESOURCEFUL, IT'S TRUE. ONE CAN NEVER BE TOO CAREFUL...
HM. IF THE MIND OF HER HUSBAND CANNOT ENTRAP HER--
--PERHAPS HIS TOUCH SHALL.

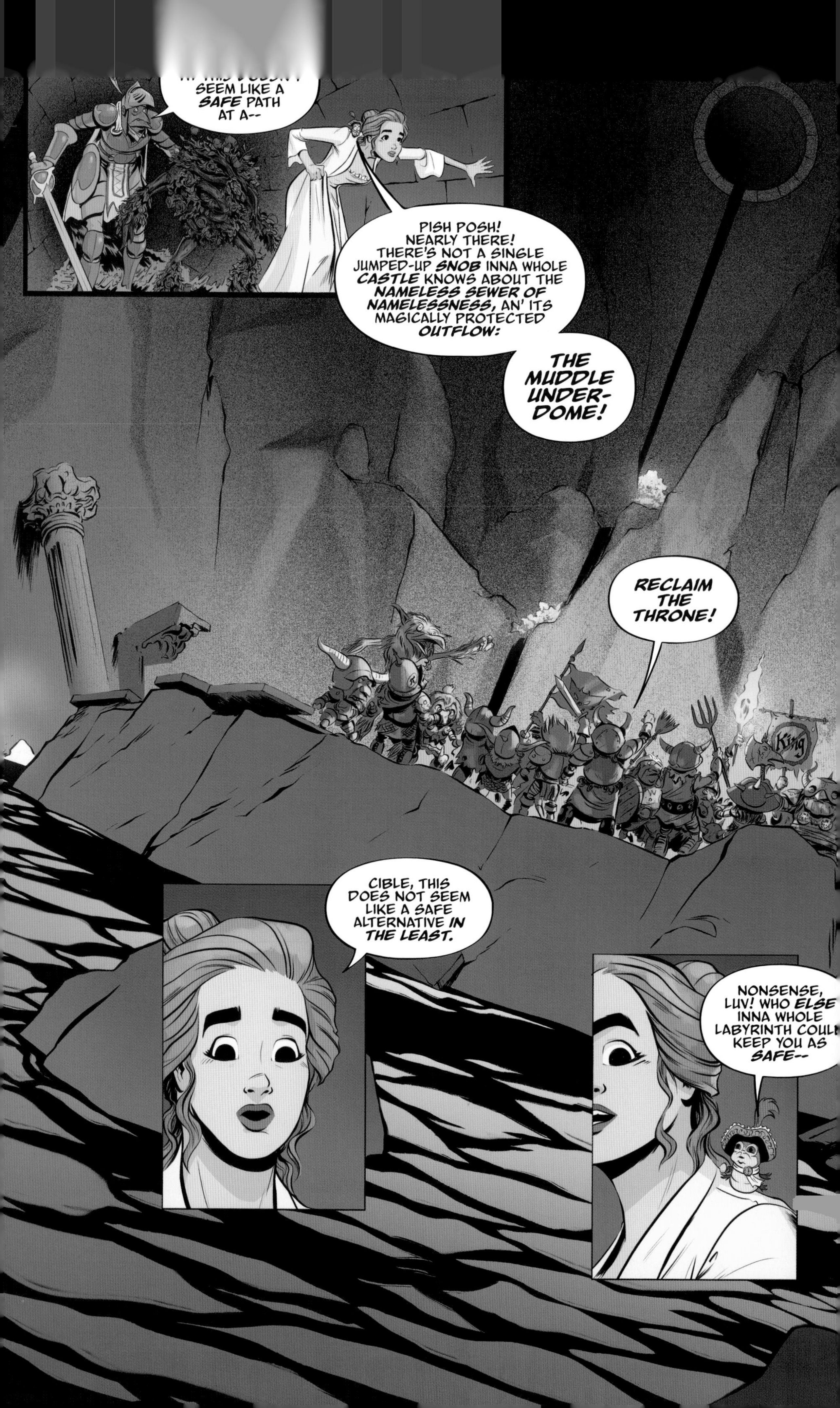

SEEM LIKE A SAFE PATH AT A--
PISH POSH! NEARLY THERE! THERE'S NOT A SINGLE JUMPED-UP SNOB INNA WHOLE CASTLE KNOWS ABOUT THE NAMELESS SEWER OF NAMELESSNESS, AN' ITS MAGICALLY PROTECTED OUTFLOW:
THE MUDDLE UNDER-DOME!
RECLAIM THE THRONE!
King
CIBLE, THIS DOES NOT SEEM LIKE A SAFE ALTERNATIVE IN THE LEAST.
NONSENSE, LUV! WHO ELSE INNA WHOLE LABYRINTH COUL
KEEP YOU AS SAFE--

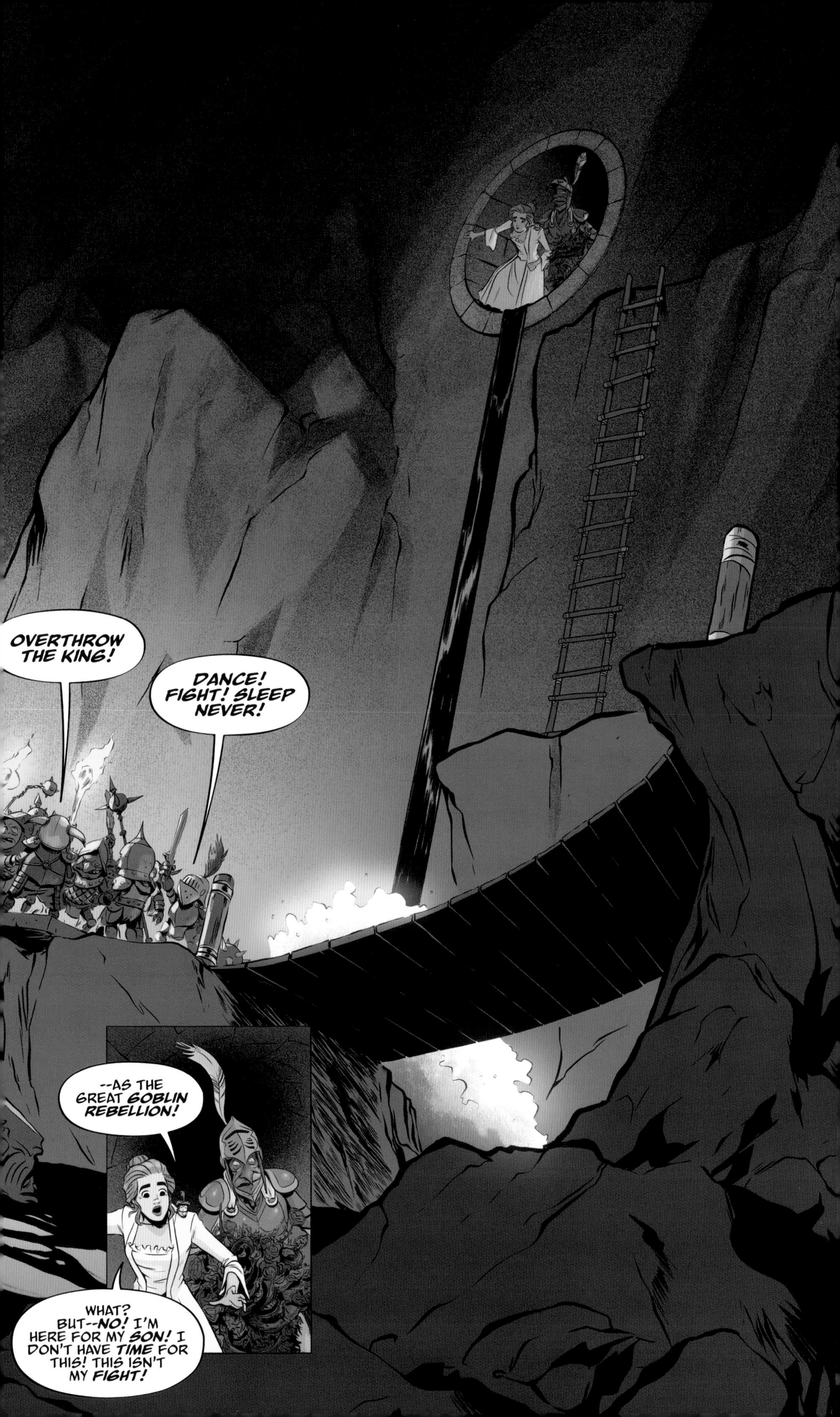
OVERTHROW THE KING!
DANCE! FIGHT! SLEEP NEVER!
--AS THE GREAT GOBLIN REBELLION!
WHAT? BUT--NO! I'M HERE FOR MY SON! I DON'T HAVE TIME FOR THIS! THIS ISN'T MY FIGHT!

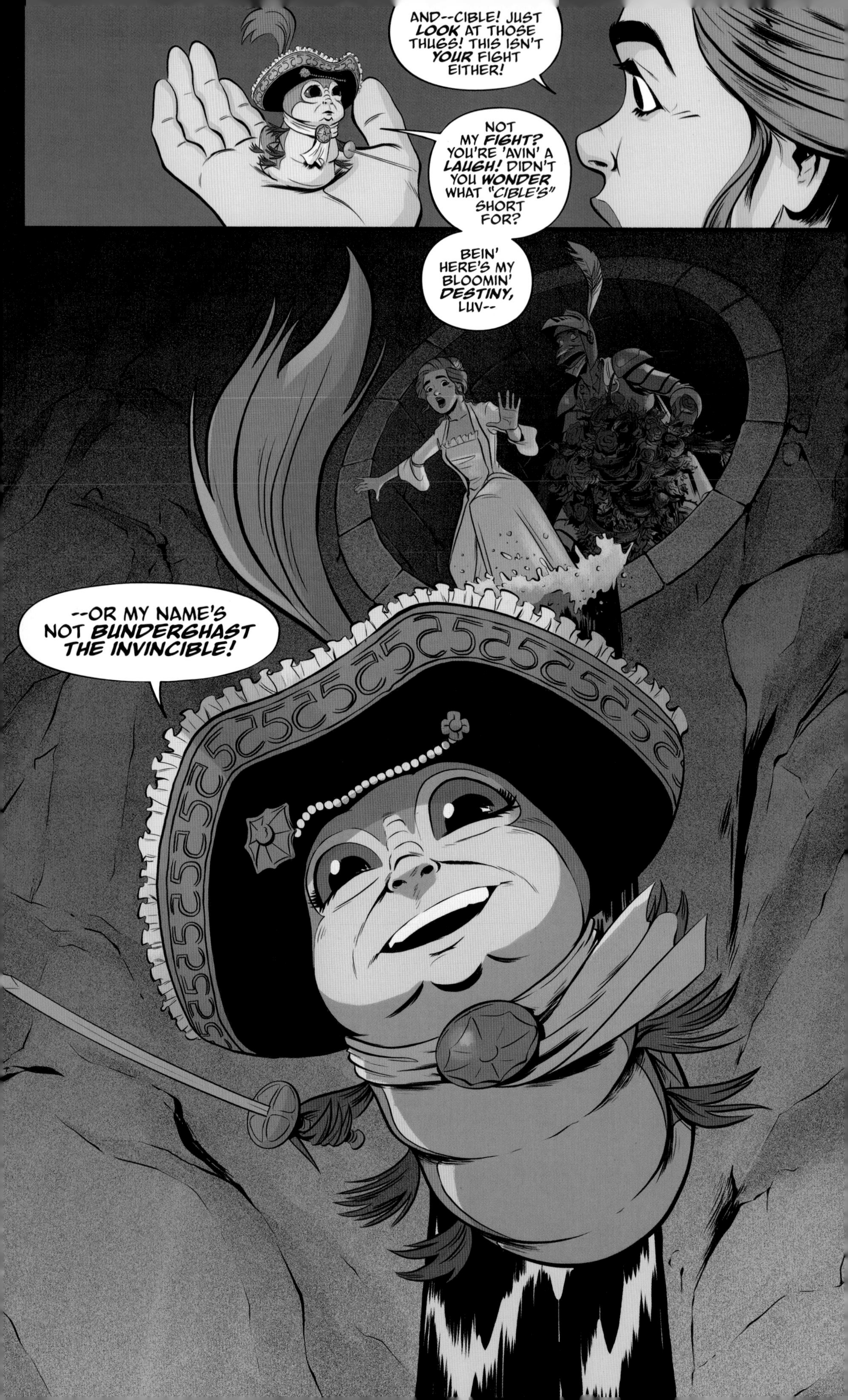
AND--CIBLE! JUST LOOK AT THOSE THUGS! THIS ISN'T YOUR FIGHT EITHER!
NOT MY FIGHT? YOU'RE 'AVIN' A LAUGH! DIDN'T YOU WONDER WHAT "CIBLE'S" SHORT FOR?
BEIN' HERE'S MY BLOOMIN' DESTINY, LUV--
--OR MY NAME'S NOT BUNDERGHAST THE INVINCIBLE!

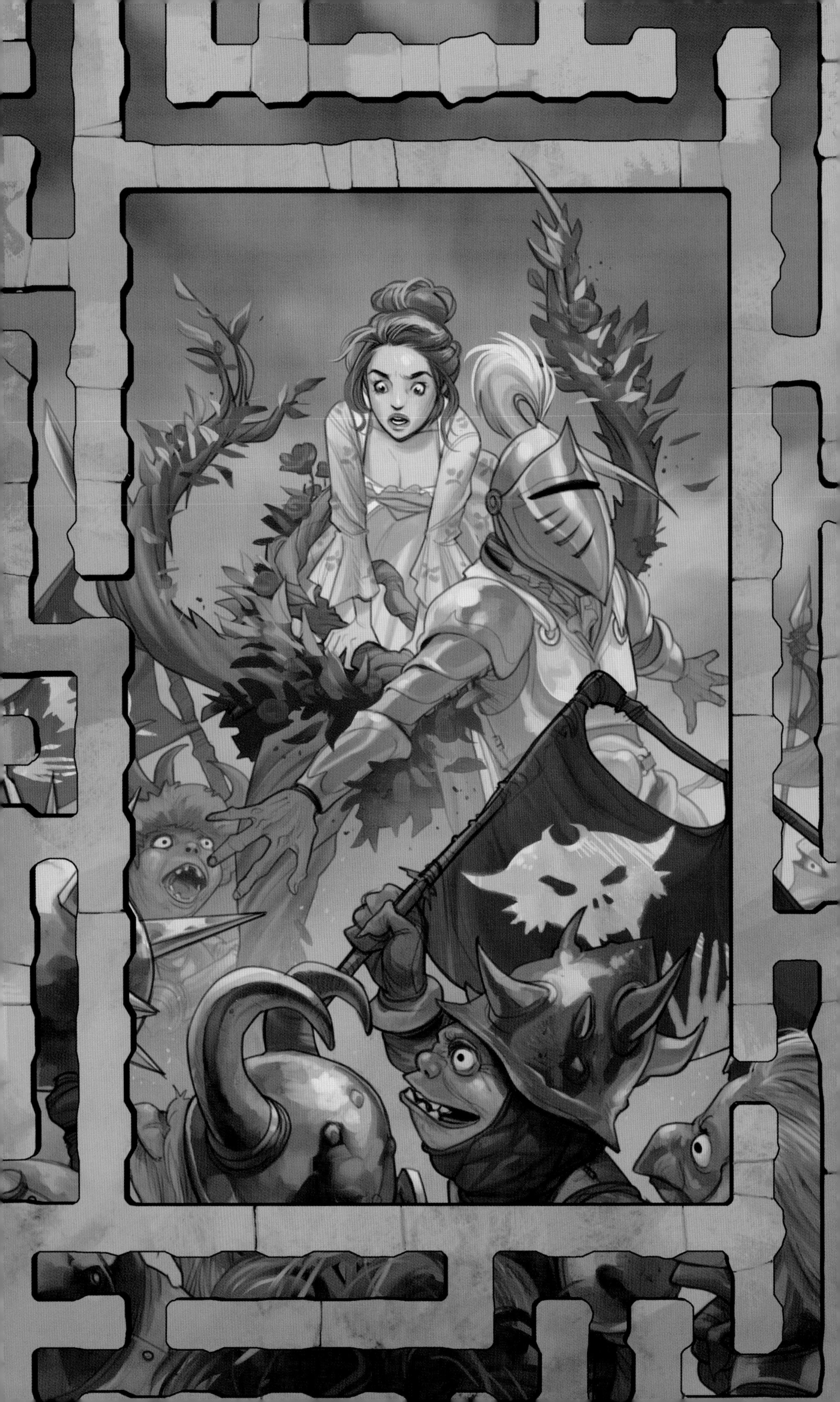

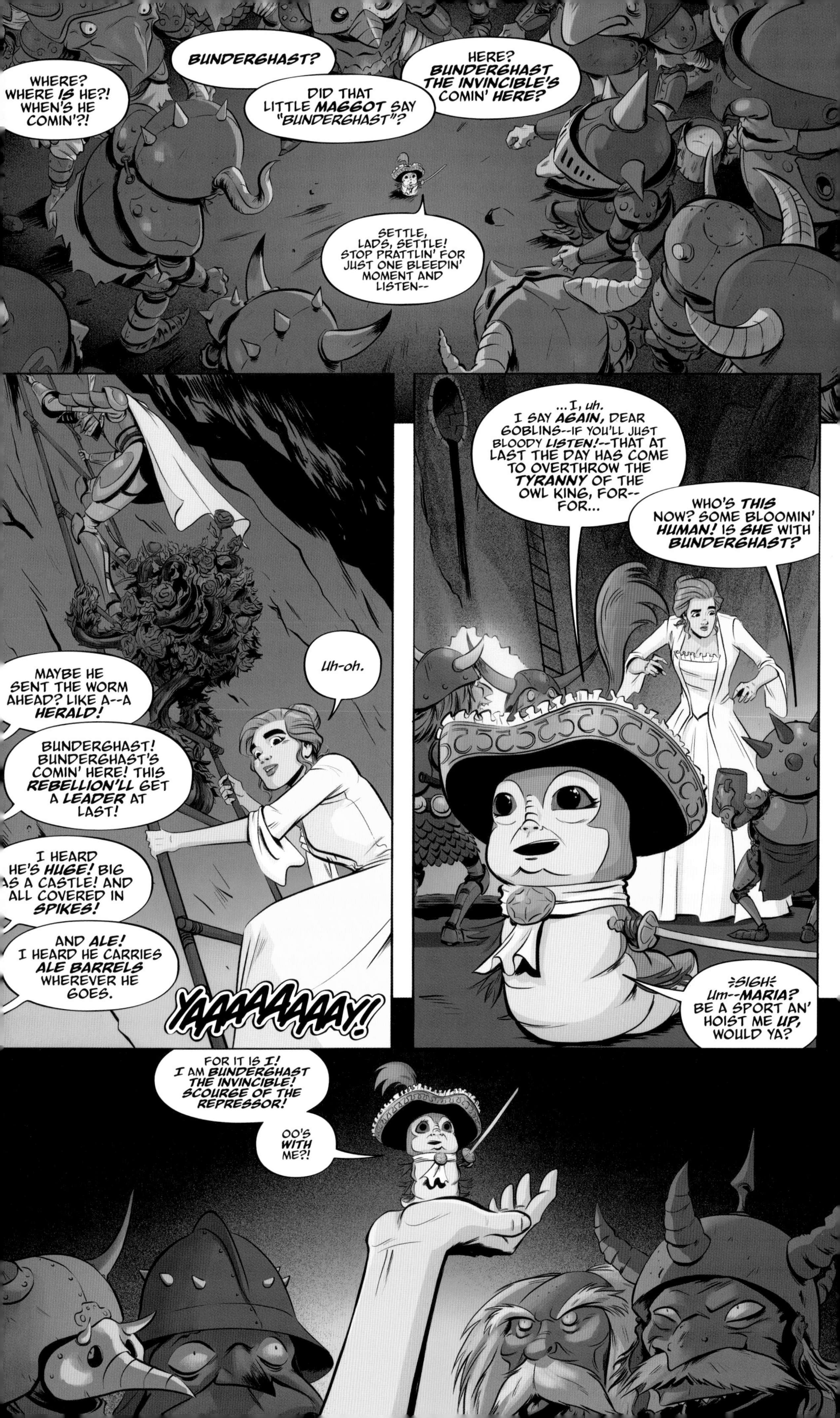
WHERE? WHERE IS HE?! WHEN'S HE COMIN'?!
BUNDERGHAST?
DID THAT LITTLE MAGGOT SAY "BUNDERGHAST"?
HERE? BUNDERGHAST THE INVINCIBLE'S COMIN' HERE?
SETTLE, LADS, SETTLE! STOP PRATTLIN' FOR JUST ONE BLEEDIN' MOMENT AND LISTEN--
MAYBE HE SENT THE WORM AHEAD? LIKE A--A HERALD!
BUNDERGHAST! BUNDERGHAST'S COMIN' HERE! THIS REBELLION'LL GET A LEADER AT LAST!
I HEARD HE'S HUGE! BIG AS A CASTLE! AND ALL COVERED IN SPIKES!
AND ALE! I HEARD HE CARRIES ALE BARRELS WHEREVER HE GOES.
Uh-oh.
YAAAAAAAAY!
...I, uh. I SAY AGAIN, DEAR GOBLINS--IF YOU'LL JUST BLOODY LISTEN!--THAT AT LAST THE DAY HAS COME TO OVERTHROW THE TYRANNY OF THE OWL KING, FOR--FOR...
WHO'S THIS NOW? SOME BLOOMIN' HUMAN! IS SHE WITH BUNDERGHAST?
SIGH Um--MARIA? BE A SPORT AN' HOIST ME UP, WOULD YA?
FOR IT IS I! I AM BUNDERGHAST THE INVINCIBLE! SCOURGE OF THE REPRESSOR!
OO'S WITH ME?!

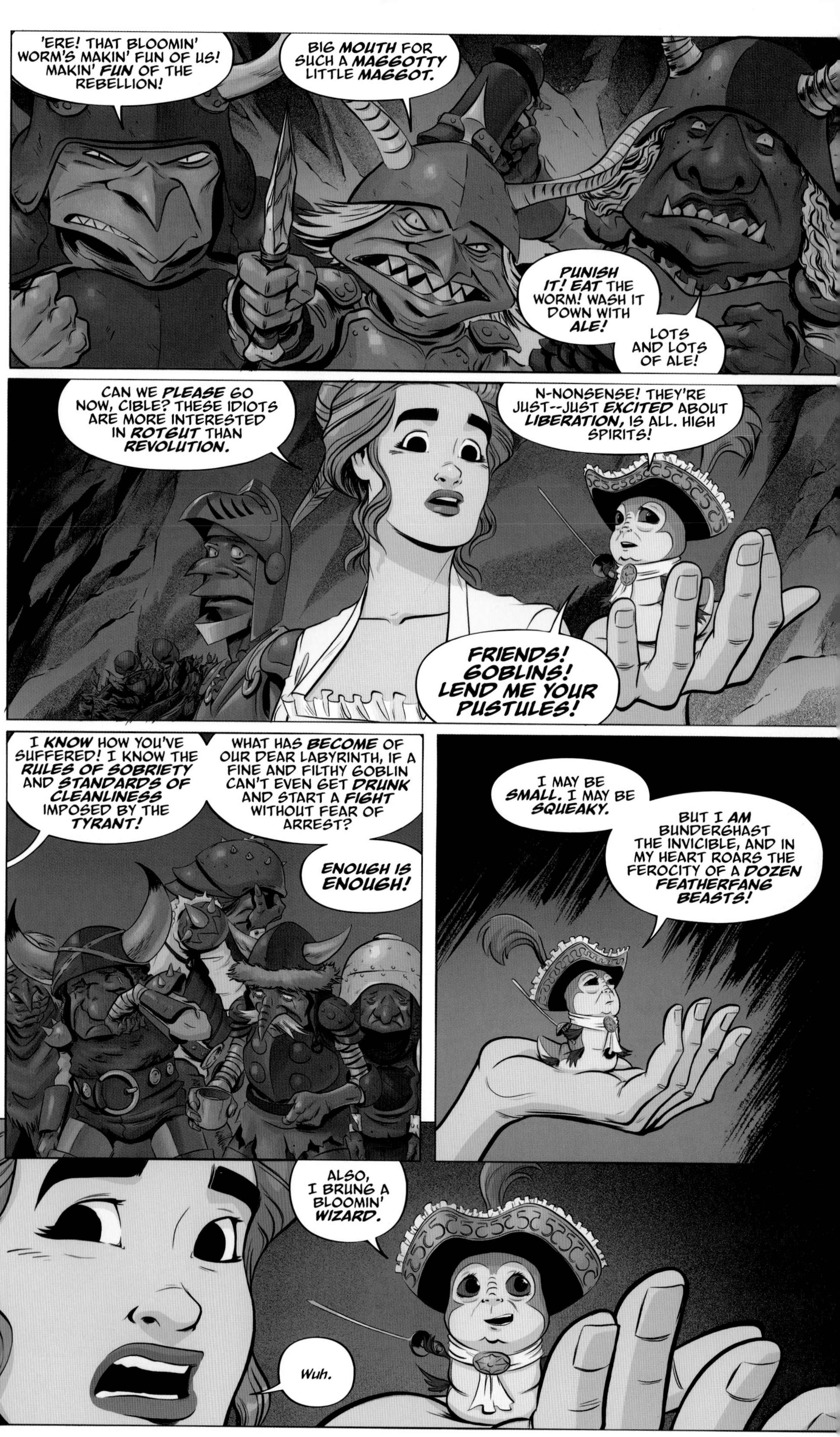
'ERE! THAT BLOOMIN' WORM'S MAKIN' FUN OF US! MAKIN' FUN OF THE REBELLION!
BIG MOUTH FOR SUCH A MAGGOTTY LITTLE MAGGOT.
PUNISH IT! EAT THE WORM! WASH IT DOWN WITH ALE!
LOTS AND LOTS OF ALE!
CAN WE PLEASE GO NOW, CIBLE? THESE IDIOTS ARE MORE INTERESTED IN ROTGUT THAN REVOLUTION.
N-NONSENSE! THEY'RE JUST--JUST EXCITED ABOUT LIBERATION, IS ALL. HIGH SPIRITS!
FRIENDS! GOBLINS! LEND ME YOUR PUSTULES!
I KNOW HOW YOU'VE SUFFERED! I KNOW THE RULES OF SOBRIETY AND STANDARDS OF CLEANLINESS IMPOSED BY THE TYRANT!
WHAT HAS BECOME OF OUR DEAR LABYRINTH, IF A FINE AND FILTHY GOBLIN CAN'T EVEN GET DRUNK AND START A FIGHT WITHOUT FEAR OF ARREST?
ENOUGH IS ENOUGH!
I MAY BE SMALL. I MAY BE SQUEAKY.
BUT I AM BUNDERGHAST THE INVICIBLE, AND IN MY HEART ROARS THE FEROCITY OF A DOZEN FEATHERFANG BEASTS!
ALSO, I BRUNG A BLOOMIN' WIZARD.
Wuh.

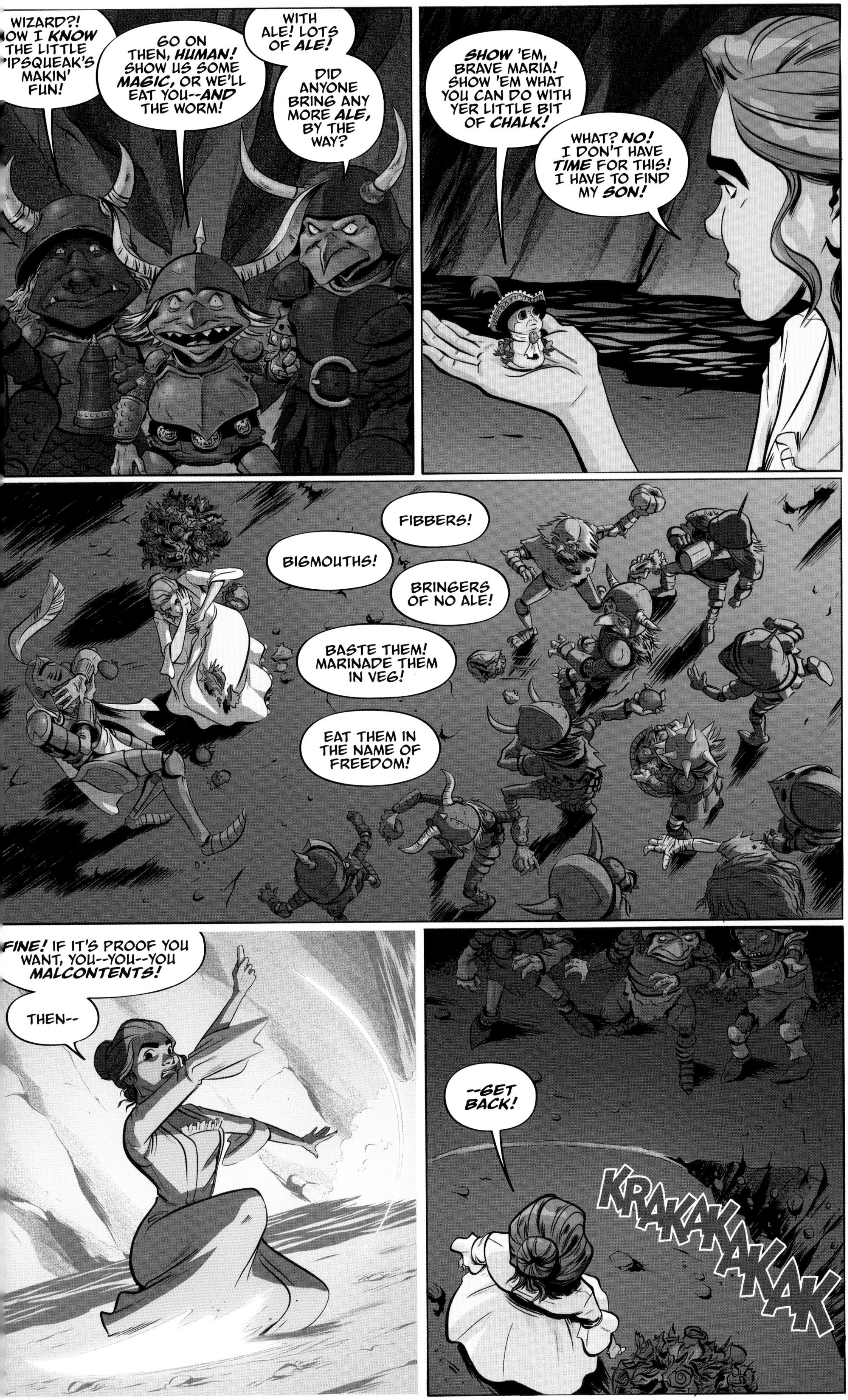
WIZARD?! NOW I KNOW THE LITTLE PIPSQUEAK'S MAKIN' FUN!
GO ON THEN, HUMAN! SHOW US SOME MAGIC, OR WE'LL EAT YOU--AND THE WORM!
WITH ALE! LOTS OF ALE!
DID ANYONE BRING ANY MORE ALE, BY THE WAY?
SHOW 'EM, BRAVE MARIA! SHOW 'EM WHAT YOU CAN DO WITH YER LITTLE BIT OF CHALK!
WHAT? NO! I DON'T HAVE TIME FOR THIS! I HAVE TO FIND MY SON!
FIBBERS!
BIGMOUTHS!
BRINGERS OF NO ALE!
BASTE THEM! MARINADE THEM IN VEG!
EAT THEM IN THE NAME OF FREEDOM!
FINE! IF IT'S PROOF YOU WANT, YOU--YOU--YOU MALCONTENTS!
THEN--
--GET BACK!
KRAKAKAKAK

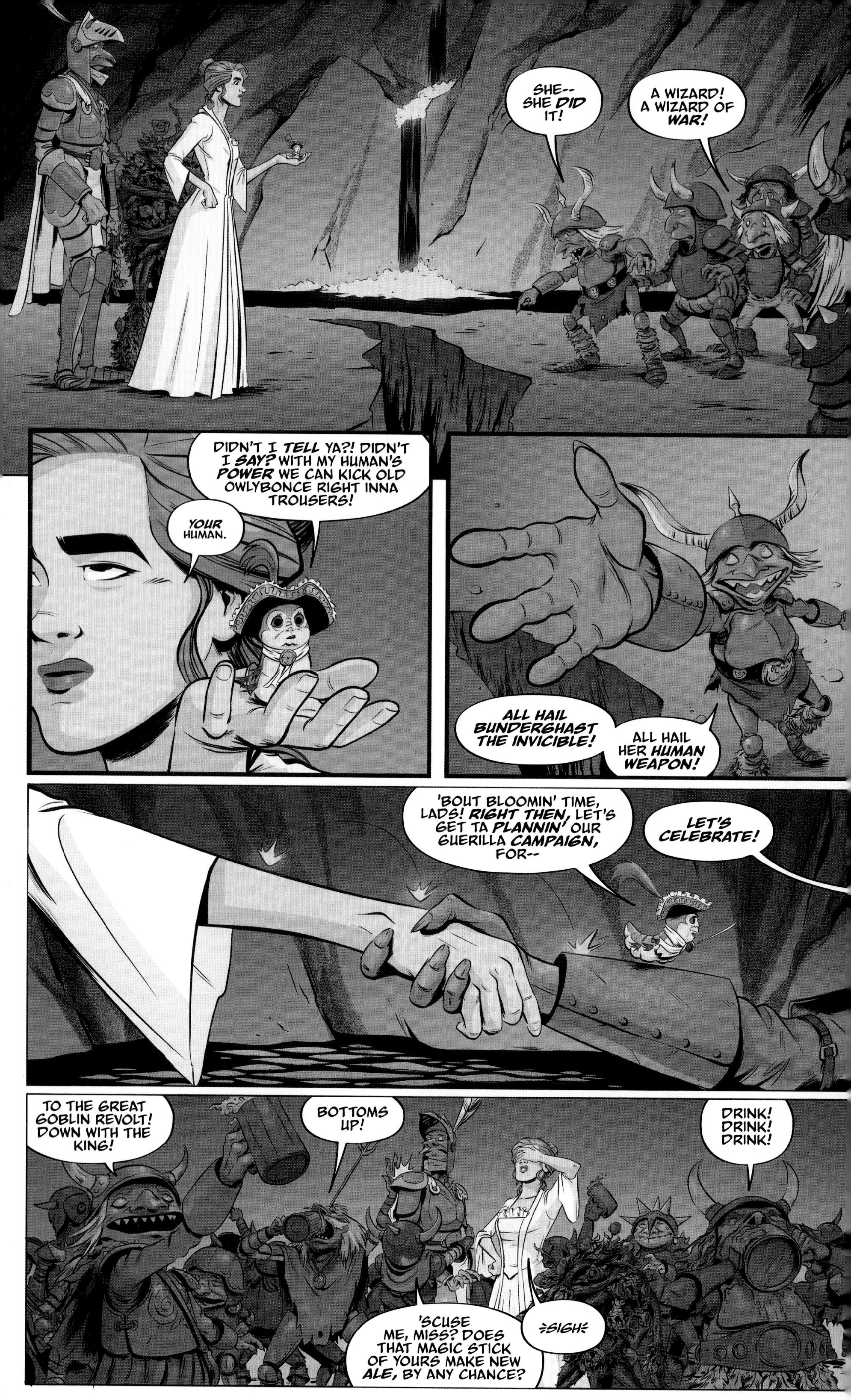
SHE-- SHE DID IT!
A WIZARD! A WIZARD OF WAR!
DIDN'T I TELL YA?! DIDN'T I SAY? WITH MY HUMAN'S POWER WE CAN KICK OLD OWLYBONCE RIGHT INNA TROUSERS!
YOUR HUMAN.
ALL HAIL BUNDERGHAST THE INVICIBLE!
ALL HAIL HER HUMAN WEAPON!
'BOUT BLOOMIN' TIME, LADS! RIGHT THEN, LET'S GET TA PLANNIN' OUR GUERILLA CAMPAIGN, FOR--
LET'S CELEBRATE!
TO THE GREAT GOBLIN REVOLT! DOWN WITH THE KING!
BOTTOMS UP!
DRINK! DRINK! DRINK!
'SCUSE ME, MISS? DOES THAT MAGIC STICK OF YOURS MAKE NEW ALE, BY ANY CHANCE?
SIGH

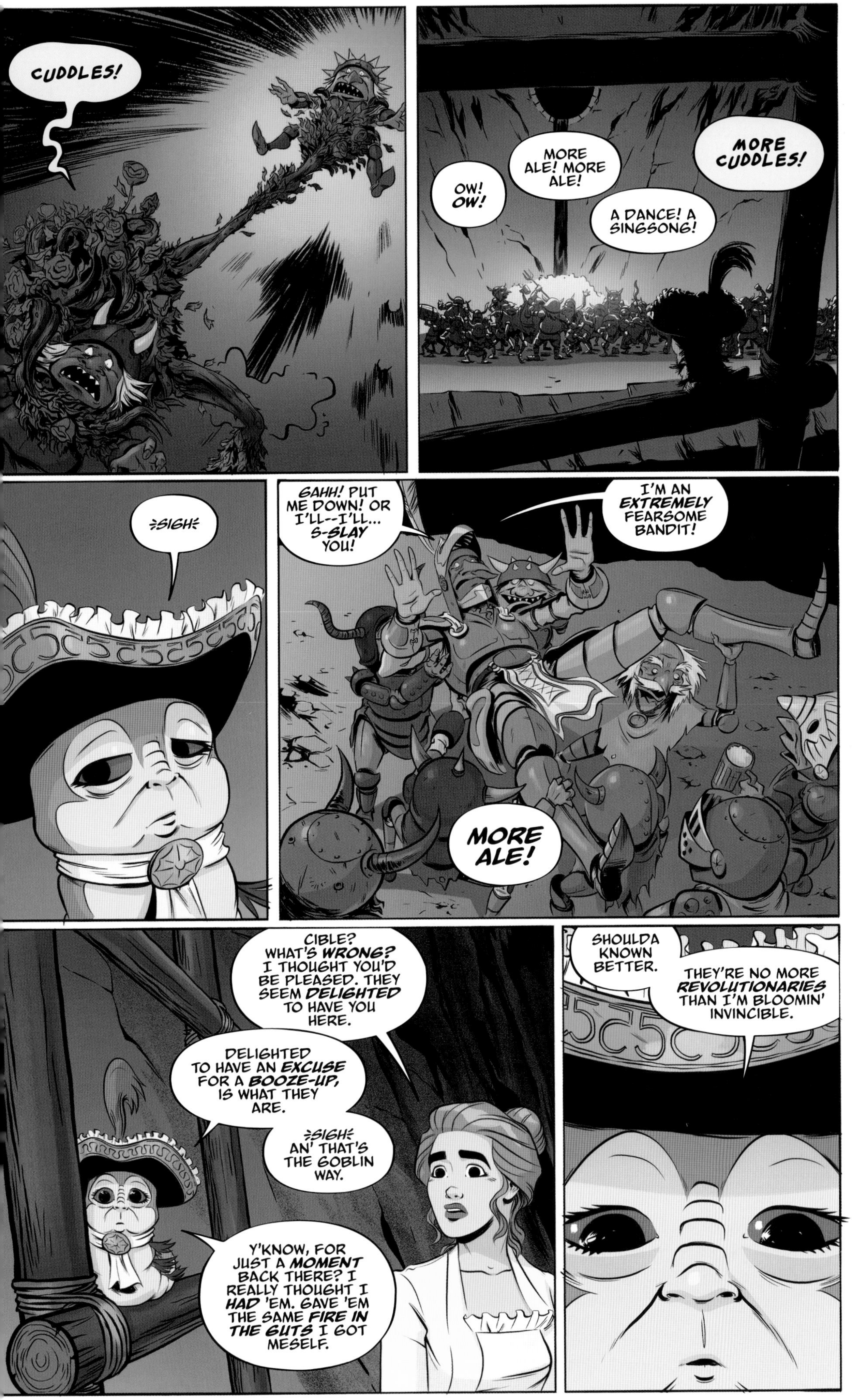
CUDDLES!
OW! OW!
MORE ALE! MORE ALE!
A DANCE! A SINGSONG!
MORE CUDDLES!
SIGH
GAHH! PUT ME DOWN! OR I'LL--I'LL... S-SLAY YOU!
I'M AN EXTREMELY FEARSOME BANDIT!
MORE ALE!
CIBLE? WHAT'S WRONG? I THOUGHT YOU'D BE PLEASED. THEY SEEM DELIGHTED TO HAVE YOU HERE.
DELIGHTED TO HAVE AN EXCUSE FOR A BOOZE-UP, IS WHAT THEY ARE.
SIGH AN' THAT'S THE GOBLIN WAY.
Y'KNOW, FOR JUST A MOMENT BACK THERE? I REALLY THOUGHT I HAD 'EM. GAVE 'EM THE SAME FIRE IN THE GUTS I GOT MESELF.
SHOULDA KNOWN BETTER.
THEY'RE NO MORE REVOLUTIONARIES THAN I'M BLOOMIN' INVINCIBLE.

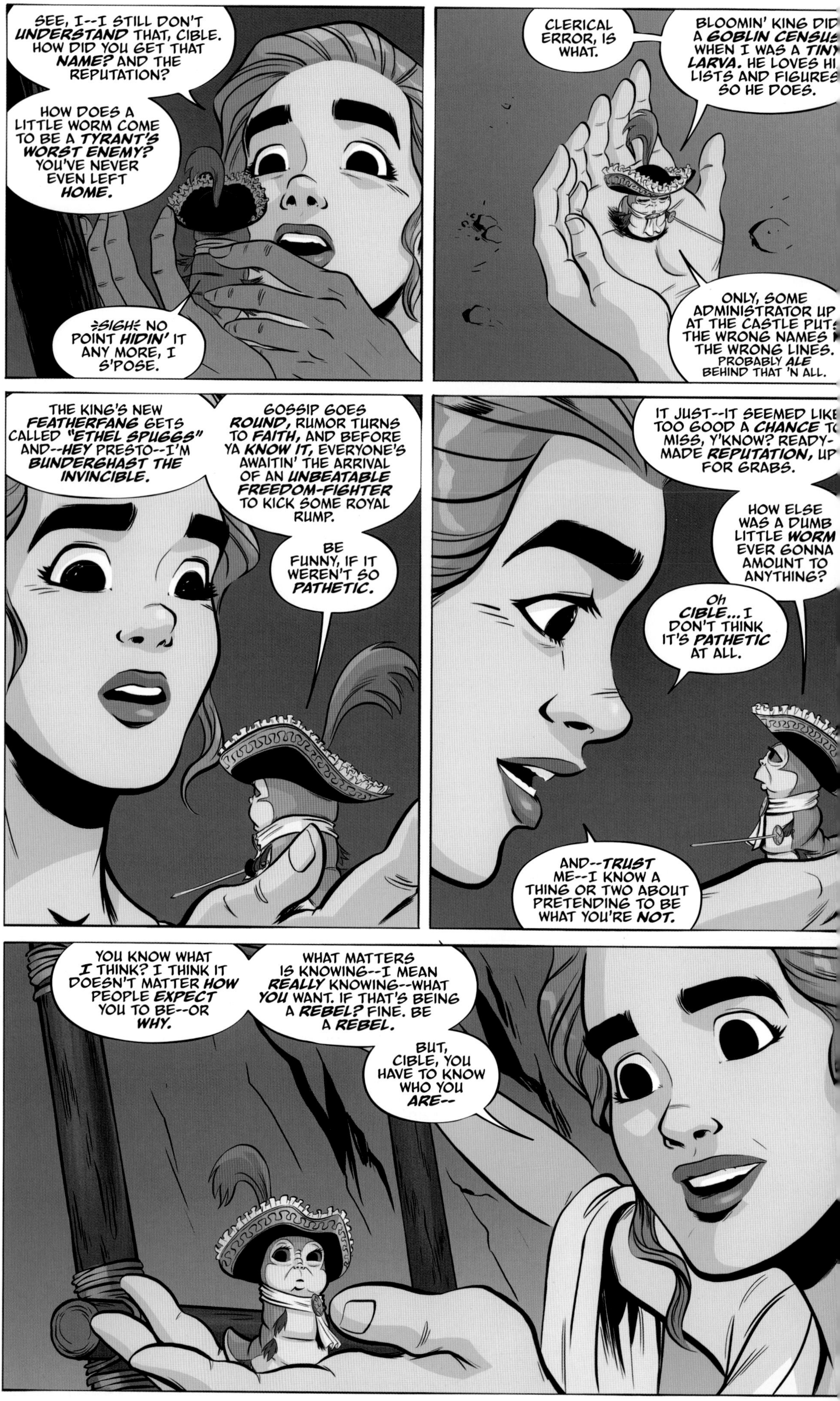

SEE, I--I STILL DON'T *UNDERSTAND* THAT, CIBLE. HOW DID YOU GET THAT *NAME?* AND THE REPUTATION?
HOW DOES A LITTLE WORM COME TO BE A *TYRANT'S WORST ENEMY?* YOU'VE NEVER EVEN LEFT *HOME.*
SIGH NO POINT *HIDIN'* IT ANY MORE, I S'POSE.
CLERICAL ERROR, IS WHAT.
BLOOMIN' KING DID A *GOBLIN CENSUS* WHEN I WAS A *TINY LARVA.* HE LOVES HIS LISTS AND FIGURES, SO HE DOES.
ONLY, SOME ADMINISTRATOR UP AT THE CASTLE PUTS THE WRONG NAMES ON THE WRONG LINES. PROBABLY *ALE* BEHIND THAT 'N ALL.
THE KING'S NEW *FEATHERFANG* GETS CALLED *"ETHEL SPUGGS"* AND--*HEY* PRESTO--I'M *BUNDERGHAST THE INVINCIBLE.*
GOSSIP GOES *ROUND,* RUMOR TURNS TO *FAITH,* AND BEFORE YA *KNOW IT,* EVERYONE'S AWAITIN' THE ARRIVAL OF AN *UNBEATABLE FREEDOM-FIGHTER* TO KICK SOME ROYAL RUMP.
BE FUNNY, IF IT WEREN'T SO *PATHETIC.*
IT JUST--IT SEEMED LIKE TOO GOOD A *CHANCE* TO MISS, Y'KNOW? READY-MADE *REPUTATION,* UP FOR GRABS.
HOW ELSE WAS A DUMB LITTLE *WORM* EVER GONNA AMOUNT TO ANYTHING?
Oh *CIBLE...* I DON'T THINK IT'S *PATHETIC* AT ALL.
AND--*TRUST* ME--I KNOW A THING OR TWO ABOUT PRETENDING TO BE WHAT YOU'RE *NOT.*
YOU KNOW WHAT *I* THINK? I THINK IT DOESN'T MATTER *HOW* PEOPLE *EXPECT* YOU TO BE--OR *WHY.*
WHAT MATTERS IS KNOWING--I MEAN *REALLY* KNOWING--WHAT *YOU* WANT. IF THAT'S BEING A *REBEL?* FINE. BE A *REBEL.*
BUT, CIBLE, YOU HAVE TO KNOW WHO YOU *ARE--*

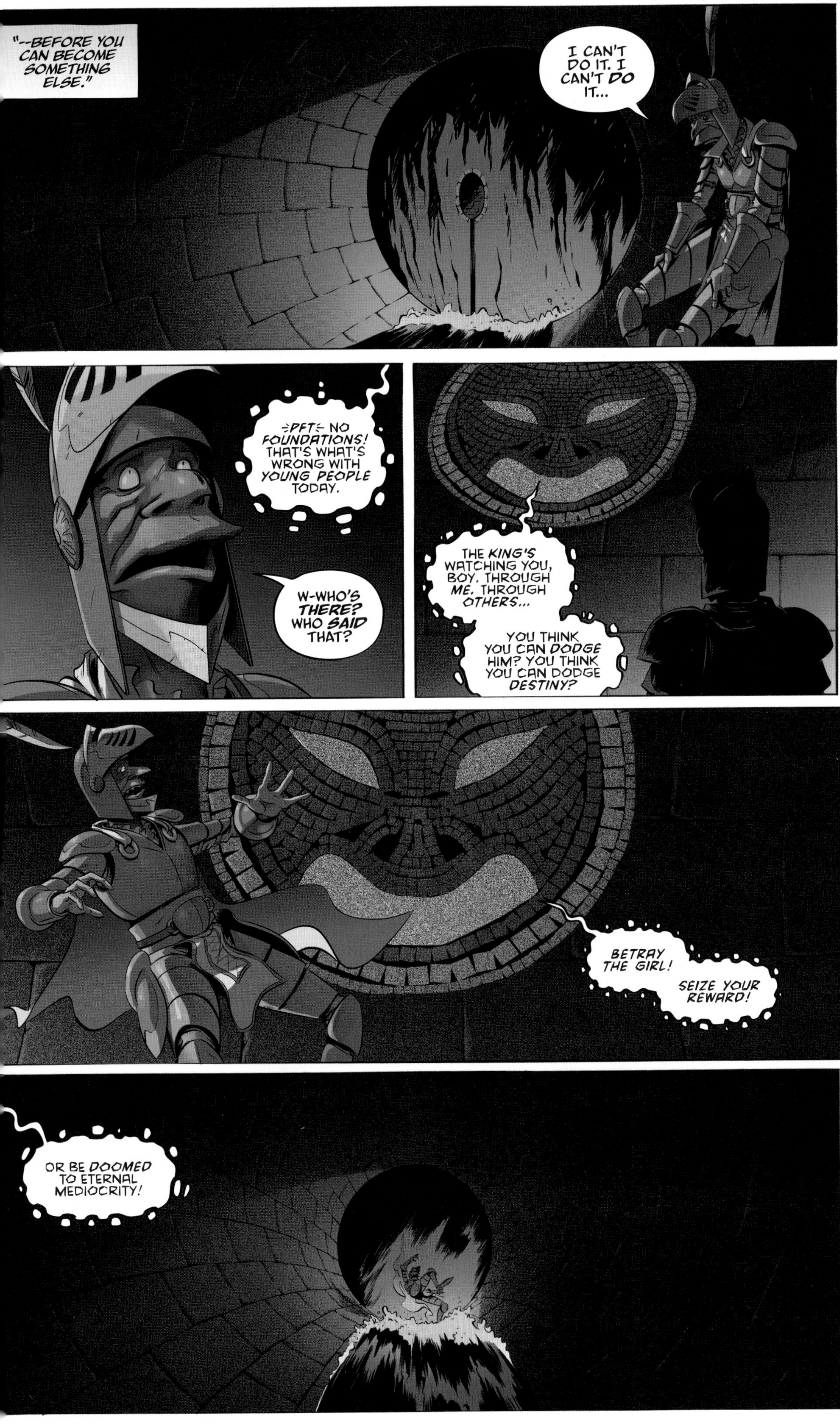
"--BEFORE YOU CAN BECOME SOMETHING ELSE."
I CAN'T DO IT. I CAN'T DO IT...
=PFT= NO FOUNDATIONS! THAT'S WHAT'S WRONG WITH YOUNG PEOPLE TODAY.
W-WHO'S THERE? WHO SAID THAT?
THE KING'S WATCHING YOU, BOY. THROUGH ME. THROUGH OTHERS...
YOU THINK YOU CAN DODGE HIM? YOU THINK YOU CAN DODGE DESTINY?
BETRAY THE GIRL!
SEIZE YOUR REWARD!
OR BE DOOMED TO ETERNAL MEDIOCRITY!

SKUBBIN? WHAT ON EARTH ARE YOU DOING IN THERE?

Oh, I--I JUST--I FELL.

C-CAUGHT UP IN THE FESTIVITIES, I EXPECT.

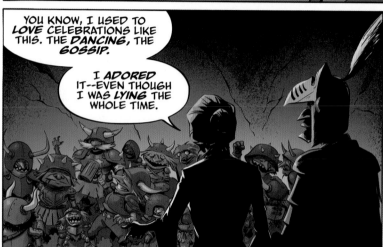

YOU KNOW, I USED TO LOVE CELEBRATIONS LIKE THIS. THE DANCING, THE GOSSIP.

I ADORED IT--EVEN THOUGH I WAS LYING THE WHOLE TIME.

WHO AMONG US ISN'T?

Mm...?

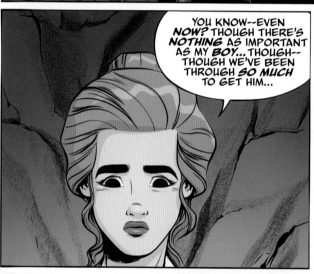

YOU KNOW--EVEN NOW? THOUGH THERE'S NOTHING AS IMPORTANT AS MY BOY... THOUGH-- THOUGH WE'VE BEEN THROUGH SO MUCH TO GET HIM...

I STILL MISS THAT LIFE.

Oh, LISTEN TO ME GO ON! WHAT A LOT OF OLD ROT!

WHAT'S THIS ABOUT YOU LYING, TOO? YOU'RE THE MOST HONEST PERSON I KNOW!

MARIA, THERE'S... THERE'S SOMETHING I NEED TO...

≶SIGH≷

Oh, IT DOESN'T MATTER. IT'S NOT A BIG DEAL.

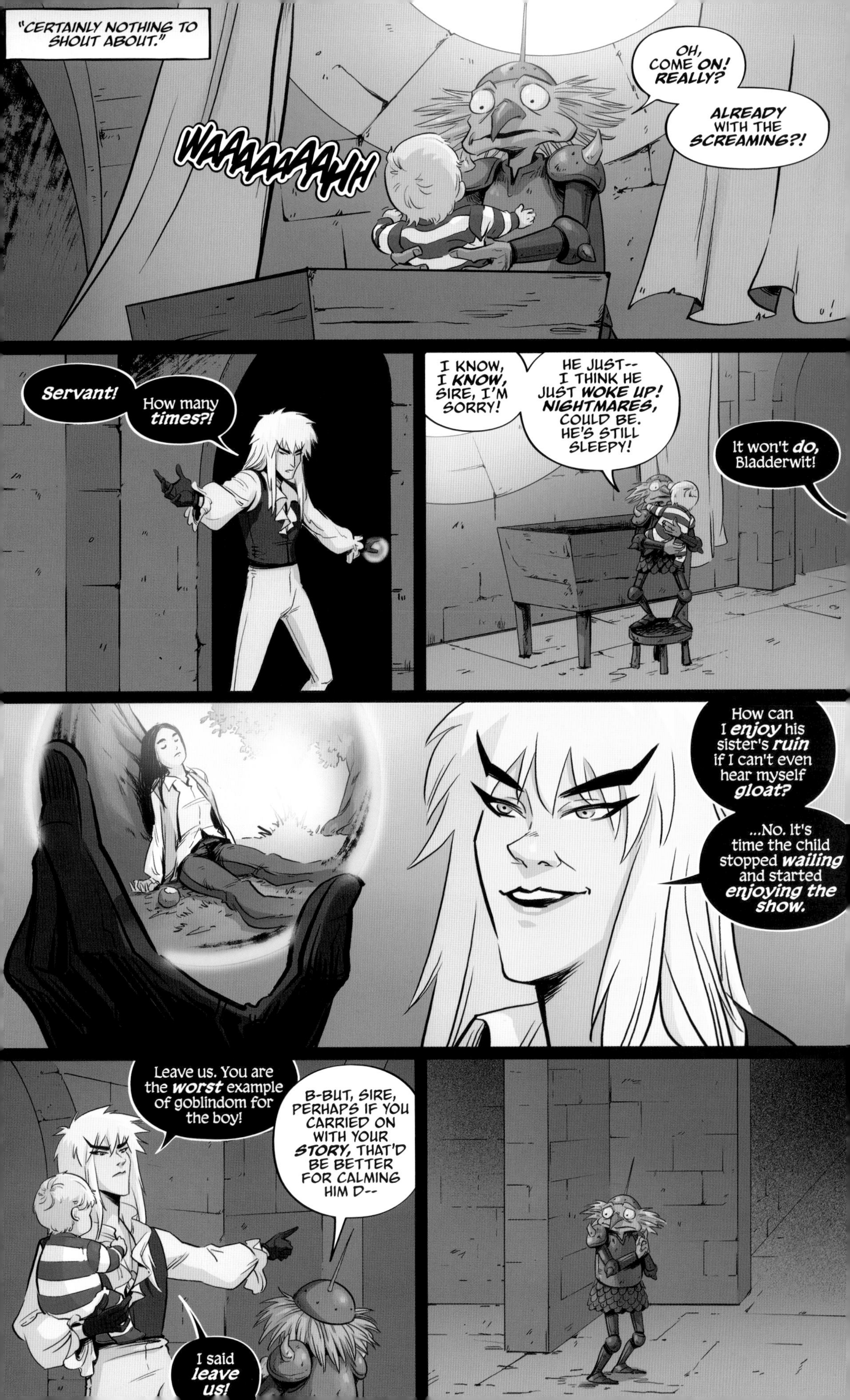
"CERTAINLY NOTHING TO SHOUT ABOUT."
WAAAAAAAAAH
OH, COME ON! REALLY?
ALREADY WITH THE SCREAMING?!
Servant!
How many times?!
I KNOW, I KNOW, SIRE, I'M SORRY!
HE JUST-- I THINK HE JUST WOKE UP! NIGHTMARES, COULD BE. HE'S STILL SLEEPY!
It won't do, Bladderwit!
How can I enjoy his sister's ruin if I can't even hear myself gloat?
...No. It's time the child stopped wailing and started enjoying the show.
Leave us. You are the worst example of goblindom for the boy!
B-BUT, SIRE, PERHAPS IF YOU CARRIED ON WITH YOUR STORY, THAT'D BE BETTER FOR CALMING HIM D--
I said leave us!

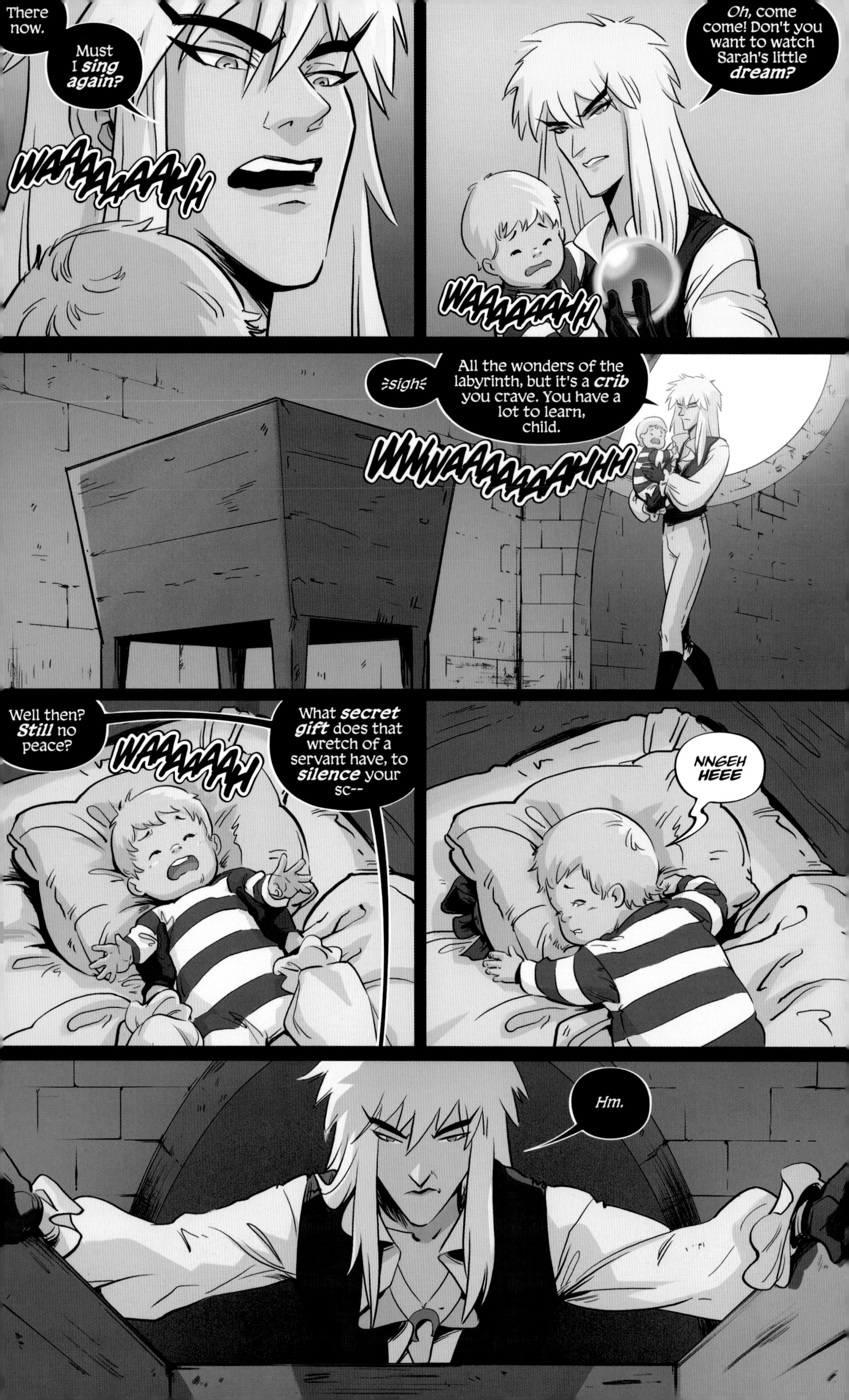
There now.
Must I *sing again?*
WAAAAAAAAHH
Oh, come come! Don't you want to watch Sarah's little *dream?*
WAAAAAAAHH
≥sigh≤
All the wonders of the labyrinth, but it's a *crib* you crave. You have a lot to learn, child.
WWWAAAAAAAAHHH
Well then? *Still* no peace?
WAAAAAAH
What *secret gift* does that wretch of a servant have, to *silence* your sc--
NNGEH HEEE
Hm.

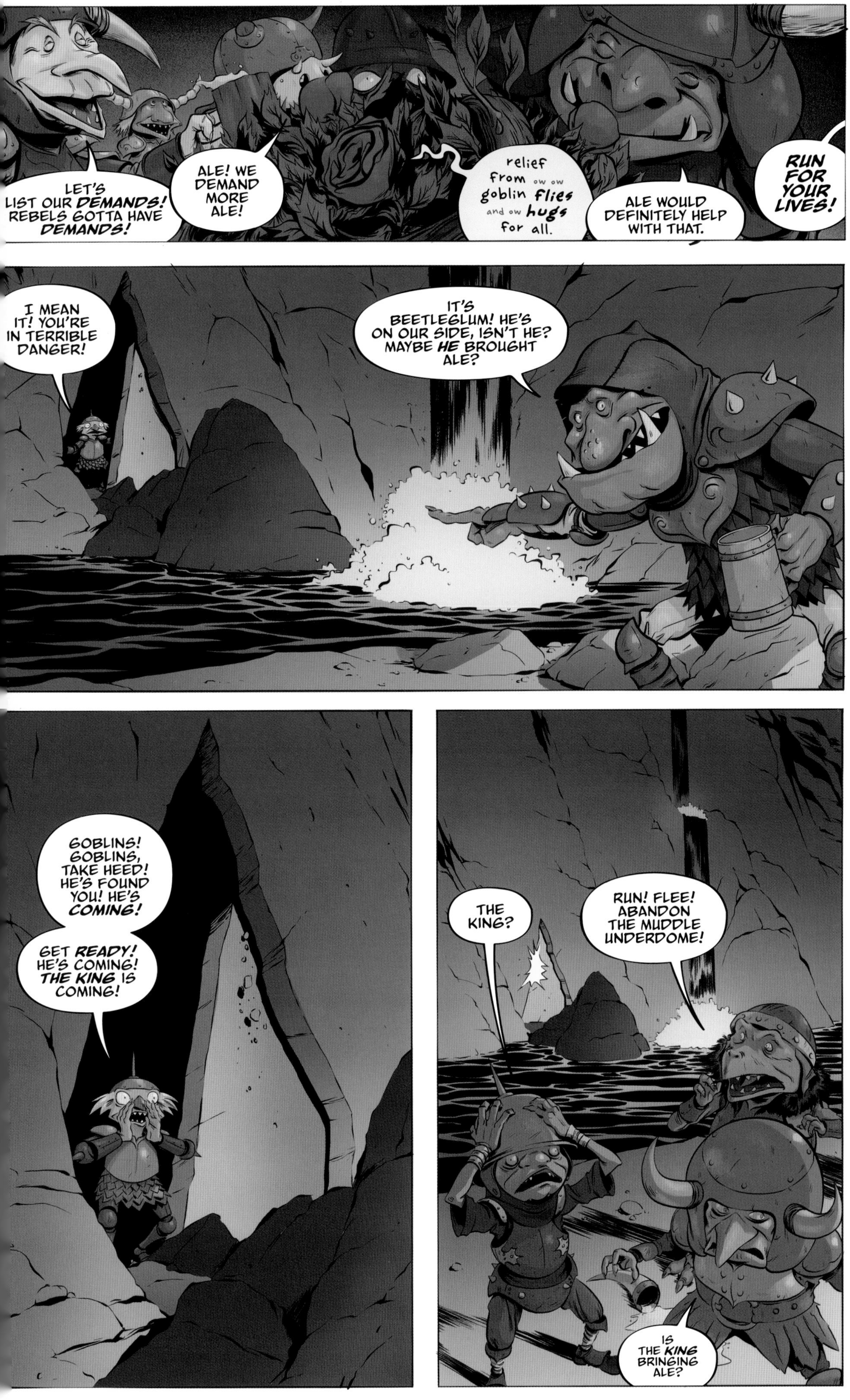
LET'S LIST OUR DEMANDS! REBELS GOTTA HAVE DEMANDS!
ALE! WE DEMAND MORE ALE!
relief from ow ow goblin flies and ow hugs for all.
ALE WOULD DEFINITELY HELP WITH THAT.
RUN FOR YOUR LIVES!
I MEAN IT! YOU'RE IN TERRIBLE DANGER!
IT'S BEETLEGLUM! HE'S ON OUR SIDE, ISN'T HE? MAYBE HE BROUGHT ALE?
GOBLINS! GOBLINS, TAKE HEED! HE'S FOUND YOU! HE'S COMING!
GET READY! HE'S COMING! THE KING IS COMING!
THE KING?
RUN! FLEE! ABANDON THE MUDDLE UNDERDOME!
IS THE KING BRINGING ALE?

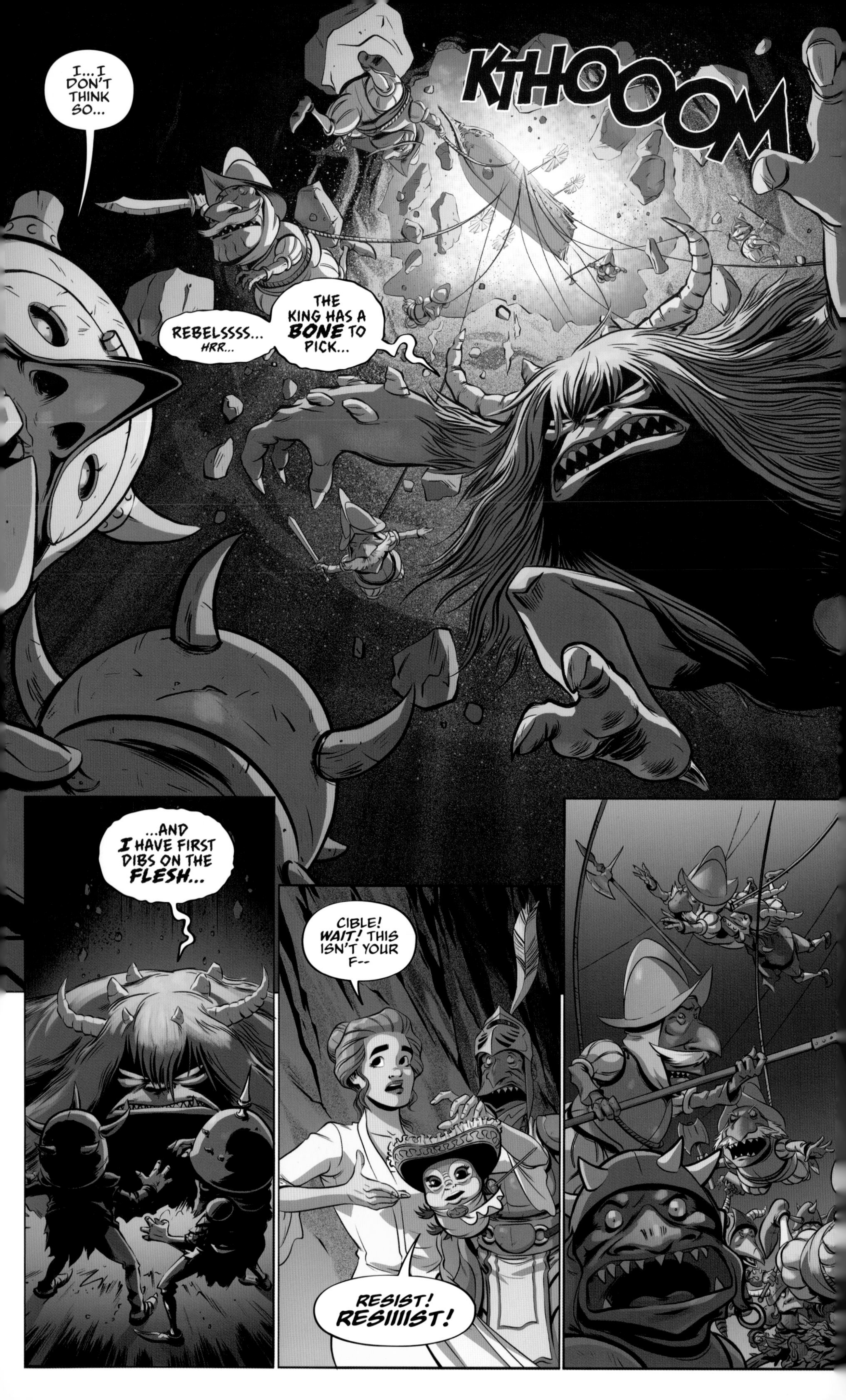
I... I DON'T THINK SO...
KTHOOOOM
REBELSSSS... HRR...
THE KING HAS A BONE TO PICK...
...AND I HAVE FIRST DIBS ON THE FLESH...
CIBLE! WAIT! THIS ISN'T YOUR F--
RESIST! RESIIIIST!

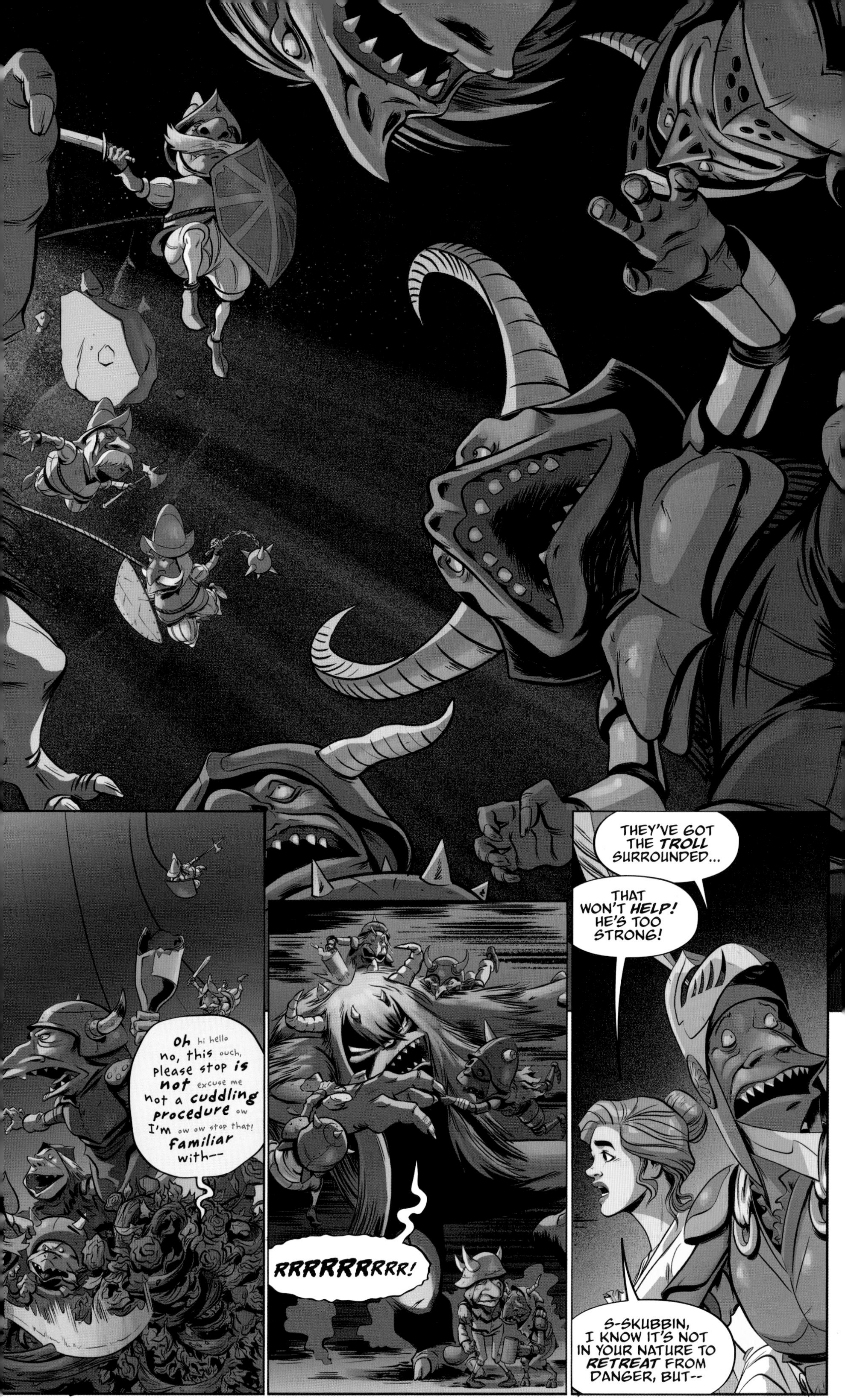
Oh hi hello no, this ouch, please stop is not excuse me not a cuddling procedure ow I'm ow ow stop that! familiar with--
RRRRRRRRR!
THEY'VE GOT THE TROLL SURROUNDED...
THAT WON'T HELP! HE'S TOO STRONG!
S-SKUBBIN, I KNOW IT'S NOT IN YOUR NATURE TO RETREAT FROM DANGER, BUT--

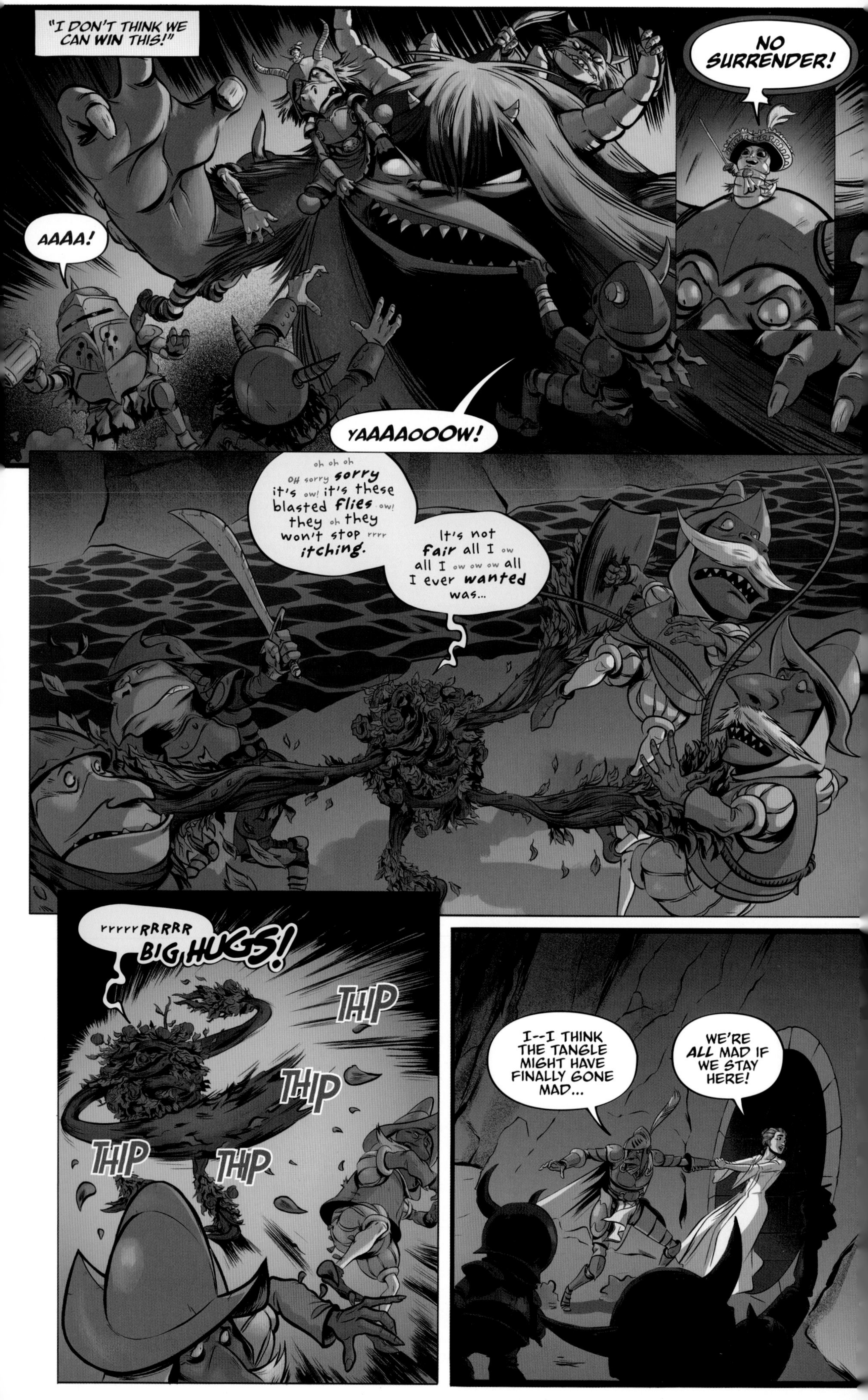
"I DON'T THINK WE CAN WIN THIS!"
AAAA!
YAAAAOOOW!
NO SURRENDER!
oh oh oh OH sorry sorry it's ow! it's these blasted flies ow! they oh they won't stop rrrr itching.
It's not fair all I ow all I ow ow ow all I ever wanted was...
rrrrrRRRRR BIG HUGS!
THIP
THIP
THIP
THIP
I--I THINK THE TANGLE MIGHT HAVE FINALLY GONE MAD...
WE'RE ALL MAD IF WE STAY HERE!

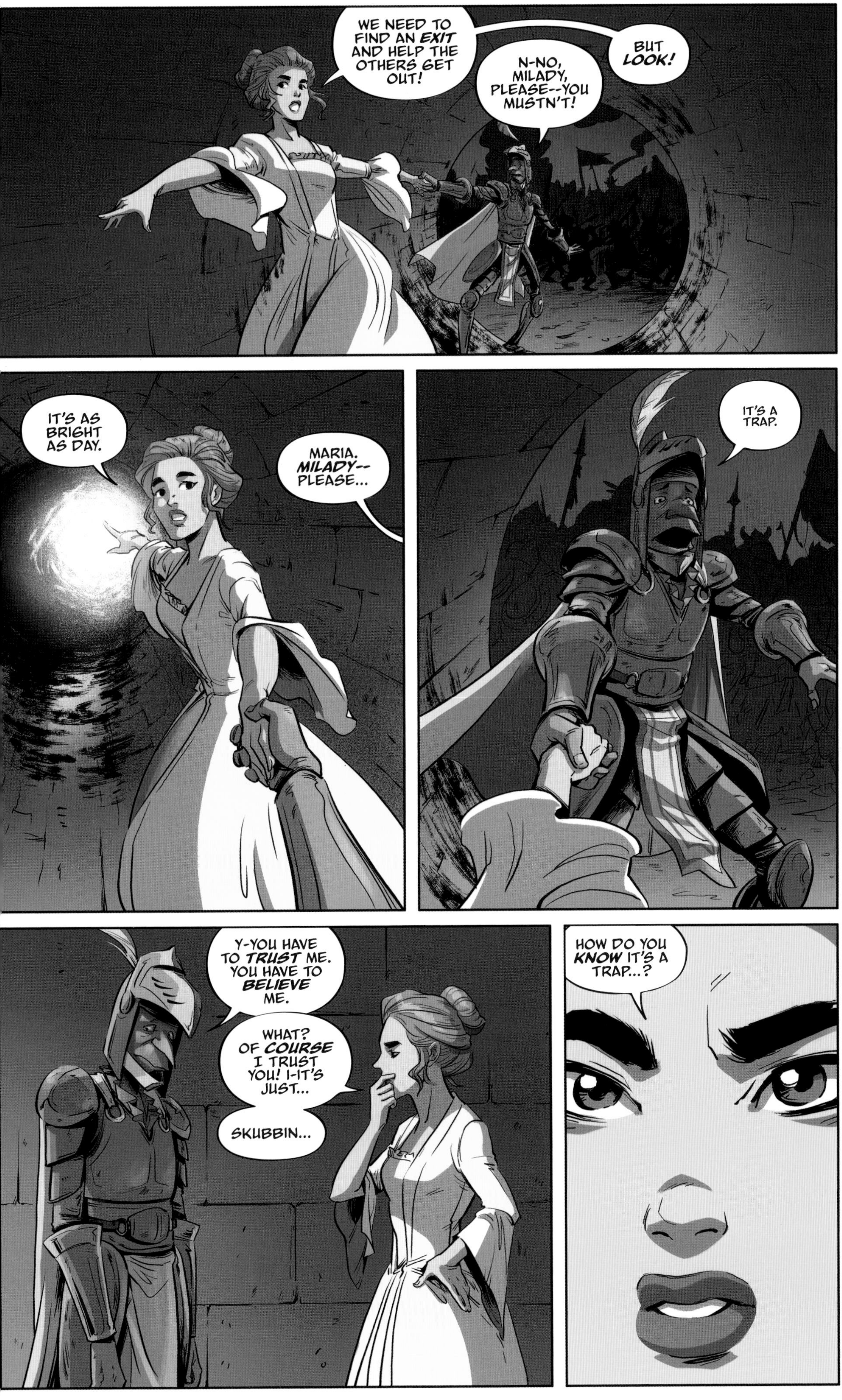
WE NEED TO FIND AN EXIT AND HELP THE OTHERS GET OUT!
BUT LOOK!
N-NO, MILADY, PLEASE--YOU MUSTN'T!
IT'S AS BRIGHT AS DAY.
MARIA. MILADY-- PLEASE...
IT'S A TRAP.
Y-YOU HAVE TO TRUST ME. YOU HAVE TO BELIEVE ME.
WHAT? OF COURSE I TRUST YOU! I-IT'S JUST...
SKUBBIN...
HOW DO YOU KNOW IT'S A TRAP...?

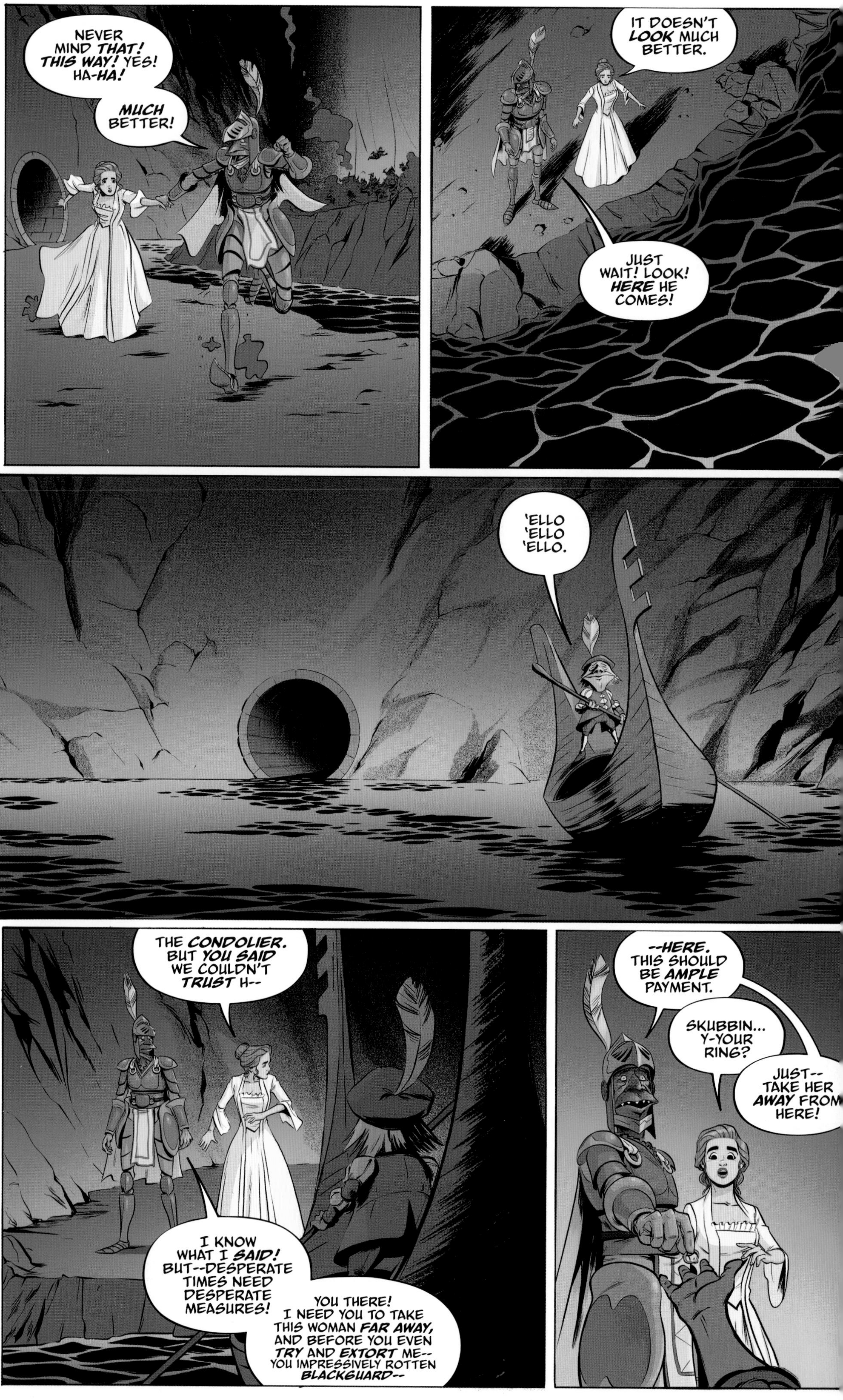
NEVER MIND *THAT!* *THIS WAY!* YES! HA-*HA!*
MUCH BETTER!
IT DOESN'T *LOOK* MUCH BETTER.
JUST WAIT! LOOK! *HERE* HE COMES!
'ELLO 'ELLO 'ELLO.
THE *CONDOLIER.* BUT *YOU SAID* WE COULDN'T *TRUST* H--
I KNOW WHAT I *SAID!* BUT--DESPERATE TIMES NEED DESPERATE MEASURES!
YOU THERE! I NEED YOU TO TAKE THIS WOMAN *FAR AWAY,* AND BEFORE YOU EVEN *TRY* AND *EXTORT* ME-- YOU IMPRESSIVELY ROTTEN *BLACKGUARD--*
--HERE. THIS SHOULD BE *AMPLE* PAYMENT.
SKUBBIN... Y-YOUR RING?
JUST-- TAKE HER *AWAY* FROM HERE!

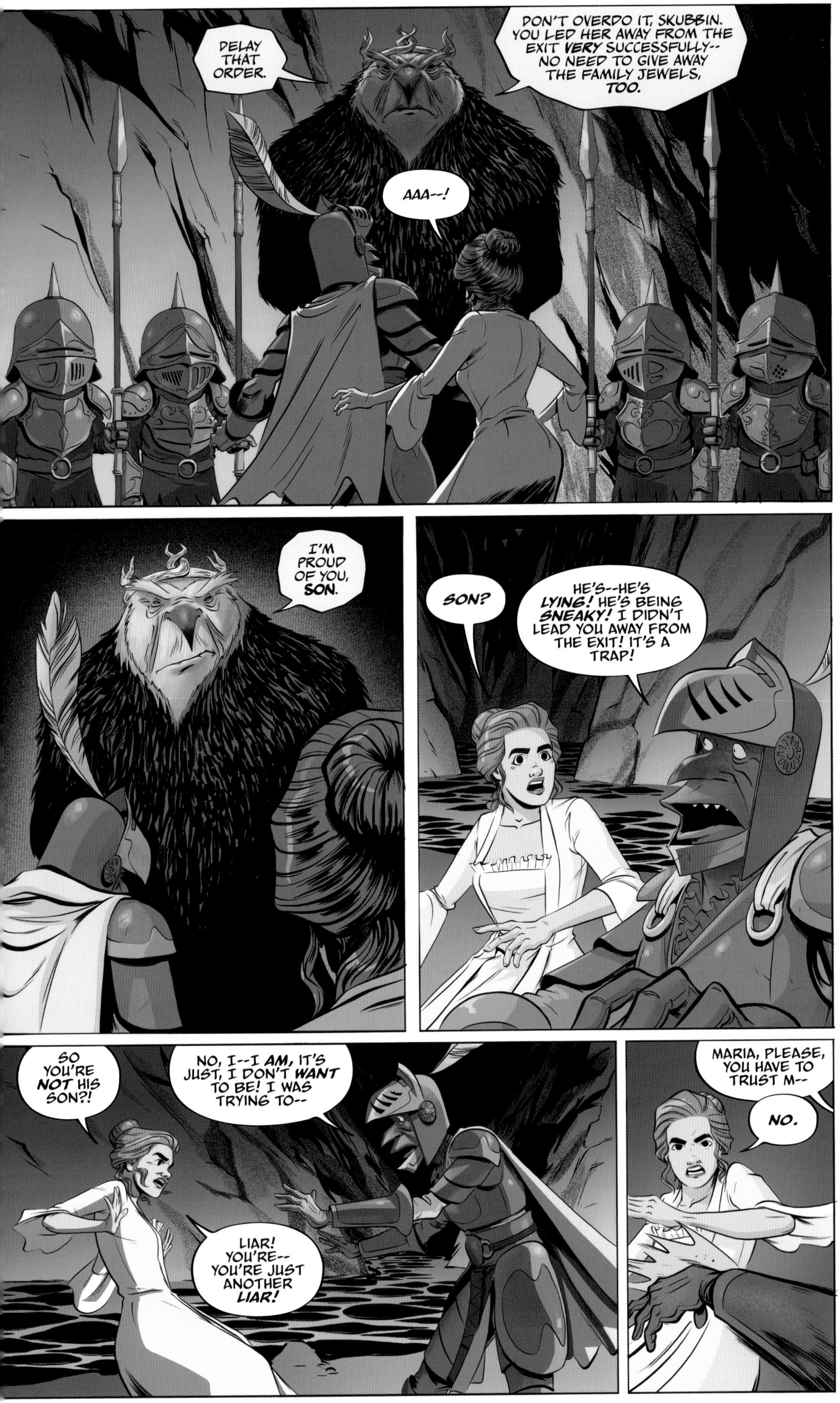
DELAY THAT ORDER.
DON'T OVERDO IT, SKUBBIN. YOU LED HER AWAY FROM THE EXIT *VERY* SUCCESSFULLY-- NO NEED TO GIVE AWAY THE FAMILY JEWELS, **TOO.**
AAA--!
I'M PROUD OF YOU, **SON.**
SON?
HE'S--HE'S *LYING!* HE'S BEING *SNEAKY!* I DIDN'T LEAD YOU AWAY FROM THE EXIT! IT'S A TRAP!
SO YOU'RE *NOT* HIS SON?!
NO, I--I *AM,* IT'S JUST, I DON'T *WANT* TO BE! I WAS TRYING TO--
LIAR! YOU'RE-- YOU'RE JUST ANOTHER *LIAR!*
MARIA, PLEASE, YOU HAVE TO TRUST M--
NO.

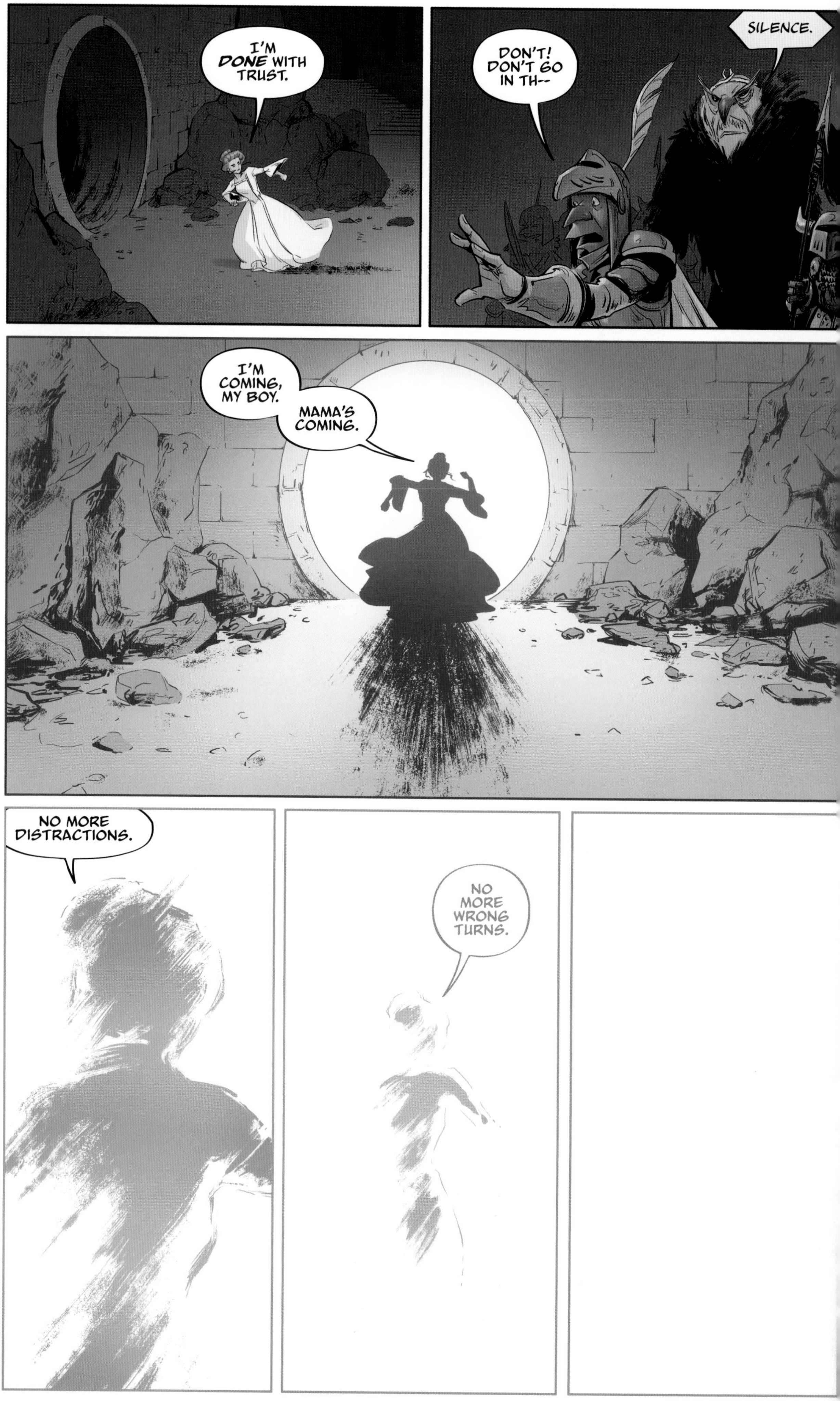
I'M DONE WITH TRUST.
DON'T! DON'T GO IN TH--
SILENCE.
I'M COMING, MY BOY.
MAMA'S COMING.
NO MORE DISTRACTIONS.
NO MORE WRONG TURNS.

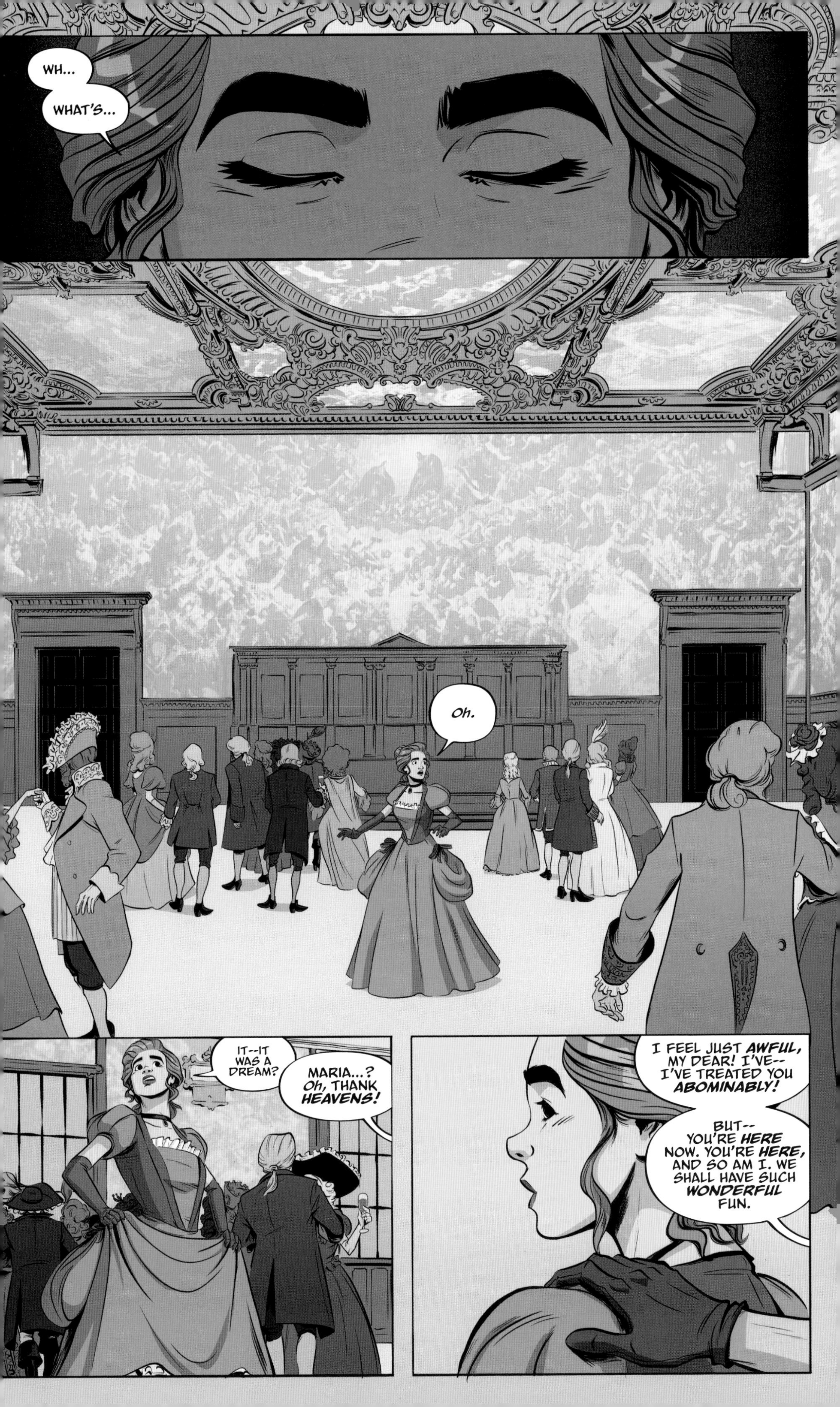
WH...
WHAT'S...
Oh.
IT--IT WAS A DREAM?
MARIA...? Oh, THANK HEAVENS!
I FEEL JUST AWFUL, MY DEAR! I'VE-- I'VE TREATED YOU ABOMINABLY!
BUT-- YOU'RE HERE NOW. YOU'RE HERE, AND SO AM I. WE SHALL HAVE SUCH WONDERFUL FUN.

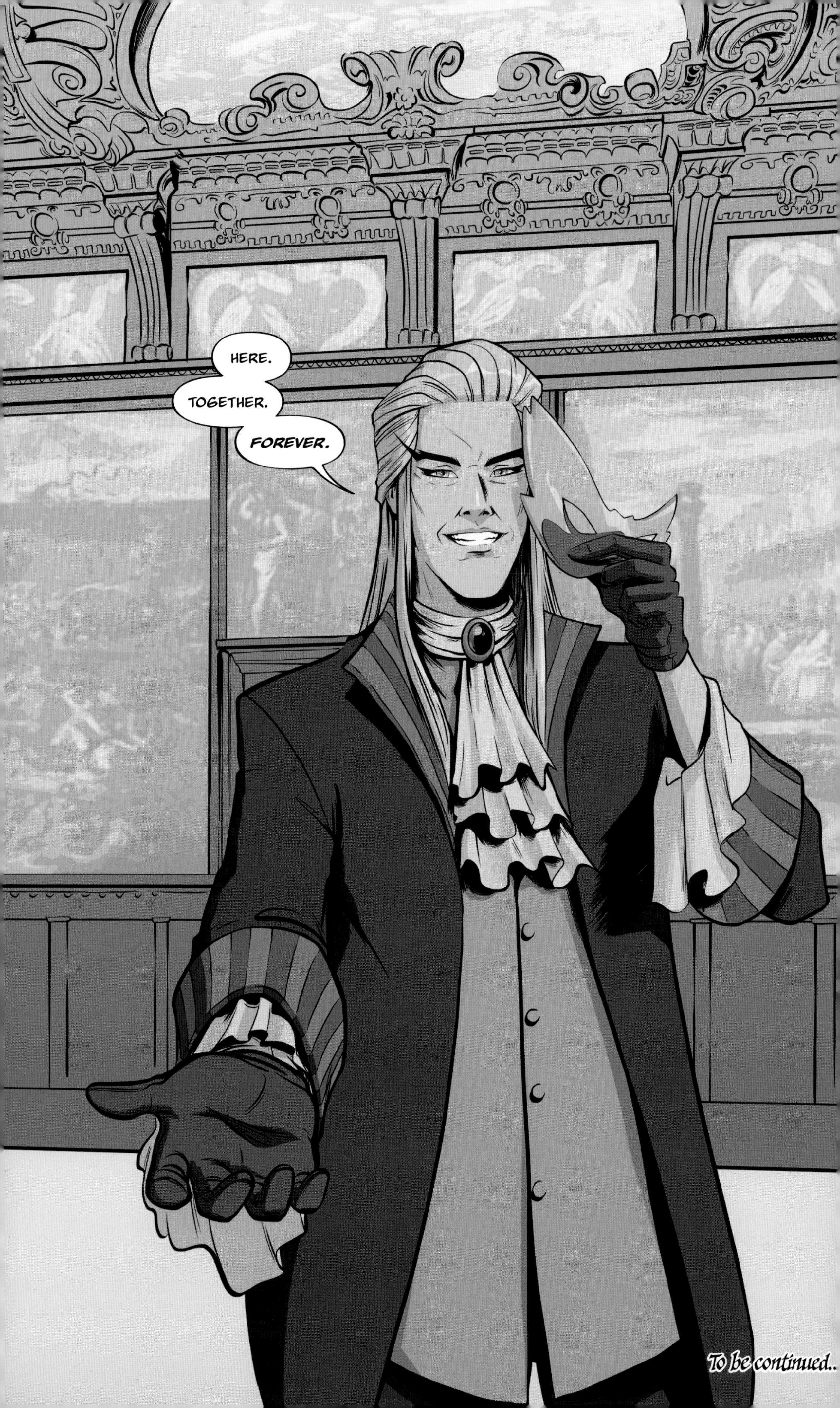
HERE.
TOGETHER.
FOREVER.
To be continued...

COVER GALLERY

Facing Page:
Issue #5 Subscription Cover by
Sana Takeda

Following Pages:
Issues #6-8 Subscription Covers by
Sana Takeda

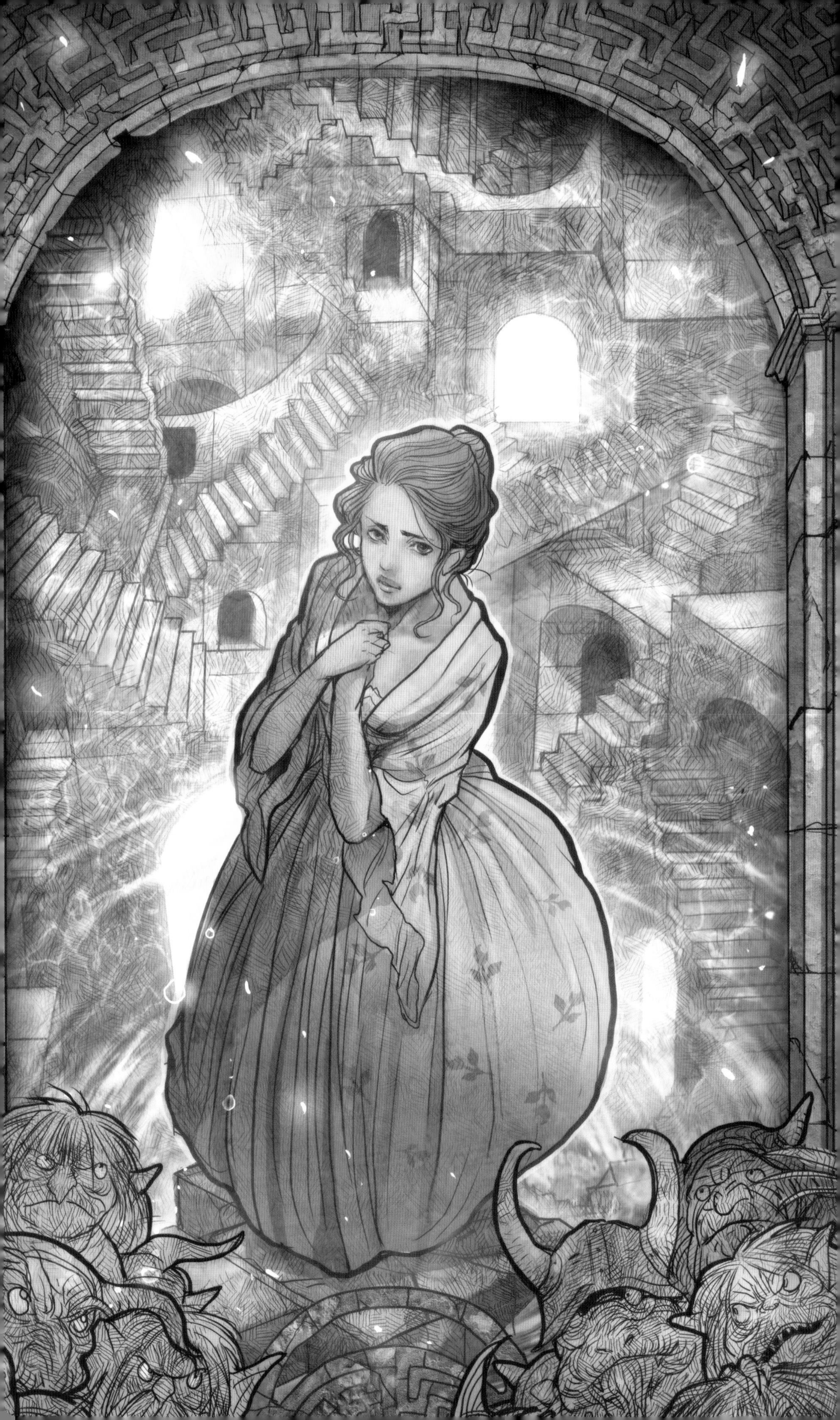

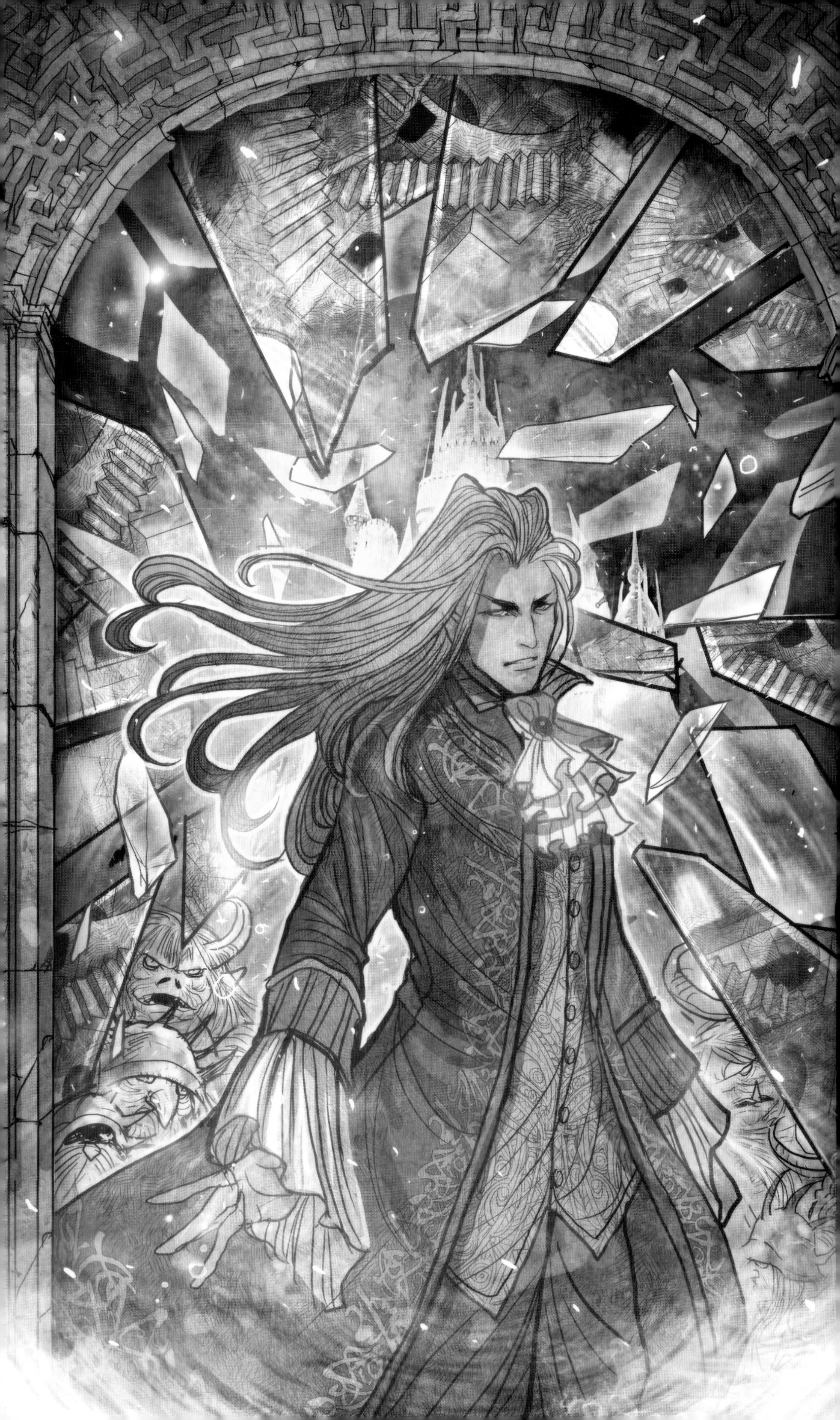

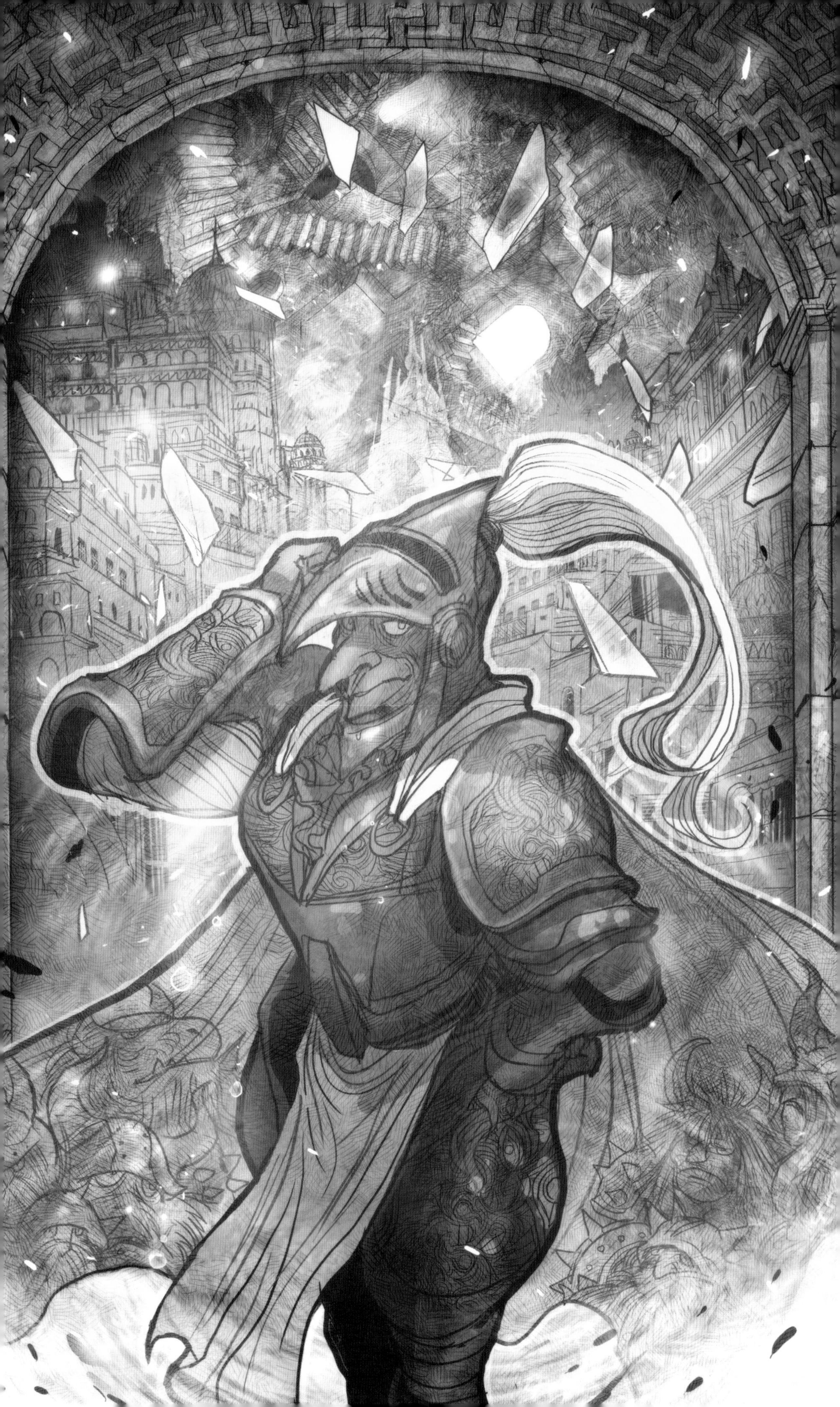

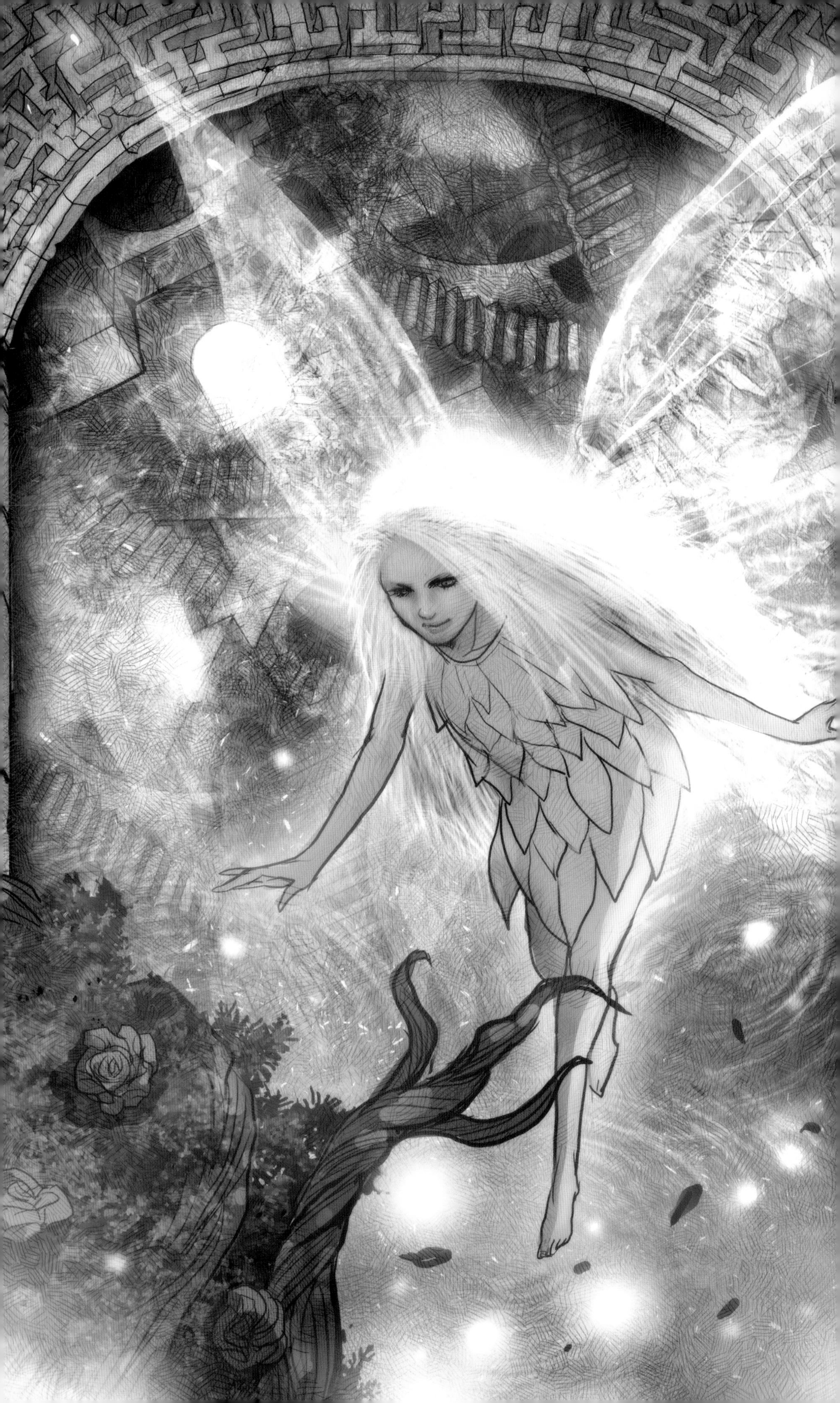

LABYRINTH
SKETCHBOOK

The following pages offer a first look at the never-before-seen characters designs for Labyrinth: Coronation *by Kyla Vanderklugt and Daniel Bayliss*

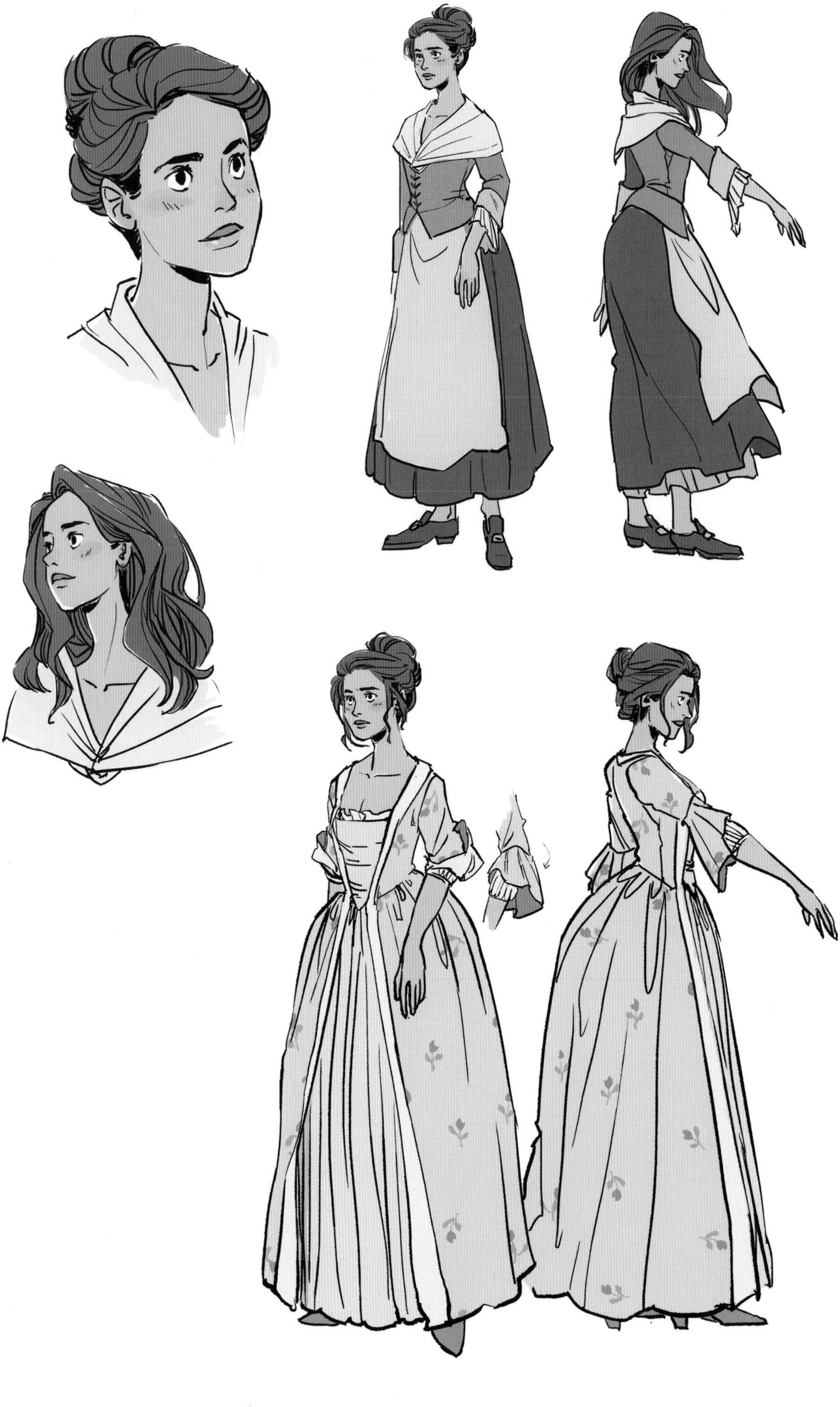

During the development stage of the series, artist Kyla Vanderklugt came up with an early take on Maria before landing on her iconic look.

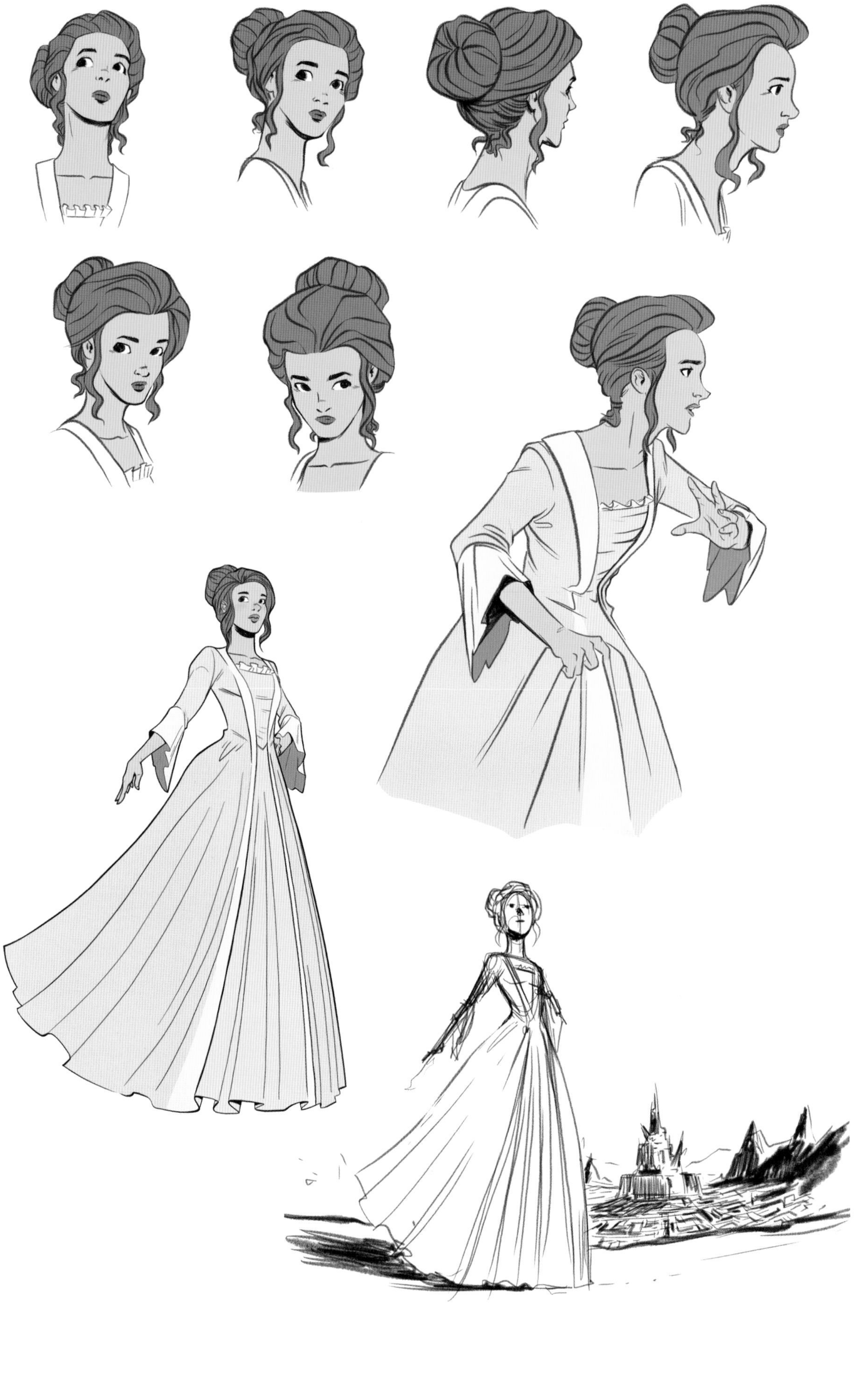

Daniel worked off of Kyla's original design, while also adding his own unique flair.

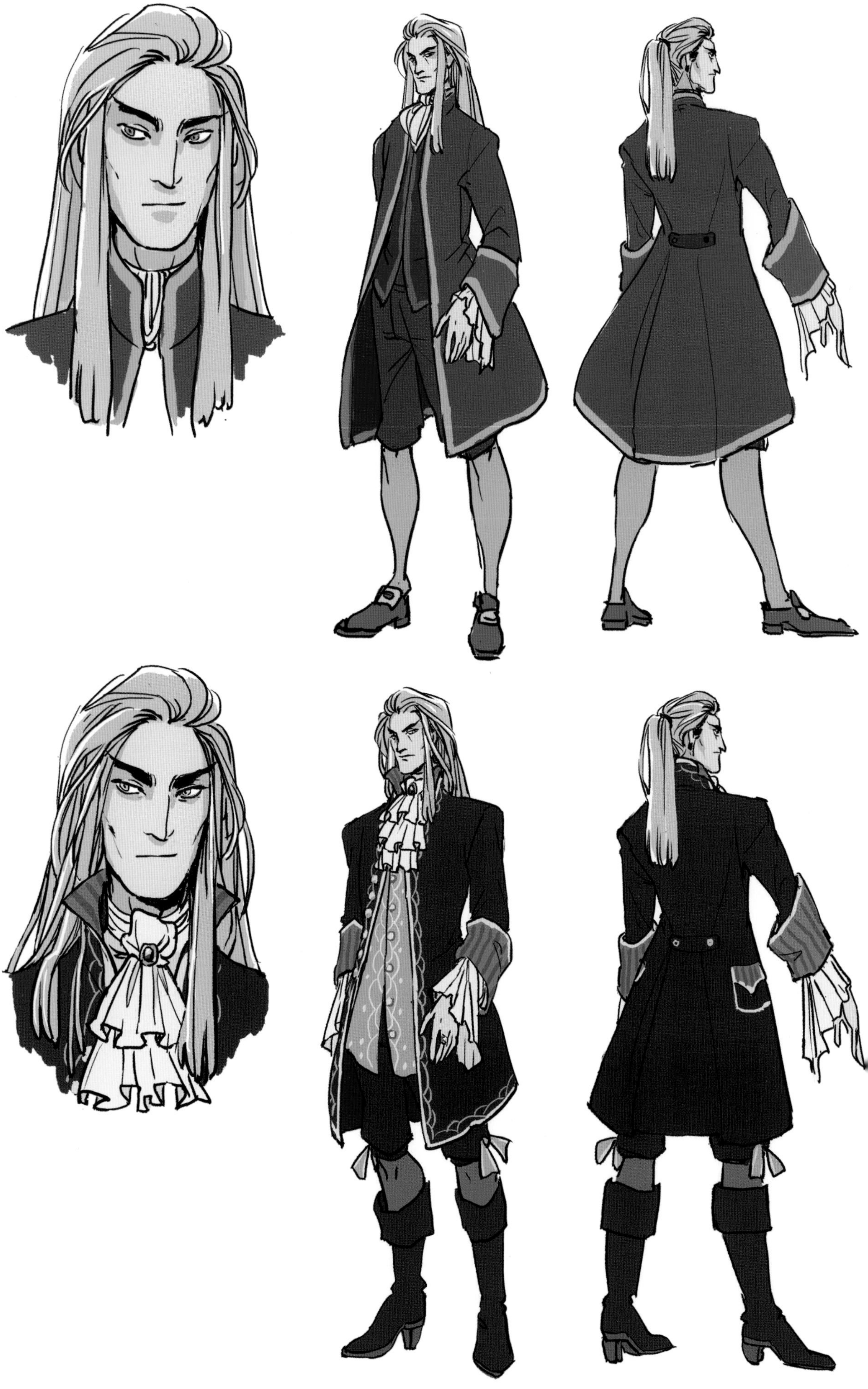

Here are Kyla's initial Albert designs along with her final version.

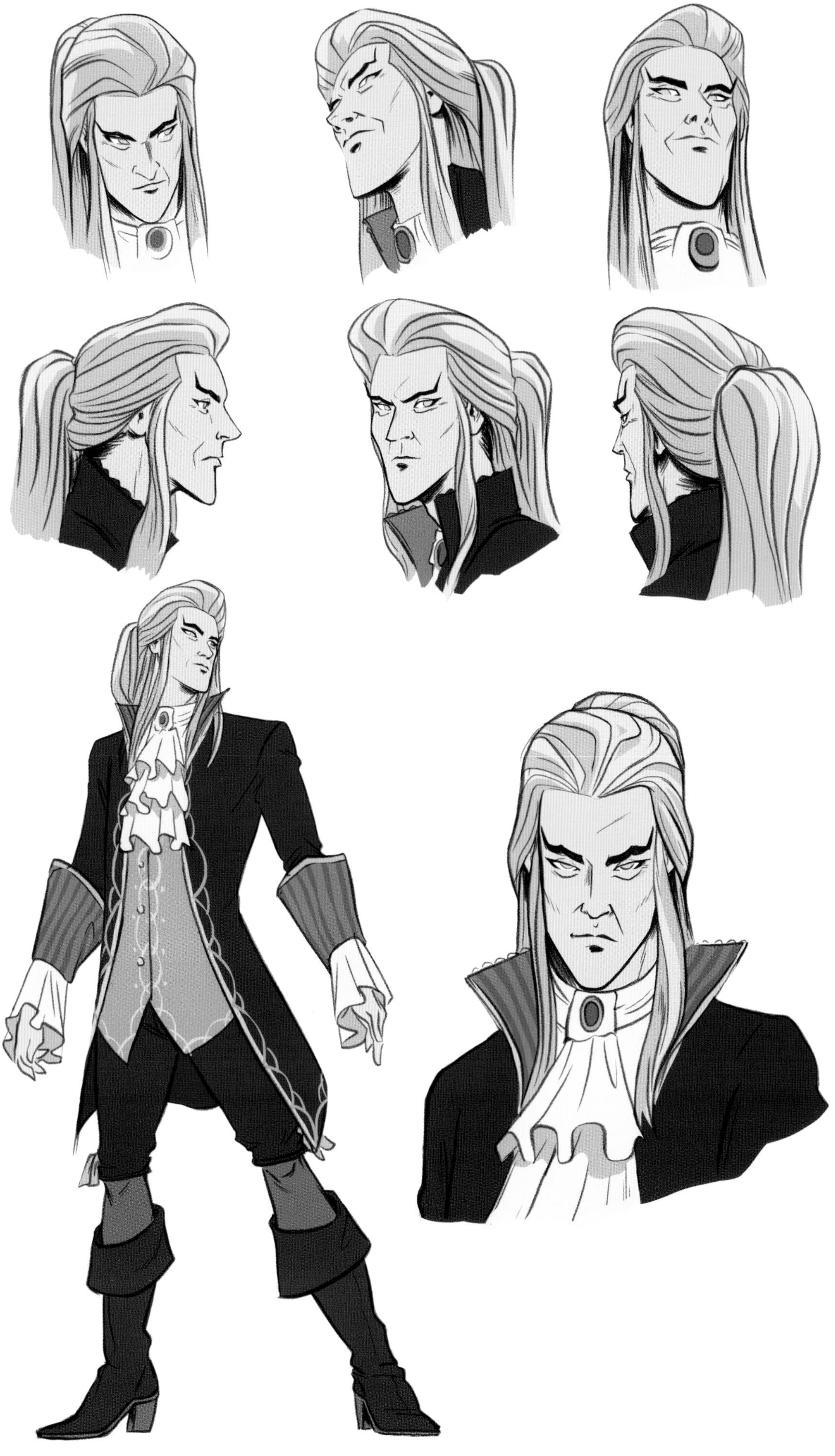

Daniel's first pass based on Kyla's work.

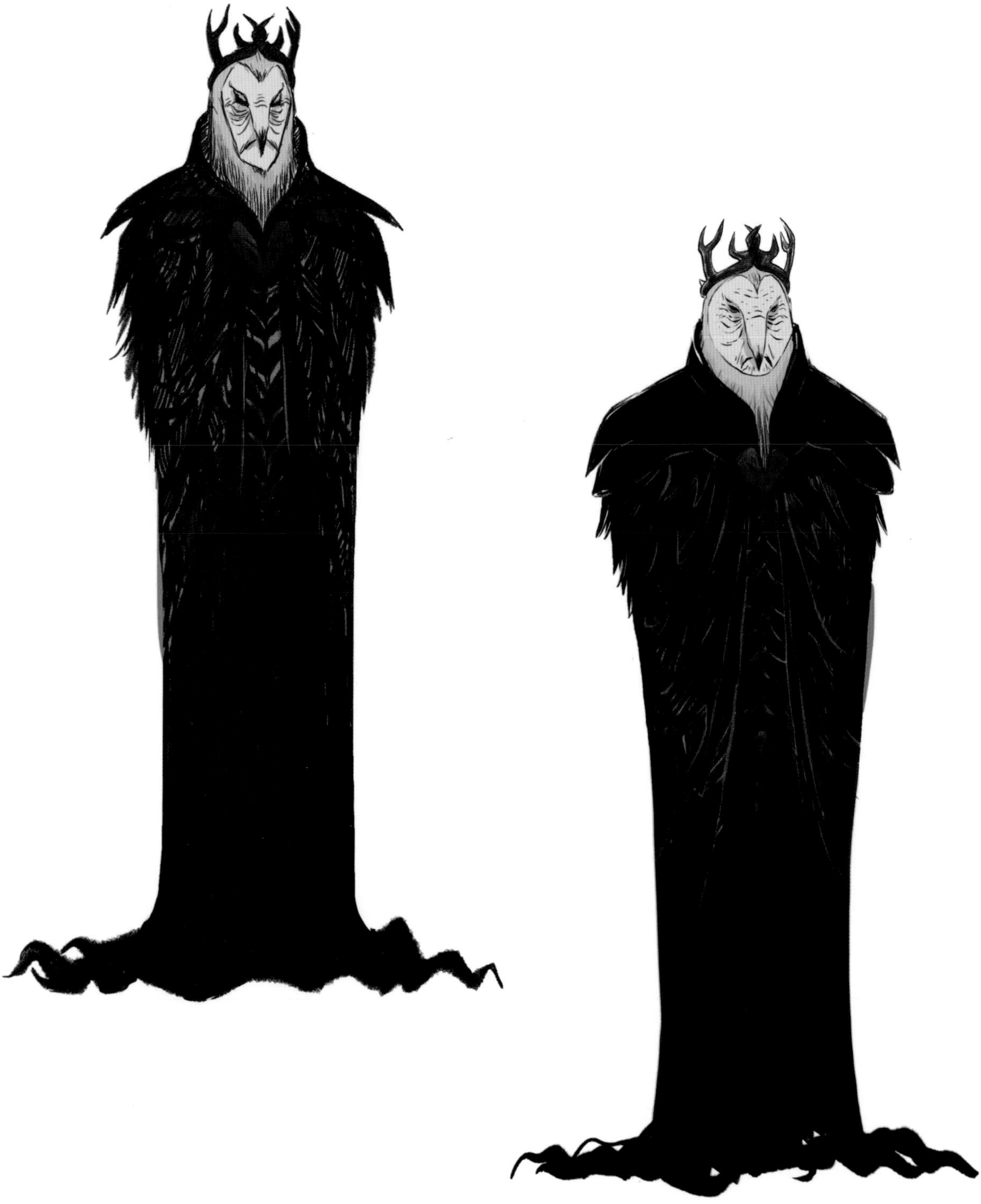

Daniel's first pass at the design for the Owl King.

Facing page: *Designs for Skubbin's helmet and face went through a few iterations before landing on his final look.*

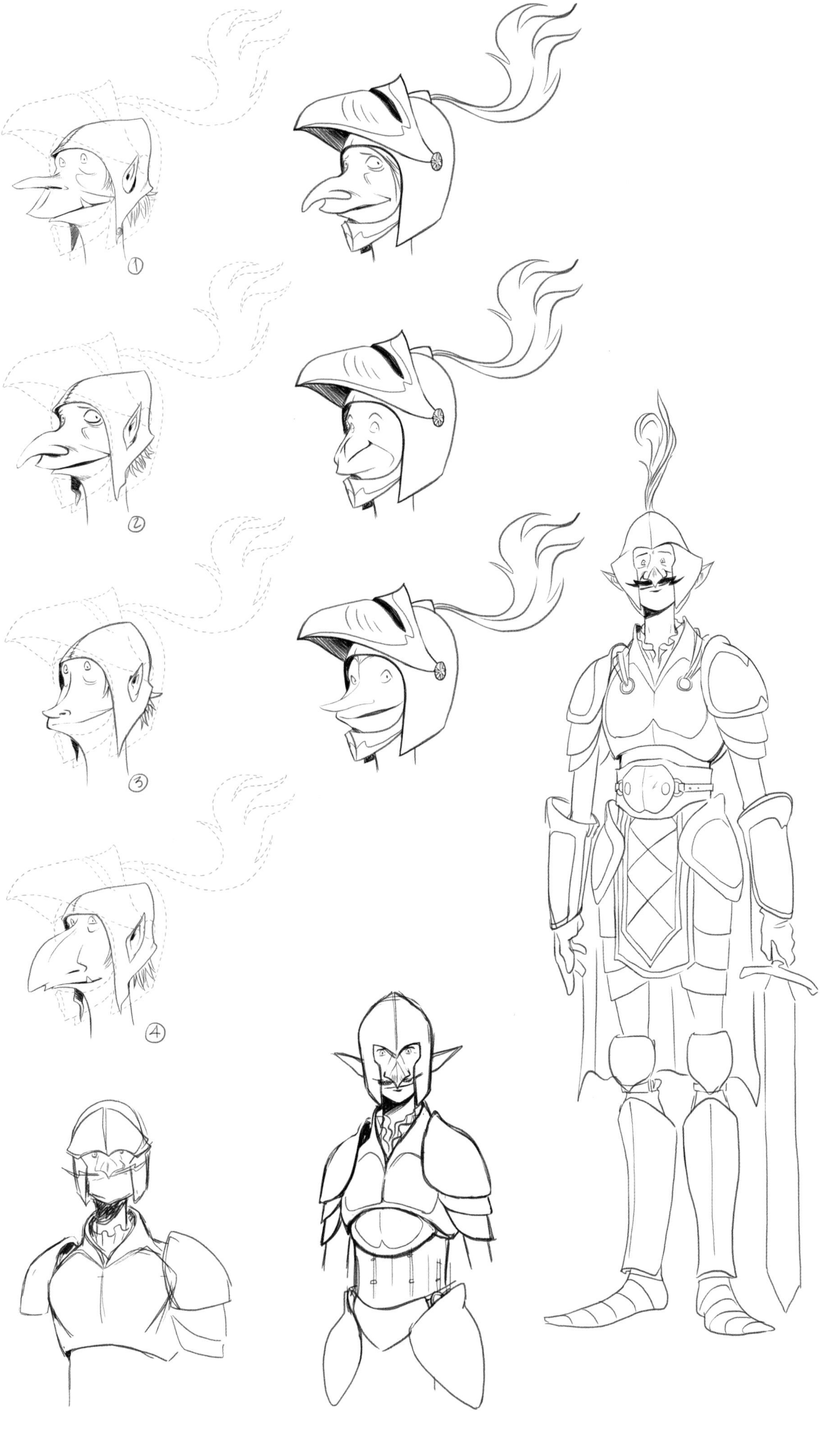
1
2
3
4

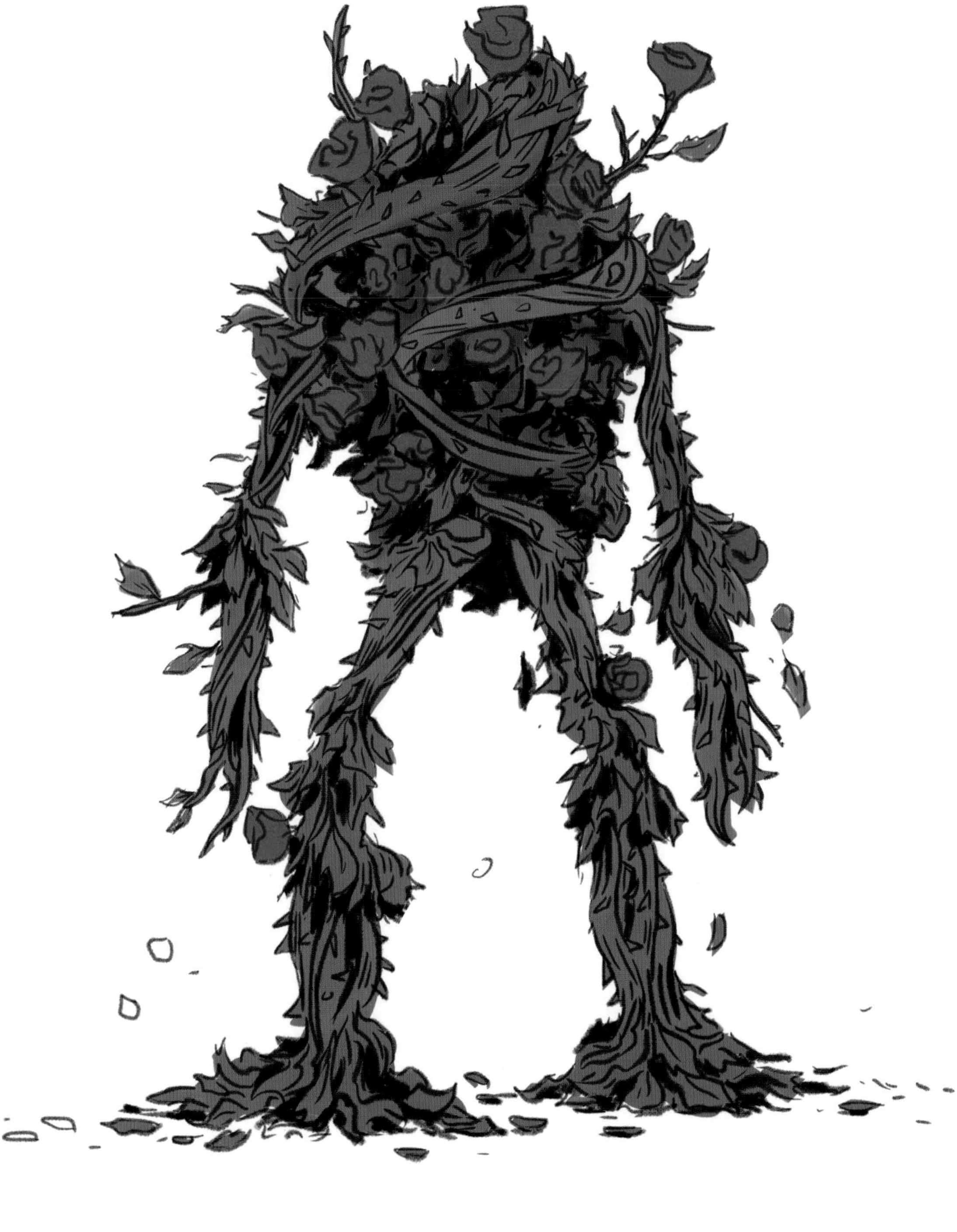

Daniel's initial character designs for the Tangle.

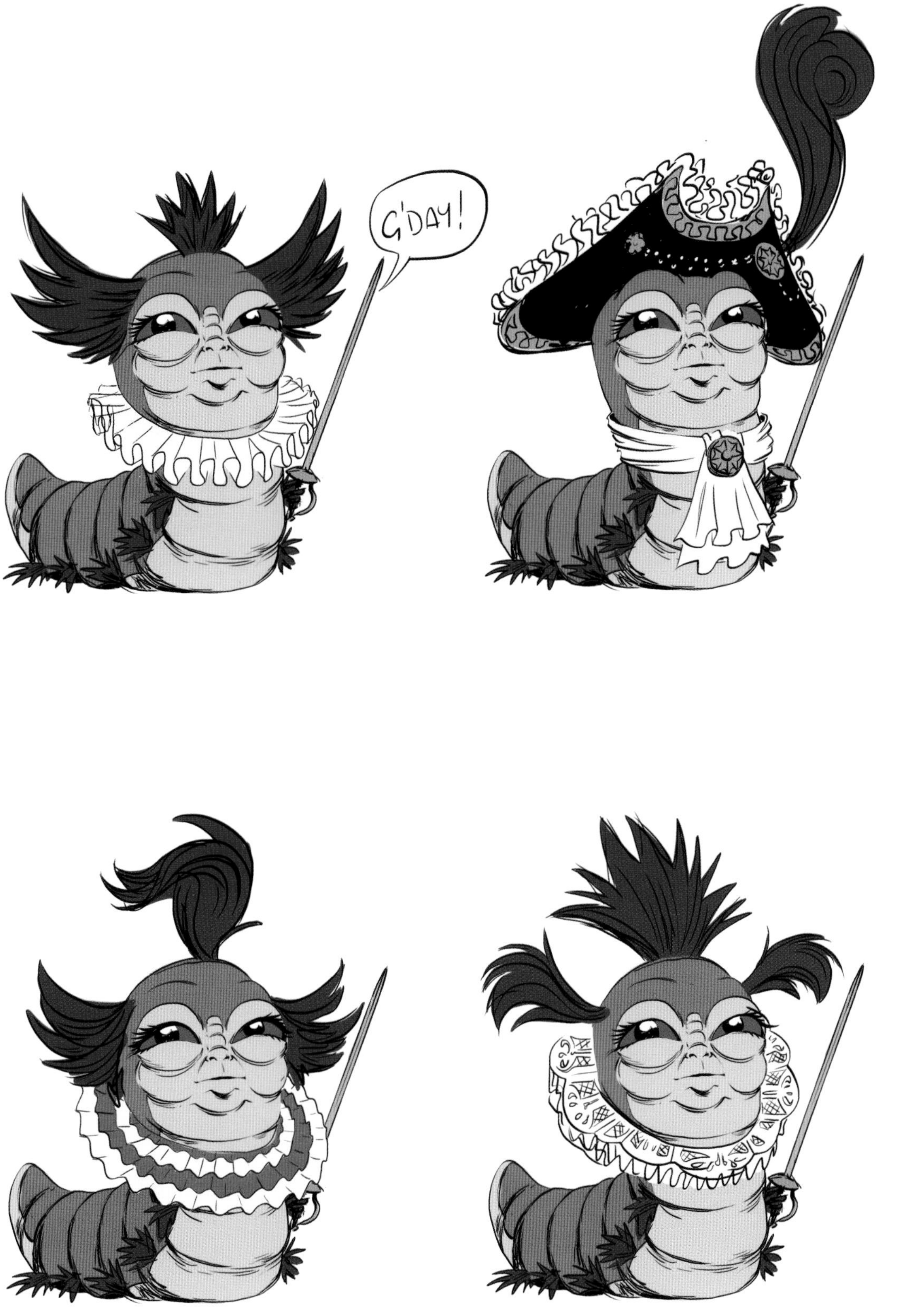
G'DAY!

Daniel put together a number of options for Cible's hair and outfit. In the final design, it's her hair that acts as the hat's plume.

Septimus the Night Troll is based on a design by Brian Froud. It was originally created for the film but never made it into the final product. Daniel reimagined him for Labyrinth: Coronation, *honoring Froud's iconic work.*

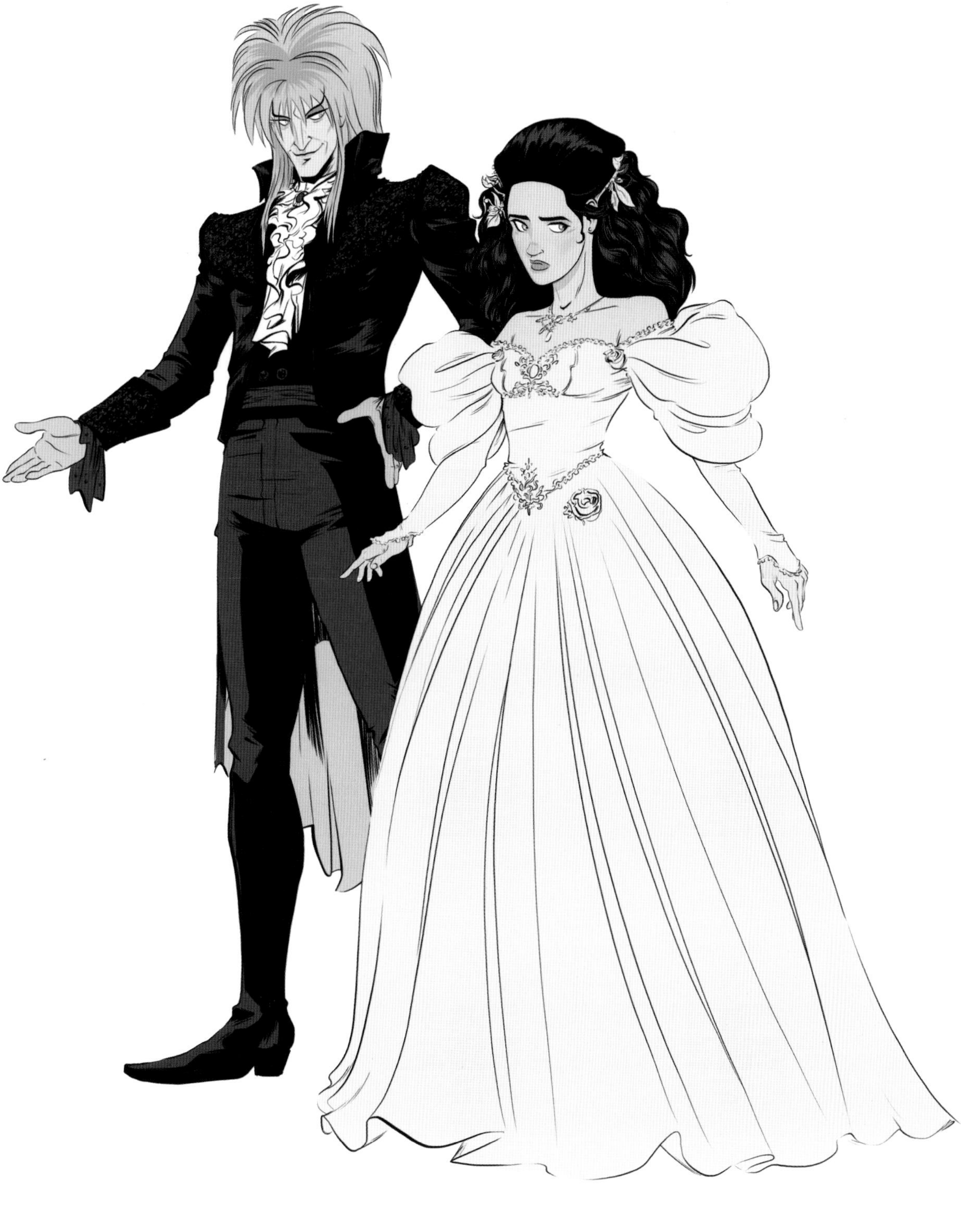

Daniel's first sketches of Jareth and Sarah.

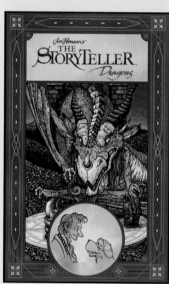

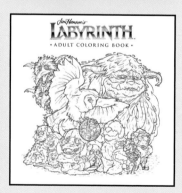